THESE
MEN
OF
BANSTEAD

THESE
MEN
OF
BANSTEAD

Lewis N Wood

Banstead History Research Group

2010

A catalogue record for this book is available from
The British Library

ISBN 978-0-9566313-0-5

Book jacket:
In Flanders Fields
Photograph by Catherine Barnes

Printed through SS Media
88 Sandy Lane South, Wallington, Surrey SM6 9RQ
Tel: 020 8404 3922 Email: info@ss-media.co.uk
Printed in the EU

CONTENTS – THE MEN

OTHER CONTENTS

ACKNOWLEDGEMENTS

This book is the product of many people's efforts. A few are my own fellow members of the Banstead History Research Group, but this record of the men of Banstead could not have been completed without all the contributions from their descendants, neighbours, colleagues in the armed forces, and local villagers, who were able to provide me with many personal memories which form such an important part of this publication.

Most of the photographs came from relatives, and to all these people, I owe my gratitude, with special thanks to those who I met personally and who often trusted me with their most precious documents and memorabilia.

The key to finding many of the descendants was to have the benefit of two genealogists who are passionate about their work, and who often spent many hours, days and sometimes weeks, in pursuit of any clue which would help to progress the research. This invaluable assistance was provided freely by Christine Kent, and Barbara Rough who also assisted greatly with the index. Mark Stanley contributed much to the RAF accounts as well as using his expertise and vast library to source additional material on squadrons, aircraft, aeroplane crashes and the like.

Many organisations provided information, sometimes on individuals and other times on battles, equipment or places, and my thanks go to all such institutions, too numerous to mention. Only one was able to provide information on all the men – The Commonwealth War Graves Commission – without whose on-line search facility, and the assistance provided by its dedicated staff, it would have been impossible to progress this research. Thanks also to Reverend David Chance, Vicar of All Saints Banstead for allowing access to the All Saints record of the Banstead men who served overseas in the Great War.

I must thank my daughter Laura, for the many long hours she spent assisting me with the production of this book, and Thomas Mayo for his assistance with the editing of the stories.

The unenviable task of helping me turn years of research into a quality publication fell to my BHRG colleague Mike Shackel, who compiled the War Year summaries, and whose expert eye for detail, and patient tuition on the book publishing process, has greatly improved the finished version.

Finally, thanks to Faith Bedford, daughter of Serjeant Clifford Remané 7928067, Royal Armoured Corps, 3rd Royal Tank Regiment, for writing such a moving Foreword.

Lewis N Wood
Banstead, September 2010

FOREWORD

by Faith Bedford (née Remané)

I feel very proud to be asked to write the Foreword to this book because I know that *These Men of Banstead* will mean a lot to its readers. Firstly many of them will, like me, have some strong family connection with the men whose courage, endurance and, sadly, their ultimate sacrifice the book commemorates. Secondly because – whether or not they have a personal interest in the lives of the men who are remembered in these pages – they will find the individual stories both moving and inspiring.

Over the years, countless thousands of people – by no means all of them residents of Banstead – will have passed its war memorial. Many of them must have speculated about the fate of those who left the village to go to war and, tragically, never came home. Among them was my father, so naturally it was to his story that I turned first. Familiar as I was with many of its details, the story again touched my heart and so too did the stories of all the other men Lewis has pieced together with such dedication and patience, and told here so vividly and sympathetically.

We relatives, descendants and friends of the Banstead men who fell in two world wars, owe Lewis and his colleagues from the Banstead History Research Group, a debt of gratitude and appreciation. We can all derive comfort and satisfaction from the knowledge that in this book, these men of Banstead have a second fine memorial.

The Banstead War Memorial

INTRODUCTION

One day, I walked the couple of hundred yards from my house to the War Memorial in High Street, Banstead, situated in the county of Surrey some fourteen miles south of London. It's something I must have done hundreds of times, but on this occasion, I did not walk past, but stopped to have a look.

The main purpose of my stroll that morning was to photograph the memorial in the run up to Remembrance Day, with the intention of adding a new image to the website of the Banstead History Research Group of which I am an active member. I had no idea how many names were on the memorial, nor any knowledge of who they were. I took my photograph and stood there for a while looking at the inscriptions carved into the Portland stone panels. It seemed odd that whilst the panel on the front mentioned the two World Wars, there was no indication of which panels related to which War.

That single observation was to become the starting point for this book as I quickly found out that, despite the good work of many dedicated historians in Banstead, nothing had been written about the memorial. So who were the men behind the names? Was it possible to find out? After all, over half of them had died over ninety years ago. Where did the memorial come from? Who erected it? When was it unveiled? I determined to find out.

Four years later, I feel I have come to know many of these men whose portraits now hang in my study. Clifford Remané, a local estate agent whose tank received a direct hit, John Peter Marley Lintott, a Spitfire pilot awarded the Distinguished Flying Cross; he shot down an enemy aircraft before he, too, crashed. Bertram Henry Ives, killed at Dunkirk on his third trip back to bring the stranded soldiers home. Jack Hillman who was under-age, but went to fight in the trenches after receiving a white feather. The list goes on.

Collecting and researching information on these men has not been an easy task as the starting point for each one was a surname and one or two initials, no rank, no service number or any other detail. Furthermore, some of the names were incorrectly inscribed, but despite this, all the men from the Great War have been positively identified and almost all the casualties from World War II are now also known. Yet there are one or two that have proved elusive; A E Stemp who seems to have no service records, and J Brown who could be any one of hundreds of J Browns on record.

This task is not finished, and perhaps it can never be finished, but too many books have remained unwritten because of a few unknown details. To some extent the research has already revealed so much, that some of the stories will have to wait for a second book.

This volume documents the stories of the thirty-four men on the memorial for whom we have photographs.

Above: All Saints Church at the turn of the century.

Below: Looking west along the narrow village High Street circa 1905, the Woolpack Inn on the left.

THE VILLAGE OF BANSTEAD

At the time of the Doomsday Book survey of 1086, the small village of Banstead, situated on the North Downs in the county of Surrey in England, boasted twenty-eight villagers, fifteen cottagers, and seven serfs, as well as one church.

Over eight hundred years later, by the early 1900s, All Saints Church was still at the centre of the village, half-way down the High Street, which by then had a public house at each end; The Victoria Hotel in the west and The Woolpack Inn in the east. Opposite the church, to the north, the ground sloped away to fields commanding a view over London, some fourteen miles away.

The village had the usual compliment of small businesses; a grocer and Post Office, a confectionery shop, a bank, and the local forge where the smithy always kept a scorching hot fire going. By 1914, a new Police Station and a Church Institute had been built on the southern side of the High Street, the latter providing an entertainments venue, a meeting place, and facilities for the local Working Man's Club. A number of smaller roads, whose names will be familiar to residents today, were already in place; Shrubland, Diceland, Ferndale and Lyme Regis to the west of the High Street, Salisbury and Park roads and Sutton Lane to the east. In these roads lived most of the young men of the village who were to fight in the Great War and die for their country.

This photograph shows the eastern end of Banstead High Street in the early 1900s, with The Woolpack Inn on the right and, further on, The Provincial Bank. The confectionery shop can be seen on the left, and beyond it, the forge. In the background is the perimeter wall of Well House, and it was immediately in front of this wall, right in the centre of the picture, that the Banstead War Memorial was to be erected in 1921.

1914

On the eve of the First World War Britain is more prosperous than ever before. Apart from prodigious incomes from banking, insurance and shipping she is still the world's biggest producer of textiles. But rising union power, increasing support for women's suffrage and the threat of civil war in Ireland give the nation a sense of unease. When a Serbian activist shoots dead Archduke Franz Ferdinand of Austria-Hungary in the streets of Sarajevo, our national worries pale in the light of belligerent postures by the leaders of Germany, Austria, Hungary, Serbia, and Russia.

While France knows it has to face up to a German threat of invasion, Britain's 'Great Power' attitude is directly challenged as German troops storm into Belgium on 4 August. This triggers an immediate declaration of war by Britain against an aggressor who expects to be victorious and have its troops 'home by Christmas'.

Our Expeditionary Force joins the fighting in Belgium and the German advance is slowed at Mons. Determined German advances threaten to carry them to Paris. Our success at the Marne leads to halting the invasion of France but this is short-lived. Successive attacks and counter-attacks lead to a race to the sea, but stalemate follows and both sides begin to dig-in. Trench warfare is about to make its entry into the lives of millions of men. The romantic adventure of 'going off to war' is now severely tested. Before the year is out Britain feels the first enemy air raid, albeit by a single German seaplane, and in France, bemused commanders witness a local truce-inspired Christmas Day football match between the Tommies and the Fritzs. It brings to those present some joy but infuriates the High Commands.

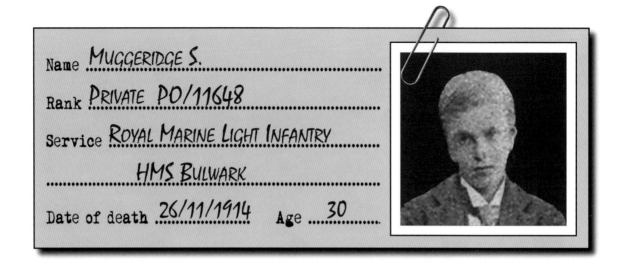

Name MUGGERIDGE S.

Rank PRIVATE PO/11648

Service ROYAL MARINE LIGHT INFANTRY

HMS BULWARK

Date of death 26/11/1914   Age 30

S TEPHEN MUGGERIDGE was the son of Robert and Elizabeth Muggeridge and was born on 1 February 1883 at 1 Sutton Lane, Banstead, where the family lived.

Private Stephen Muggeridge enlisted on the 12 April 1901 and was described as being five feet five inches tall, with a fresh complexion, brown hair and grey eyes. He served with the Royal Marine Light Infantry and over the next thirteen years he worked on many different vessels including the *Duke of Wellington*, the *Illustrious*, and the *Superb*. In November 1914 he was on board HMS *Bulwark*, a battleship of 15,000 tons which was one of the ships forming the 5th Battle Squadron. It was moored in Kethole Reach on the River Medway, almost opposite the town of Sheerness on the Isle of Sheppey in Kent. At 7.30am on 26 November, the ship's usual routine was interrupted by a roaring and rumbling sound, and a huge sheet of flame and debris shot upwards. The ship lifted out of the water and fell back, and this was followed by further explosions and a thick cloud of grey smoke. When the smoke eventually cleared, the *Bulwark* had disappeared, having sunk without trace. Only fourteen men from the ship's complement of approximately 760 men survived that initial explosion.

The ship had been moored on the Medway for some days, and many of her crew had been given leave the previous day. They had returned to the *Bulwark* early that morning, tragically ensuring that everyone was on board at the time of the explosion.

The scene was described by an eye witness, who was aboard another nearby ship:

'I was at breakfast when I heard an explosion, and I went on deck My first impression was that the report was produced by the firing of a salute by one of the ships, but the noise was quite exceptional. When I got on deck I soon saw that something awful had happened. The water and sky were obscured by dense volumes of smoke. We were at once ordered to the scene of the disaster to render what assistance we could.

'At first we could see nothing, but when the smoke cleared a bit we were horrified to find the battleship Bulwark had gone. She seemed to have entirely vanished from sight, but a little later we detected a portion of the huge vessel showing about four feet above water. We kept a vigilant look-out for the unfortunate crew, but only saw two men.

'Boats of all kinds were launched from the nearby ships and shore to pick up survivors and the dead. Work was hampered by the amount of debris which included hammocks,

furniture, boxes and hundreds of mutilated bodies. Fragments of personal items showered down in the streets of Sheerness. Initially fourteen men survived the disaster, but some died later from their injuries. One of the survivors, an able seaman, had a miraculous escape. He said he was on the deck of the Bulwark when the explosion occurred. He was blown into the air, fell clear of the debris and managed to swim to wreckage and keep himself afloat until he was rescued. His injuries were slight.'

At the inquest, the first witness was Lt. Benjamin George Carroll, who was assistant coaling officer at Sheerness. He stated that he was passing down the River Medway on the day in question and saw the *Bulwark* in Kethole Reach. He was looking at a signal she was flying, indicating the amount of coal onboard, when he saw a spurt of flame abaft the after barbette turret. *'Then the flame seemed to rush towards the after funnel and the whole interior of the ship blew into the air and everything seemed on fire.'*

The deposition of Sgt. John Albert Budd, RM, who was still in hospital suffering from burns and a fractured leg, was read out to the court. He said that he was serving on the *Bulwark* at the time of the explosion and had been with her since mobilization. At 7.30am he was finishing his breakfast on the portside second mess deck, when he saw a sudden flash aft. He turned and then the deck seemed to open up under him and he fell down. He recalled coming to the surface of the water and saw the *Bulwark* had disappeared.

All the evidence pointed towards the explosion being internal. A juror wanted to know how the ignition had occurred. The Coroner replied, *'That is precisely what we cannot solve!'* The Coroner, clearly not quite satisfied with the evidence, summed up the findings. He said it was impossible to discover exactly how the ignition was caused. The theory of external explosion could be discounted. If the jury were prepared to endorse the views placed before them, then their duty would be very simple. A verdict

H.M.S. BULWARK. BLOWN UP IN SHEERNESS HARBOUR NOV 26 1914.

of accidental death was returned and the inquiry on the fate of the crew of HMS *Bulwark* was closed.

During January 1915 many more bodies of the *Bulwark's* crew were washed up on the Kent shoreline. The body of Stephen Muggeridge may have been one of these but like so many others, it was never identified. Stephen was the first of the Banstead residents to die in WWI, and his name heads the list on the first panel of the Banstead War Memorial in the High Street.

Peter Whiting, the son of the young curly haired little girl in the photo says *'Stephen was killed long before I was born, but his memory was kept alive in the family long after his death.'*

The page from the All Saints Church book of men who served overseas, shows the entry recording Stephen's death. The second entry down records the service of Stephen's brother, Frederick; his entry, in black ink, indicates that he survived the Great War.

Stephen is shown in this family picture which was taken about 1895. He stands behind his mother, Elizabeth, and looks to be a shy, retiring young man of about twelve. He was the second child of the marriage and stands next to Frederick his older brother. In front of his father, Robert, is George Muggeridge.

Muggeridge, Benjamin.   Well Cottages,
                                      High Street.
Corporal, 19th Middlesex Regiment.
Served in France and Italy.
Muggeridge, Frederick Robert. 1, Sutton Lane.
    Private, R.A.S.C.[M.T.]. Served in France.
Muggeridge, George Albert.   5, Devonshire
    Private, R.A.S.C.[M.T.].   Cottages
Served in Salonica.
Muggeridge, Harold.   High Street.
    L/Corporal, R.A.S.C.   Served in France.
Muggeridge, John.   High Street.
    Rifleman, 12th Rifle Brigade.
    Served in France. (Wounded; prisoner
    of war.)
Muggeridge, Richard.   High Street.
    Private, R.A.S.C.[M.T.]. Served in France.
Muggeridge, Stephen.   Sutton Lane.
    Private, Royal Marine L.I.
    H.M.S. Bulwark.   Killed.

The All Saints Church record of the men of Banstead who served overseas is recorded in a leather bound book entitled *The Names of those of this Parish who served Oversea in the War 1914-1918* . This page shows the two Muggeridge brothers, Frederick and Stephen. Black ink indicates 'survived' and red ink indicates 'died'.

HMS *Bulwark* which had only been commissioned in 1907, was not the only ship that exploded during the early 1900s and throughout the Great War period, seemingly without explanation. Unexplained explosions were also recorded at munition dumps; the cause may have been poor quality control during the manufacturing process, resulting in volatile explosive compounds. The whole process of manufacturing and storing explosives was to become the subject of several official investigations and these must have led to improvements which saved lives. Sadly they came too late for Private Stephen Muggeridge of the Royal Marine Light Infantry, the first Banstead casualty of the Great War.

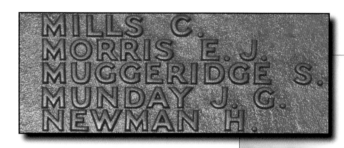

The Muggeridges have a long association with Banstead village, evidenced by the many tombstones with the family name, just to the west of All Saints Church.

Stephen Muggeridge is one of the 10,000 sailors with no known grave, commemorated on the Portsmouth Naval Memorial which is located on Southsea Common overlooking the promenade.

Private Stephen Muggeridge
Portsmouth Naval Memorial
Hampshire
Panel 6

Sources:

Commonwealth War Graves Commission. Naval Historical Collectors and Research Association. Article written by Richard Stacpoole-Ryding/Published by Medal News© September 1991.The full article including the statement by Winston Churchill can be found at HMS Bulwark - NHCRA (Naval Historical Collectors and Research Association) http://www.battleships-cruisers.co.uk/bulwark.htm. Photograph of the Muggeridge family provided by Peter Whiting. Royal Marine Light Infantry Service record from the national Archives. Photographs of Portsmouth Memorial and inscription courtesy of Melissa Channe.

itals/

1915

Attacks by the British Expeditionary Force at Neuve Chapelle lift morale but this is quickly set back by the Germans shock use of poison gas around the Belgian town of Ypres. French troops fall back but Canadian and British hold fast. A see-saw of gains and losses for both sides. A 'shuffling' of commanders brings little relief to the troops.

At sea the U-boat menace is ever-present and neutral shipping becomes a target. On 7 May the British liner *Lusitania* is sunk with the loss of nearly 1200 lives. The USA is shocked at this reckless act but Germans say the liner was munitions-running.

In the air there is some reconnaissance and sparring between the belligerents but the Germans are first to field a fighter aircraft. The zeppelin makes an appearance over East Anglia killing nine in a raid on four towns. The Royal Flying Corps is anxious to get new aircraft to challenge the Germans in the air.

Our seaborne invasion against Turkey in the Dardanelles is a disaster and as a result the main supporter of the attack plan, First Lord of the Admiralty Winston Churchill, resigns. Heavy loss of life, including many Australian and New Zealand troops, forces withdrawal at the end of the year.

Germany's preoccupations with her battles against Russia lead to some quiet periods on the Western Front which aids our training of fresh troops. Allied attacks at Champagne, Artois and Loos, but our casualties worryingly seem always to exceed those of the enemy. French General Joffre's plan to attack towards Vimy Ridge loses impetus due to lack of artillery support, heavy rain and fog. This all adds to inevitable entrenchment by both sides which points towards more prolonged warfare.

Name DAVIS F.G.

Rank PRIVATE 2768

Service LONDON REGIMENT 15TH BATTALION

PRINCE OF WALES'S OWN CIVIL SERVICE RIFLES

Date of death 2/9/1915. Age 21

FREDERICK GEORGE DAVIS was the son of Frederick and Eleanor Davis, of *Dehra Doon*, Lyme Regis Road, Banstead and he attended Sutton County Secondary School from 1905 to 1911. Soon after the outbreak of war he joined the 15th (County of London) Battalion Prince of Wales's Own Civil Service Rifles which moved to billets at Watford in November 1914.

The battalion landed at Le Havre on 18 March 1915 and on 11 May, the formation became the 140th Brigade in the 47th (2nd London) Division. The London Regiment was the largest infantry regiment in the army, initially with twenty-six battalions, but increasing to eighty-eight battalions during the Great War. Unusually, the battalions wore their own individual badges, as the London Regiment was the only one in the army not to have its own badge.

Frederick became batman to an officer, meaning that he was an officer's uniformed servant or orderly, supposedly taken on as a voluntary extra duty, with the officer paying for the service. In addition to his normal duties, Private Davis would have been responsible for the officer's clothing and kit, and probably also for preparing and serving his meals. In the trenches, he would have carried his officer's personal weapon and often acted as a bodyguard, while the officer carried out his duties as a platoon, company or battalion commander. This position of trust often built up a continuing close relationship between officers and their batmen, sometimes putting their own lives at risk to save the other.

Private F G Davis
WWI medal group.
1914/15 Star
The British War Medal
The Victory Medal

This partnership was not to last; on the morning of 2 September Private Frederick Davis was killed by a German shell. He was buried close to where he fell in the little churchyard of Bully Grenay.

LA GUERRE DANS LE NORD
164 GRENAY – L'Eglise

A diary from a soldier in the area at the same time records how *'The Germans shell the villages of Labourse, Bully Grenay, and Mazingarbe every day, and as soon as the guns of the French and English open fire here, they retaliate on the villages.'* These places were industrial areas behind British lines, where coal mining was the predominant activity and where numerous slag heaps called Fosses could be found.

The Grenay Churchyard, was damaged by shellfire and was closed; three graves had to be moved to the cemetery at Maroc – after the Armistice – where Frederick's remains rest to this day. This location was just behind the firing line during the conflict, and during the greater part of the war it was a front-line cemetery used by fighting units and field ambulances, and protected from German observation by a slight rise in the ground.

Private Frederick George Davis
Plot III. D. 13
Maroc British Cemetery
Grenay
France

Sutton County Secondary School WWI Roll of Honour

**Fred Davis is one of the eighty-one men listed on the Old Suttonians' War Memorial
which still hangs proudly at the School.**

Frederick George Davis was the first son in the family to die during WWI; his step-brother
Charles Edward Couchman died two years later, in September 1917. Thus both are listed
on the Banstead War Memorial.

Sources:

Commonwealth War Graves Commission. The Long, Long Trail – The British Army of 1914-1918 for family
historians at www.1914-1918.net/london.htm. Diary entry from The Great War Diary of Cpl Brumfitt Atkinson of
Addingham 26 May 1915 to 15 July 1916. *The Suttonian* magazine from Sutton Grammar School's archives. Issue
no. 33-34 dated November 1915. Photographs of Private Frederick Davis' actual medals, and headstone, kindly
supplied by Michael Huggett. Photograph of Grenay church courtesy of Paul Reed's website. Batman duties from
an article by Iain Kerr.

1916

In February, Germany's plan to bring the French army into battle is launched against the fortified city of Verdun. Huge casualties are suffered on both sides as the struggle goes on throughout the year. The defence of the city is vital to French morale and the Germans apply relentless pressure to force the French to over-commit men and material.

British and German fleets clash in the North Sea off the Danish coast of Jutland. Over 450 warships take part in a furious but inconclusive battle resulting in heavy losses on both sides. However, as a result, the German navy stays in port for the rest of the war.

The British Expeditionary Force yield near Belgium's Vimy Ridge after a bloody battle, but the Allies will be back. On 1 July British and French guns open the battle of the Somme but the week-long shelling of German positions fails badly to prepare the way for Allied infantry. There is a hideous slaughter of men, mown down by an aware and well-equipped enemy. First-day casualties include 20,000 British dead. Before the battle is over, in November, more than one and a quarter million casualties are recorded. The Allies advance five miles.

Our Royal Flying Corps is hard pressed in the early part of the year and it is not until they receive two new fighter aircraft types that the scales are tipped in their favour. Aerial support is provided more regularly and is sorely needed at the battle of the Somme.

Name HUNT G.

Rank PRIVATE 3950

Service THE QUEEN'S

(ROYAL WEST SURREY REGIMENT)

Date of death 19/2/1916. Age 31

GEORGE WILLIAM HUNT was the son of George and Isabella Hunt. He was born in 1884, in the North-West Frontier of India at Nowshera, where his father was a sergeant in the Duke of Wellington's, West Riding Regiment of Foot. On return to England, the family lived in the School Cottage at School Lane, East Clandon. In 1911, George, a carter, married Martha Edith Brackpool who worked as a servant in a house in Back Lane, East Clandon. Later, the family moved to Ferndale Road, Banstead and the photo below shows the terraced houses on the left-hand side of the road, where three generations of the Hunts lived. George and Martha had four children, Edith, William, Albert and Alfred.

Private George Hunt enlisted at Guildford and served with the 1st Battalion of The Queen's Royal West Surrey Regiment, often referred to as The Queen's.

FERNDALE ROAD   BANSTEAD

In early August 1914 The Queen's, then part of the 3rd Brigade, 1st Division, were at camp in Bordon. On 13 August they landed at Le Havre and on 14 November they transferred to 1 Corps. Eight months later, in July 1915, they were transferred to 5th Brigade, 2nd Division and shortly before Christmas that year, they were transferred yet again, this time to the 100th Brigade, 33rd Division.

The Regimental war diary shows the regiment was in the area of Bethune in January 1916, then Annequin la Fosse, and later, Beuvry. The diary records a relatively quiet period with *'ordinary routine'* shown against quite a few days. Other entries record patrolling the trenches and occasional shelling. The enemy line was reported to be very thick and *'unpassable even by a single man'*.

In the first eighteen days of February, a total of six men were killed, and five wounded. On the day that Private George Hunt was killed, the diary records the following:

'Shelling caused at about 10.30am, 600x behind our trenches (front line). Sergt. ARCHER A. H. recommended for bravery and helping mechanic under heavy shell and M.G. [machine-gun] fire....2 killed, 10 wounded.' It was normal practice not to name the lower ranks killed, but it is likely that George Hunt was one of the two men killed on that day.

PRIVATE GEORGE HUNT

This coloured picture has been handed down the generations of the Hunt family and is displayed proudly by his granddaughter Katherine Barnard. It is not known who coloured it, but it remains a precious reminder of a much loved grandfather who has never been forgotten.

The helmet and plume, along with the riding gauntlets all point to George being attached to a mounted unit earlier in his military career.

George is buried in the village of Cambrin at the Military Cemetery 'behind the Mayor's House.' The village was only 800 metres from the front-line trenches and the Military cemetery is often called Cambrin Chateau Cemetery.

George Hunt left a widow, Martha, and four children, Edith, William, Albert and Alfred shown in this old family photograph taken outside their house in Ferndale Road.

Private George Hunt
Cambrin Military Cemetery
Pas de Calais
France
Grave Reference: F7

Sources:
Commonwealth War Graves Commission. Regimental war diary entries from The Queen's Royal Regiment archive. Census details from Ancestry.co.uk. Headstone photograph adapted from an original supplied by the The War Graves Photographic Project. Family pictures supplied by granddaughter Katherine Barnard.

Fact*file*

The small site chosen for the memorial was common land

In March 1919 the Epsom Rural District Council received a letter from Mr Ralph Neville DL JP OBE, of Banstead Place, stating that it was desired to erect a Celtic cross in the village as a memorial to those who had fallen in the 1914-1918 war.

It was thought that unquestionably the best site was the piece of waste land at the east end of the village and the Banstead War Memorial committee hoped that they might have the help and sympathy of the Council. The surveyor reported that the ground was not part of the highway and was planted with laurel and fenced in, and no objection would be raised so long as the monument did not cause an obstruction to the highway.

A year later, on the 11 November 1920, Mr Neville asked for permission to remove the fence and laurel bushes and this was granted.

The memorial was to remain in the same spot for seventy-five years.

Banstead Village.

Taken from Park Road, this photograph shows the High Street veering off to the left and Sutton Lane to the right. The War Memorial replaced the laurel bushes and signpost in the middle of the junction.

Name **BUCKLE A. S.**

Rank **BRIGADIER-GENERAL**

Service **ROYAL ARTILLERY**

17TH DIVISION

Date of death **18/08/1916** Age **47**

ARCHIE STEWART BUCKLE was the son of Archibald Lewis Buckle (Captain, Royal Engineers), and Louisa Catherine Rose who were married in Epsom in 1864. Archie was born in India on 24 November 1868. He was educated at Clifton College and was commissioned in the Royal Artillery on 17 February 1888. At the time of the 1891 census, he was recorded as visiting with Reverend Northey at Woodcote, Epsom, and not long afterwards, he married the Reverend's daughter, Mildred Louisa Northey.

Archie and his battery took part in the Sudan expedition in 1898, and he also fought at the Battle of Omdurman which was the Dervish capital across the river from Khartoum. British forces had superior Lee-Enfield rifles, Maxim machine-guns and gunboats against the swords, spears and single-loading muskets of the Dervishes. On 2 September 1898, the army commanded by General Sir Horatio Kitchener, defeated the army of Abdullah al-Taashi, despite being outnumbered two-to-one by al-Taashi's forces. The Mahdists sustained thousands of casualties at the hands of the artillery, machine-guns and trained soldiers of the British and Egyptian armies, who only lost forty-eight men killed, and took total casualties of less than five hundred.

The engagement was a clear demonstration of the superiority of a highly disciplined European-led army equipped with modern rifles and artillery, over tribesmen with older weapons, and marked the success of British efforts to re-conquer the Sudan. It was here that Archie Buckle earned the Queen's and the Khedive's medals along with the bar for Khartoum. A young cavalry officer wrote at the time:

Khartoum clasp awarded with the Khedive's Sudan medal.

'The white flags [of the Mahdi's army] *were nearly over the crest. In another minute they would become visible to the batteries. Did they realize what would come to meet them? They were in a dense mass, 2,800 yards from the 32nd Field Battery and the gunboats. The ranges were known. It was a matter of machinery . . . About twenty shells struck them in the first minute. Some burst high in the air, others exactly in their faces. Others, again, plunged into the sand, and, exploding, dashed clouds of red dust, splinters, and bullets amid the ranks . . . it was a terrible sight, for as yet they had not hurt us at all, and it seemed an unfair advantage to strike thus cruelly when they could not reply.'*

That cavalry officer was Winston Churchill.

The still below shows the Battle of Omdurman from the film

THE FOUR FEATHERS

A little known fact regarding this film is that the soldiers shown on the firing line in this photo, were actually members of the East Surrey Regiment, who were stationed in the Sudan in 1938, at the time of filming. It is thought that the *'costumes'* used were actually British uniforms left over from Kitchener's expedition some forty years earlier. These had been in storage in Egypt until they were reissued for the production of this film which starred Ralph Richardson.

This illustration is most likely a still from the Classic Films Inc. 1947 re-release of the film. It depicts the Dervishes attacking the British Formation.

In September 1898 when the real Battle of Omdurman took place, Archie Stewart Buckle listed on the Banstead War Memorial was there, along with Winston Churchill.

By the end of September 1898, Archie Buckle was gazetted Captain, and went on to Aden as an instructor of Gunnery. He served all through the South African war, was twice mentioned in Despatches, receiving the Queen's medal with three clasps, and the King's medal with two clasps. For most of this time, Archie's wife Mildred, was left behind to live with her parents.

In 1903 he went to India as captain of a Royal Field Artillery battery, and the following year he returned to England where he graduated at the end of 1905. In January 1906, he went back to India, this time as a major of a battery, which he brought home to England three years later, in January 1909. By this time he had acquired experience and expertise in the issuing and handling of explosives.

From June 1909 until June 1913, he acted as General Staff Officer 1st grade to the General Commanding in South Africa and during this period, Mildred had a son, Archibald Courtenay C. Buckle, who was born in London. Mildred then moved to

Royal Field Artillery Cap badge

Capetown where the family lived in married quarters at *The Castle,* HQ staff, Cape of Good Hope Division. Late in 1913 Archie returned to India to command a Royal Field Artillery battery which he took to the front in 1914. Shortly afterwards, he was promoted Lieutenant-Colonel. In October, Archie Buckle was wounded in the face and invalided home.

Following his recovery, in January 1915, he was made Chief-of-Staff with the 19th (Western) Division, a new army formation. He deployed to France with the Division in July 1915 and helped plan its costly and abortive baptism of fire on 25 September, in the action at Piètre, part of the Battle of Loos. The 19th Division was employed three times on the Somme in July 1916, each time as a holding division.

On 9 August, Buckle was promoted Brigadier-General and posted to 17th (Northern) Division as its Commander, Royal Artillery. The CRA was the senior artillery officer in the division and commanded the regiments of field, anti-aircraft and anti-tank artillery, and provided specialist artillery and offensive support advice to the divisional commander. Buckle arrived in the middle of the battle of Delville Wood. A week after his appointment he was suddenly taken ill and died two days later of meningitis.

Archie spent all of his career in the army and was involved in numerous battles. Despite all these dangerous assignments, and his final battle at the Somme, the enemy were never to be the cause of his death.

Brigadier-General Archie Stewart Buckle was married to Mildred Louisa Northey daughter of the Reverend E W Northey, of Woodcote House Epsom and had one son, Archibald Courtenay Buckle born in May 1909. Archie Stewart Buckle left an estate of £4749 2s 9d, a substantial sum at the time.

Archie Buckle is remembered on no less than three War Memorials. Banstead – where the Buckle family were major land owners – Epsom, where his wife came from and Byfleet. At the time of writing, the connection to Byfleet has yet to be established.

All Saints Church at Banstead, houses the Buckle family vault, but Archie is remembered on his own family headstone in the south-east section of the churchyard. The memorial is in need of some attention and the cross no longer tops the memorial but has been carefully laid against it. The inscription is not clear but is still readable:

ARCHIE

STEWART BUCKLE

THEIR SON

ROYAL FIELD ARTILLERY BRIGADIER GENERAL

BORN 24TH NOVEMBER 1868

DIED 18TH AUGUST 1916 IN FRANCE

BATTLE OF THE SOMME

The Buckle family headstone in All Saints Churchyard.

The inscription is barely legible and the top stone above has been digitally enhanced to reveal Archie's name.

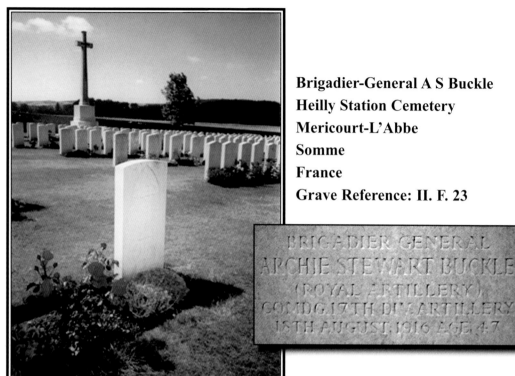

Brigadier-General A S Buckle
Heilly Station Cemetery
Mericourt-L'Abbe
Somme
France
Grave Reference: II. F. 23

As always, the Commonwealth War Graves Commission keep the headstone and cemetery well-maintained and looking at their best and the photograph above shows Archie's headstone in the foreground.

At the time of Archie's death, the cemetery was being used by the 20th Casualty Clearing Station. There are now 2,890 Commonwealth servicemen of the First World War buried or commemorated in this cemetery which also contains eighty-three German graves. The burials in this cemetery were carried out under extreme pressure and many of the graves are either too close together to be marked individually, or they contain multiple burials. Some headstones carry as many as three sets of casualty details.

Archie is one of two Buckles on the Banstead War Memorial, the other being Second Lieutenant Cuthbert Charles Corbett Buckle, a distant relation from the USA. The Buckles have a long association with Banstead starting with Sir Cuthbert Buckle, Lord Mayor of London in 1593, who bought the Great Burgh Estate in 1614.

Sources:

Commonwealth War Graves Commission. Career information from the *Times* obituary dated 28 August 1916 supplied by Clive Gilbert and from 'Lions Led by Donkeys' www.firstworldwar.bham.ac.uk. Edited personal history from the Centre for 1st WW studies. Film still from Edward Garcia www.soldiersofthequeen.com from an album originally owned by William Quinnell. Information about the battle of Omdurman from www.fitzmuseum.cam.ac.uk. Portrait photograph supplied by David Stanley a distant relation. Heilly cemetery photo courtesy of David Collins www.ww1wargraves.co.uk. Personal information from Robert Wildon and Elizabeth Hewson both descendants of Archie Stewart Buckle.

1917

A turbulent yet inconclusive year. Russia's Tsar Nicholas quits and the wind of revolution gathers force. America enters the war. Germany pins her hopes of victory on unrestricted U-boat attacks. This brings serious supply problems to our war effort but the introduction of the convoy system starts to reduce shipping losses.

Agreed plans for a Franco-British offensive on the Western Front are delayed by politicians. Lloyd George's dismay at the cost in lives on the Somme in 1916 is rooted in criticism of Earl Haig, British Commander-in-Chief. The French act and replace their supremo, Joffre. The BEF attacks at Arras as a preliminary to a French offensive on the Aisne. British attacks along their entire front are surpassed by the Canadians at Vimy Ridge. A poorly coordinated attack by the Australians, on the Hindenburg Line around Bullecourt, leads to 2258 casualties out of 3000 officers and men.

Battles at Messines, Ypres and Cambrai bring some successes but at a huge cost in lives. Tanks at last prove their worth. Ground gained is slight and heavy attacks by the Germans, reinforced by troops from the Russian Front, keep our forces pinned down. News that America is entering the war is especially welcomed by the hard-pressed French army. They are beset by some mutinous units and morale is low.

The scale of land fighting promotes increased activity in the air. Germany's von Richthofen commands larger formations over the battlefields but they are challenged by two new outstanding British aircraft, the SE5 and the Sopwith Camel. The allies gain air superiority until the end of the war.

A new star rises in the East – Lawrence of Arabia organises Arab tribesmen against the Turks and they capture the port of Aqaba. Jerusalem falls to British troops at the year's end.

Name .BALDWIN J.H..

Rank ..PRIVATE 231043..

Service ..LONDON REGIMENT..

............ROYAL FUSILIERS 2ND BATTALION...............................

Date of death ...28/2/1917.......... Age ....24............

John Henry Baldwin was the son of Harry and Anna Bella Baldwin, of 3 Devonshire Cottages, Banstead. Three years before the start of WWI, his mother was recorded as the head of the household as his father was an inmate at the Guardians Institution, Dorking Road, Epsom. This institution housed men and women in need, and also had an infirmary for the sick. John Henry was a gardener in Banstead, and his father worked as a cowman on a local farm whilst at the Institution.

John Henry enlisted at Westminster and his secondary regiment is recorded as the London Regiment (Rangers) attached to the 12th Battalion.The Rangers were a Territorial Force unit which existed before the war. Those men who agreed to go overseas on the outbreak of war – not all did – formed the first line battalion, known as the 1/12th London Regiment (The Rangers). Subsequent new recruits and anyone left over from the original battalion in Britain, formed a second line battalion, the 2/12th based in the UK for training purposes, and from this unit, men would have been sent out to replenish losses in the 1/12th. Later, the second line battalions were also sent out, so a third UK based training battalion was formed. Up until the summer of 1916 the drafts of men sent for active service would normally have gone to their own first line battalion but, such were the losses in the first days of the Battle of the Somme, that this policy was abandoned. In the 56th (1st London) Division, of which the 1/12th London Regiment was part, men from the various reserve battalions in the UK were split up across the whole division and some went to completely different divisions. This was a cause for great complaint when men from, say, The Rangers saw drafts from their reserve battalion marching past their billets to join a completely different unit.

Exactly how John Henry Baldwin ended up with the 2nd Battalion Royal Fusiliers is not known, but they landed on the Gallipoli peninsula in Turkey on the 25 April 1915, as part of the invasion force sent out to open up the Dardanelles which is a thirty-eight mile long narrow strait in north-western Turkey, connecting the Aegean Sea to the Sea of Marmara. The regiment was subsequently evacuated to Egypt in January 1916 and landed at Marseilles in March. The following account is taken from one surviving page of the All Saints Banstead Parish Magazine for December 1917:

'Private John Henry Baldwin joined the London Regiment soon after war broke out.
He had from the outset a strenuous experience. He served three months at the

Dardanelles, and saw much terrible fighting, but came through all safely, being one of the force which took part in that skillful but melancholy evacuation. He spent a short time in Egypt and then was sent to France, where he was soon in the thick of it again. In the Battle of the Somme in July 1916 he was wounded and taken prisoner by the Germans.'

John ended up at a Prisoner of War camp called Langensalza, in Thuringia, Germany. Prisoners in this camp were generally expected to work at nearby mines but their lot seems to have been somewhat better than their counterparts in Silesia. When not engaged on mining activities, most of the day was spent trying to find any alternative activity to avoid getting bored, sometimes playing cards or listening to music or both. Prisoners reported that the German sergeant in 1917 was quite amiable and he was often able to provide the prisoners with items they requested.

On Saints' days the prisoners were sometimes taken to the Lutheran church in the village and they were also marched there when their parcels were due to arrive. It is clear that security at the camp was not particularly tight. Another POW, Private Preston who spent some time there recalled how he was able to sneak out into the local woods every Sunday and read a book under cover of the pine forest not far from the camp.

The news of Private Baldwin's death arrived in Banstead via a letter from a fellow prisoner, an Australian. It said, '. . . *the German doctor did all that was possible to relieve his sufferings but he died of disease which evidently he contracted in camp'*.

This was reported in the Parish magazine which finished as follows:

'He has done his duty manfully and has now joined many another hero in the unseen spiritual world, where fighting is no more. May the Risen Prince of Peace give him eternal rest.'

John Henry Baldwin shown here in a photograph retained by the family.

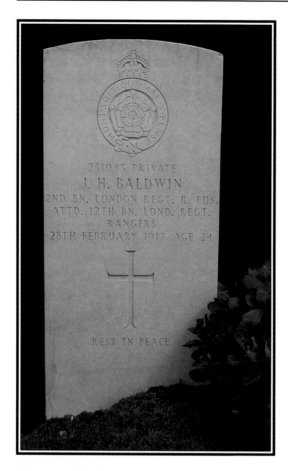

Private John Henry Baldwin
Niederzwehren Cemetery
Kassel
Hessen
Germany
Grave Reference: VI. G. 11

Private Baldwin was initially buried in one of the two cemeteries at Langensalza and it was several years later that his remains were moved to Niederzwehren Cemetery. This cemetery was begun by the Germans in 1915 for the burial of prisoners of war who died at the local camp. During the war almost 3,000 Allied soldiers and civilians, including French, Russian and Commonwealth, were buried there.

In 1922–3 it was decided that the graves of Commonwealth servicemen who had died all over Germany should be brought together into four permanent cemeteries. Niederzwehren was one of those chosen and in the following four years more than 1,500 graves were brought into the cemetery from 190 burial grounds in Baden, Bavaria, Hanover, Hesse and Saxony. Private John Henry Baldwin is one of 1,796 First World War servicemen buried or commemorated in the Commonwealth plot at Niederzwehren.

Sources:

Commonwealth War Graves Commission. All Saints Church Memorial, Banstead, Surrey. Enlistment details from Soldiers Died in The Great War CD. The Rangers – Great War Forum. Headstone photograph adapted from one supplied by The War Grave Photographic Project. All Saints article from All Saints Banstead Parish Magazine dated December 1917. John Henry Baldwin's photograph provided by Edna Touzel. 1911 census.

Fact*file*

The Memorial was unveiled on 5 June 1921

The Banstead War Memorial was unveiled by General Sir Charles Carmichael Monro on Sunday 5 June 1921. The General addressed the gathered crowd and sixty names of men lost were read out. This was followed by The Last Post before the memorial was *'handed over to the care of the schoolchildren for all time'*.

Prayers followed, and afterwards a hymn was sung to the accompaniment of The Banstead Silver Band. There followed a minute's silence and the ceremony ended with one verse of *God Save the King*.

At that time, the names of the fallen were inscribed on the topmost panels of the Memorial. The Union Flag was removed revealing the following inscription:-

THESE MEN OF BANSTEAD FELL IN THE WAR
1914-18

The unveiling ceremony in June 1921

Name .... COUCHMAN C.E. ....

Rank .... PRIVATE 2813 ....

Service .... ROYAL INNISKILLING FUSILIERS ....

.... 2ND BATTALION ....

Date of death .... 26/9/1917 .... Age .... 36 ....

CHARLES EDWARD COUCHMAN was the son of Charles and Eleanor Couchman who were married in 1879, the marriage being registered in Kensington. In 1881 they lived at 22 Neal Street in the parish of St Giles-in-the Fields, Finsbury, Middlesex. Charles senior – who was forty-nine at the time – was employed as a Brewer's servant. Eleanor, was much younger, just twenty-two years old. Charles Edward Couchman was born on the 18 March 1882 in Long Acre in Middlesex, and at the age of nine was still at school, as was his younger brother, Herbert; his older brother William was an errand boy. Their father, now aged fifty-nine, was a storekeeper foreman.

Charles senior died, and his widow Eleanor, married Frederick Davis in 1894. By 1901 they had moved to Park Road Cottage, in Park Road, Banstead, shown in-between the two smaller properties in the photograph below. It is now Grade II listed.

PARK ROAD, BANDSTEAD.

The family included two of Eleanor's children from her first marriage, and another two children that she had with Frederick.

Sometime in the late 1890's Charles Edward Couchman left England and went to live in Ireland. On the 7 June 1904, Charles married Mary Anne Coyle in Ballyshannon in County Donegal. His profession is given as '*Soldier*' and it is very likely that he served with the Royal Inniskilling Fusiliers, an Irish infantry regiment of the British Army, formed in 1881. The regiment recruited mainly from the counties of Donegal, Londonderry, Tyrone and Fermanagh, with its garrison depot located at Omagh. Charles enlisted at Londonderry and his place of residence at the time was recorded as Castlederg, County Tyrone.

By 1911 Charles, then aged 29, was a pedler and is recorded as a Roman Catholic who could read and write. Mary Anne aged 24, was unable to read. The couple now lodging at McKays Court, Castlederg, County Tyrone, had two sons, Charles aged five, and Hugh aged two, both born in County Donegal, and a baby daughter Mary, born in County Tyrone.

By the time their daughter Bridget was born on the 16 January 1916, Charles Edward was again a soldier serving with the 4th Battalion, Inniskilling Fusiliers, which was the extra reserve battalion.

Charles eventually joined the ranks of the 2nd Battalion Inniskilling Fusiliers which became part of 96th Brigade of the 32nd Division in January 1916, and was involved in forcing the German retreat to the Hindenburg Line in March and April 1917. Later the same year, it took part in operations on the Flanders Coast [Flanders is a region located in parts of present-day Belgium, France and The Netherlands. WWI battlefields in this region are most commonly referred to as Flanders fields]. It was during this time that Private Charles Edward Couchman was killed – on the 26 September 1917.

Private Charles Couchman
Coxyde Military Cemetery
Koksijde
West-Vlaanderen
Belgium
Grave Reference: IV. B. 21

Charles Edward was the second son in the family to die during WWI, as his step-brother Frederick George Davis died two years earlier, in September 1915. Thus both brothers are listed on the Banstead War Memorial. Charles' mother, Eleanor, and her husband Frederick Davis, were still in Banstead, but had moved to *Dehra Doon* in Lyme Regis Road.

In June 1917, Commonwealth forces relieved French forces on six kilometres of front line from the sea to a point south of Nieuport (now Nieuwpoort), and held this sector for six months. Coxyde (now Koksijde) was about ten kilometres behind the front line. The village was used for rest billets and was occasionally shelled, but the cemetery, which had been started by French troops, was found to be reasonably safe. It became the most important of the Commonwealth cemeteries on the Belgian coast and was used at night for the burial of the dead brought back from the front.

THEIR NAME LIVETH FOR EVERMORE

Coxyde Military Cemetery

Sources:

Commonwealth War Graves Commission. Portrait photograph courtesy of Des Cronin. Headstone photograph adapted from one supplied by the by The War Graves Photographic Project. All Saints Church WWI record of the local men who served overseas in the Great War.

Fact*file*

To all whom it may concern . . . Greeting

Whereas *a Memorial has now been erected at the east end of the* **Village of Banstead** *to commemorate those Villagers who have given their life for Freedom in the recent war with Germany_____*

And whereas *it is desirable that the said monument shall be carefully preserved for all time in order that each succeeding generation may be inspired by the example of those who have preceded them_____*

And whereas *the children of* **Banstead School** *from time to time are the continuing representatives of each generation to come*

Now we the undersigned do consign into their faithful charge and guardianship the said Memorial_____

And *do solemnly desire and require that they shall carefully, piously and lovingly guard and keep it in good order from one generation to another_____*

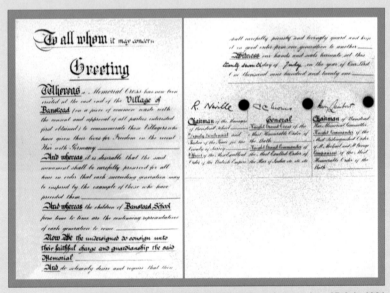

The Memorial schoolchildren's directive witnessed on 27 July 1921

Name	LEE E.
Rank	GUNNER 276904
Service	ROYAL GARRISON ARTILLERY
	114TH HEAVY BATTERY
Date of death	29/12/1917 Age 34

EDWARD LEE was the son of William and Ellen Lee who had seven children. William was a cowman and domestic gardener and in 1891 the family lived at Apsley Cottages in Park Road. Edward, started work as an agricultural labourer when he left school. In 1901, the family lived in Woodmansterne but later moved to Winkworth Cottages in Banstead. In 1911, Edward married Bessie Lock whose family lived at Devonshire Cottages by Garratts Hall, and together they moved to Court House Cottages in Woodmansterne.

Edward enlisted at Kingston-upon-Thames and joined the Royal Garrison Artillery. From 1914, when the service possessed very little heavy artillery, the Royal Garrison Artillery grew into a very large component of the British army. The Heavy Batteries were equipped with guns, capable of firing large calibre high-explosive shells in a fairly flat trajectory. The usual armaments were 60-pounder (5-inch) guns, although some had obsolescent 5-inch howitzers. They were usually positioned some way behind the front line and their power of destruction was immense. Their targets were strongpoints, dumps, stores, roads and railways behind enemy lines. Often they fired at their unseen targets by co-ordinates on a map, calculated using geometry and mathematics. As the war continued, the heavy artillery and the techniques of long-range artillery were significantly improved.

In WWI, the Mk I gun developed in 1904, could fire a 60-pound shell nearly six miles. Weighing 4 tons, this heavyweight piece of military equipment required a team of eight horses to tow it, with a maximum of twelve possible in difficult conditions, and the 114th Heavy Battery is recorded as having four 60-pounder guns.

Whilst the use of heavy artillery was extremely effective, and the guns could be camouflaged in many ways, the act of firing the gun immediately gave away its position, making it a target for enemy fire.

Edward's battery, the 114th Heavy Battery Royal Garrison Artillery went to the Western Front on 3 October 1914 and initially joined the 5th Division before being transferred to the Meerut Division at the end of the month. This was an Indian Division sent to reinforce the British Expeditionary Force fighting in France. The bulk constituted an infantry division as part of the Indian Corps. At the end of 1914 the 114th Heavy Battery was transferred yet again, this time to the 2nd Division. It was attached to several artillery brigades until November 1915, and over the following two years to no less than twelve Heavy Artillery Groups.

The Division then joined XV Corps Heavy Artillery Detachment and 6 Heavy Artillery Group in November 1917, remaining there for the rest of the war.

The exact circumstances of Edward's death are not known, but it seems likely that he was wounded by enemy shelling of his gun position, as records show that he died from wounds on 29 December 1917.

The next of kin of those who lost their lives needed some form of memorial to remember their loved ones by, and just a few months before Edward was killed it was determined that a bronze plaque would be appropriate. The final design would be chosen from those submitted in a public competition, with a prize of £250 for the winner. It was Edward Carter Preston, who designed the 4¾ inches diameter (121 mm) Memorial Plaque, sometimes known as the Death Plaque.

The plaque shows the standing figure of Britannia, classically robed and helmeted, standing facing right, holding a modest laurel wreath crown in her extended left hand and with her right arm and hand, supporting a trident by her right side. To the right of Britannia's head and by the side of her right arm is a small sinuous dolphin, a reference to British sea-power. In the foreground, a male lion stands facing right. The inscription around the edge says – HE [or she] DIED FOR FREEDOM AND HONOUR. In symbolic

confrontation, a lion is depicted pouncing on an eagle at the bottom of the plaque, this being a reference to the desired destruction of the Central Powers. Records at the Imperial War Museum show that there was a concern at the last meeting of the General Committee that the German eagle should not appear too hopelessly humiliated. It was argued that *'the imagery was anticipatory and potentially unhelpful with regard to future, post-war relations'*.

A rectangular panel below the wreath on the plaque, records the name of the casualty, and a technique was used to cast the name into each medallion, rather than having it engraved afterwards.

Over a million were produced, to commemorate the sacrifice of men and women who died between 4 August 1914 and 30 April 1920. Accompanying Edward's Memorial Plaque, was the letter from Buckingham Palace.

Private Edward Lee posing for the typical WWI full-length photograph
(Image digitally enhanced due to poor quality of the original)

The letter from the King:

'I join with my grateful people in sending you this memorial of a brave life given for others in the Great War.'

George R.I.

The original cast held by the Imperial War Museum.

Edward's Memorial Plaque

Gunner Edward Lee

Tincourt New British Cemetery

Somme

France

Grave Reference: IV. C. 13

Sources:

Commonwealth War Graves Commission. All Saints Church Memorial, Banstead, Surrey. http://www.1914-1918.net/heavy-battery-index.htm. Artillery units from Invision zone - Dick Flory. All Saints book of *Men who served Oversea*. Headstone photo adapted from one supplied by The War Graves Photographic Project. Memorial Plaque and photograph of Edward Lee courtesy of Ted Bond. Memorial Plaque information from the website of the Imperial War Museum and photograph of original by permission of The Imperial War Museum HU_053982.

1918

At the start of the year stringent food rationing is introduced at home but the Royal Navy's blockade of German ports is causing severe hardship in the Fatherland.

On the Western Front it seems certain that one side or the other is about to try to impose its will. Mindful of the build-up of American forces, the Germans are the first to move by a series of attacks. Their first, against the British, almost overwhelms them but hurried reinforcements from England help steady the line. A second attack drives the BEF from Passchendaele but again they rally. By the end of May, a third German attack pushes French battle-weary troops back ten miles in one day. Paris, now within the 56-mile range of Big Bertha, Germany's monster gun, is shelled.

Allied forces regroup and fiercely counter-attack, supported by 456 tanks. The Hindenburg Line is breached and the German forces have little more to give. Their President Hindenburg and his Commander-in-Chief Ludendorff foresee a disaster for their army, so send out armistice feelers. They hope to secure a halt in hostilities, giving the Germans time to recover whilst still in control of most of their homeland. The Kaiser flees the country. The German nation is stunned by this turn of events but their troops have had enough and at Kiel some sailors mutiny. An armistice comes on 11 November and the guns fall silent.

'Whites' and 'Reds' fight a bitter civil war in Russia, and the Communists, fearful of a rescue attempt and re-instatement of the Tsar, shoot all the Romanoffs, the Russian Royal Family.

America's President Wilson's peace plan looks leniently at a postwar Germany but does the reaction to it by France and Britain sow the seeds of a future conflict?

Name NASH W.J.

Rank PRIVATE 31863

Service NORTHUMBERLAND FUSILIERS

12/13TH BATTALION

Date of death 27/5/1918.   Age 21

WILLIAM JOHN NASH was the son of William and Elizabeth of 17 Shrubland Road, Banstead. William Nash senior was a coal porter. William John Nash was born in Banstead and had one brother Herbert, and one sister Winifred, both younger than he was. As a young man, William worked as a grocer's assistant at Pushman's grocery store, run by Cherrie, Geoff Pushman's mother. Geoff, then a small child, well remembered Willie. He recalled, *'We had a young man working for us in the shop called Willie Nash. I took to him at once, and he was very fond of me. Most fellows of his age wouldn't have wanted to be seen with a child, but he often wheeled me up the road in my pushchair.'*

Willie used to sing the songs of the day, while weighing up sugar, and taught Geoff all the words. They would both sing whilst doing the little jobs in the shop, like weighing the yellow crystals. One day, Willie announced excitedly that he had bought a gramophone and asked Geoff to go round to his house and see it. How thrilled they both were.

Geoff continues, *'Willie was my first friend and partner in singing comic songs. Two of our speciality numbers were "Hold Your Hand Out, Naughty Boy" and "Hello Hello Who's Your Lady Friend?" '*

When the war broke out in 1914, Willie was one of the first to volunteer. He was only seventeen, but signed up as being eighteen. Initially Willie Nash joined the Army Service Corps as No. 1302. Their initials led them to be known as 'Ally Sloper's Cavalry' based on a popular cartoon character of the time. Despite this, the men of the ASC were the unsung heroes of WWI.

Soldiers cannot fight without food, equipment and ammunition and it was the responsibility of the ASC to ensure that the fighting units received everything they needed. In August 1914 there were 120,000 men at the Western Front (increasing to three million men by November 1918). Willie was no doubt used to serving a few hundred customers in the shop but he had never had to serve over three million pounds (weight) of meat and over four million pounds of bread – every month. This was the job of many thousands of men who served with the ASC, and who transported all the supplies, the majority from a base in England.

Using horses and motor vehicles, railways and waterways, the ASC undertook incredible feats of logistics, and were one of the great strengths of organisation which helped to win the war.

Willie did occasionally get back home on leave and one day he stood against the door as Geoff recalls, they scratched his height on it, so they could check whether he'd grown next time they saw him. He never came back.

Willie had joined the Northumberland Fusiliers as Private 61863 William John Nash. On 27 May 1918, Willie was a member of the 12/13th Northumberland Fusiliers, two battalions which had merged during the previous year. The 27th was the first day of the Third Battle of the Aisne (river) which was a German offensive during WWI that focused on capturing the Chemin des Dames Ridge, before the American Expeditionary Force could arrive in France.

On that morning, the Germans began a bombardment of the Allied front lines with over 4,000 artillery pieces. The British suffered heavy losses, as they had been ordered to mass together in the front trenches, which made them easy artillery targets. There was worse to come as the bombardment was followed by a poison gas drop. A short edited extract from 8th Division 1914–1918, by Lt-Colonel J H Boraston graphically describes the events of the day on which Private William Nash was killed.

'It was one o'clock in the morning of 27 May, punctual to the predicted time, that the German bombardment was loosed. The whole of IX Corps front, and many back areas – railheads, ammunition dumps and the like – were drenched with gas shell. Outpost lines were assailed in addition by trench mortars of every calibre, and the Battle Zone received the terrible bombardment from artillery of all natures.

'Our artillery positions were also violently attacked with gas shell and High Explosives and had area shoots carried out upon them, with the result that by 6am most of our guns North of the river were out of action. A mist which rose into being with the opening of the bombardment, as though evoked at the will of the German Higher Command and in fact accentuated by the enemy's gas and smoke shells, grew steadily thicker as the night proceeded, and made the task of defence additionally difficult.

Private William John Nash

'It was indeed, almost uncanny how in this spring of 1918 the luck of the weather favoured the Germans in attack. On each preceding night spent on the new front, the weather had been clear and when, for the third time, the troops of the division found their defence hampered by a dense blanket of fog, men and officers began firmly to believe that the enemy had discovered means to put down a mist whenever it was wanted.

'Once the gas had lifted the main infantry assault by 17 German Sturmtruppen divisions commenced, led by Crown Prince Wilhelm, son of Kaiser Wilhelm II.'

Taken completely by surprise and with their defences spread thin, the Allies were unable to stop the attack, and the German army advanced through a forty km gap in the Allied lines. Reaching the Aisne in under six hours, the Germans smashed through eight Allied divisions on a line between Reims and Soissons, pushing the Allies back to the river Vesle and gaining an extra fifteen km of territory by nightfall. Private 31863 William John Nash was one of the many men killed on that day.

Willie died at the age of twenty-one. He was very popular locally and well-known to so many people in the village who used Pushman's grocery store. When news of his death reached Banstead, everyone in the shop, as well as all the customers were grief-stricken.

Willie Nash is remembered on the Soissons Memorial, along with almost 4000 officers and men who died during the battles of the Aisne and the Marne, and have no known grave. Names are listed on the memorial by regiments in order of precedence, under the title of each regiment by rank, and under each rank, alphabetically.

Private William John Nash
Soissons Memorial
Aisne
France

Sources:

Commonwealth War Graves Commission. All Saints Church Memorial. All Saints WWI book of *Those Men Who Served Oversea*. A book of poems by Cherrie Almond called *'With Best Wishes'*. Shelagh Jones provided the photograph of Willie Nash. Records of the battle from Invisionzone.com. Details of the ASC from *The Long, Long Trail - The British Army of 1914-1918* - for family historians. Geoff Pushman's recollections from a book called *'Geoff's Banstead'* Royal Army Service Corps record from *Soldiers Died in the Great War* CD.

Fact*file*

The 'White Feather' – a sign of cowardice in World War One

Mr Basil Reynolds wrote to the *Manchester Guardian* 1 September 1914:

'It is announced that a party of foolish women in Folkstone, incited by a retired Admiral who ought to know better, intend to go about the town and present a "white feather" (the emblem of cowardice) to young men lazing on holiday in the neighbourhood.

Now on the question of patriotism I will give way to none, but this form of insanity should be checked at the start, lest other misguided persons follow suit. Doubtless these ladies are able at a glance to distinguish whether a man is married or single, whether he has responsibilities or not, and so avoid gratuitously insulting and publicly branding with cowardice the wrong man. Possibly they are experts in these matters in Folkstone!

But even should the victim be single, by what right are these people to be permitted to judge? Is every young man in the country, however healthy he may look outwardly, fit to pass the army medical test? Those who have tried and failed (nearly 50 per cent) know only to well. And have all single men no responsibility?

What about widowed mothers, families of sisters and little children dependent on them? Is it better for a young man to rush to the front, and leave several behind who, having no resources of their own, will be thrown on the country and charity for the rest of their lives? Is he not doing his duty equally well by working patiently and quietly to keep them as best he may in these days of trouble? Let each do quietly and unostentatiously what little he can to help, or if he can do nothing at least keep quiet, and "judge not, that ye be not judged." '

Source: *Manchester Guardian* dated 2 September 1914

Name HILLMAN J.

Rank PRIVATE G/82083

Service ROYAL FUSILIERS

26TH BATTALION

Date of death 14/7/1918   **Age** 19

JOHN HILLMAN was the son of Alfred and Helen Hillman of Park Farm, Banstead, and he was born on 13 July 1899, at Park Farm Cottages in Holly Lane. His birth certificate shows the name John but he was always called Jack. His father, Alfred, was employed as a carter and ploughman by Mr and Mrs Garton, who owned the Banstead Wood Estate, which included Park Farm and the cottage where the Hillman family lived.

Jack had an elder brother William, and in January 1905 a sister, Helen, was born. All three children attended the village school in Banstead High Street which usually involved a walk along Holly Lane until just past Chipstead Road where they turned right up a path and across the fields which emerged at The Mint public house in Park Road. The route then continued along Park Road until another footpath took them across the village cricket green to the school at the corner of Avenue Road and the High Street.

Helen, or Nellie to Jack, had fond memories of Jack giving her a lift on the crossbar of his bike, part of the way to school. When Jack left school at fourteen, he joined his elder brother William, to work as a gardener at Banstead Place, in Park Road.

Jack was musically gifted; Helen always said that he could get a tune out of anything! He was a choir boy at Banstead Church and helped and encouraged Helen when she struggled to master the violin.

Jack became a member of the Banstead Silver Band, playing the trumpet, and he practised with the band in a barn located in the Court Road area. The early members were described as *'being pretty poor in terms of wealth – but not in playing prowess'*. Most of their engagements were at local fêtes and parks, and they often provided the music for open-air dances at the Lady Neville Recreation Ground.

Jack, aged sixteen in 1915, in his Banstead Silver Band uniform. This photo was taken at Park Farm Cottages. The wall in the background remains in situ, although the dwelling was demolished around 1950.

Jack was a lively and likeable character and according to his sister, popular with the girls. In 1915, his brother William reached the age of enlistment, (18) and off he went to join the East Surrey Regiment.

Jack would not reach eighteen until July 1917 but before that time, a white feather arrived anonymously by post. The white feather was bestowed on *'slackers'* sometimes by chauvinist women in the First World War. The notion of a white feather representing cowardice goes back to the 18th century, arising from the belief that a white feather in the tail of a game bird denoted poor quality. To *'show the white feather'* was therefore to be *'unmanly'*.

Jack was a healthy lively lad and someone evidently thought he was older than he was, and should be in the forces like all the other eligible men. Jack's parents were stunned and saddened the day that he announced he was no coward and had enlisted, months before his 18th birthday, by lying about his age. This was not unusual in WWI.

Jack became a private in the Royal Fusiliers, and the photograph below shows him carrying a trench bugle which he must have been very proud of. His particular battalion also had a band, but of course the battalion had more important work to do at the time. Buglers had more of a practical use on the field of battle, but they were used sparingly in WWI.

A copy of *Trumpet & Bugle Sounds for the Army, with Instructions for the Training of Trumpeters and Buglers*, dated 1914 states that:

'The following trumpet and bugle sounds are to be strictly adhered to on all occasions, and no others used in His Majesty's Service. General Officers Commanding, may at their discretion, order all or any of the peace calls to be used on active service.'

Examples include:

'Continue or Commence Firing'

'Stand Fast or Cease Fire'

'Execute Orders Received'

Bugle calls were sometimes used to inspire the men as they made their attack. It was usual that once their training in England was completed, and they arrived ready for war in France, the bandsmen put away their instruments and became stretcher bearers or riflemen.

Private John Hillman in full uniform including his cap with the Royal Fusiliers cap badge.

It is not known when Jack arrived in France but the likelihood is that it was in March 1918, having travelled from Italy with the Division. A card sent back home before he got to the front shows his full confidence in the ability of the Royal Fusiliers who were attached to the 41st Division.

This Division was comprised of three brigades each of which had four battalions. Jack was attached to the 26th Battalion of the London Fusiliers known as *The Bankers*. Originally this was a large battalion of some 1500 men formed in 1915, and made up of bank clerks and accountants from all over the country. The battalion formed part of the 124th Brigade which operated in the Ypres salient, the scene of much savage fighting where troops sought shelter in underground tunnels when not engaged in an actual attack or defence.

The more elaborate dugouts, as these tunnels were known, were often forty feet deep with a main shaft descending through the layer of blue clay well below the surface.

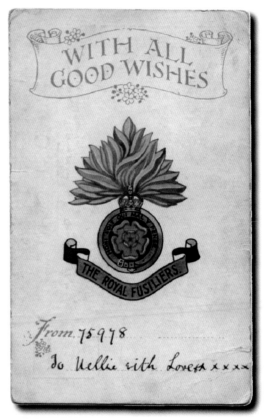

This card was sent to Helen, Jack's sister, and shows the Royal Fusilier's cap badge. The Service number belonged to Private Frederick J Evans.

This is believed to be a short note from Jack.

'Go Boys' were the Canadian Military personnel.

The term *'K,Nuts'* was WWI slang for young men who paid particular attention to their appearance, and was sometimes used to describe young officers.

Other references make mention of *'Knuts'* referring to Kitchener's recruits.

The message is unsigned and undated and rather reflects Jack's rudimentary education.

The blue clay was impermeable to water and was the cause of so much mud on the battlefield, as the heavy rain had nowhere to go. The Royal Engineers built the tunnels below the blue clay and sufficiently deep to avoid damage from the shells of the German heavy guns. Each tunnel had basic sleeping bunks where weary soldiers, probably officers, could get some respite from the dangerous, noisy and wet conditions up above.

Jack made it to his nineteenth birthday on 13 July 1918 but was to die just one day later. He lies buried with over 800 others, at La Clytte Military Cemetery in Belgium.

His parents never saw his grave but amongst the items returned to them was a small pencil sketch of Park Farm, Jack's home in Banstead. It is something he carried with him to remind him of 'HOME, SWEET HOME' and was almost certainly retrieved from his pocket after he was killed.

Jack's brother William survived the war, but not without serious injury. He was gassed at the Somme and returned to England for treatment. He went back to the front where he later suffered serious wounds to his back, and had to have one leg amputated. After months of treatment and the fitting of an artificial limb, he became the caretaker at Banstead Church Institute.

La Clytte Military Cemetery

The area around the hamlet of La Clytte served as the Brigade Headquarters, and the cemetery here was started in November 1914. It is a long strip of land in an exposed position on the crest of a ridge and was used by Infantry, Artillery and Engineering Units for the burial of their dead.

Private John Hillman
La Clytte Military Cemetery
Heuvelland
West-Vlaanderen
Belgium
Grave Reference: IV. F. 12

Sources:

Commonwealth War Graves Commission. All Saints Church Memorial, Banstead. Personal details and photographs contributed by Roy Nicholson, son of Jack's sister, Helen Hillman. Details of Bugler's duties and instructions from a discussion on The Great War Forum. Horn identification by *The Horn Collector*. Photograph of La Clytte Military Cemetery by courtesy of Brent Whittam of www.ww1cemeteries.com

Fact*file*

World War One statistics from the Banstead War Memorial

There are sixty-two names on the Memorial

(D R Baple recorded on a WWI panel was a WWII casualty)

The first died on 26 November 1914

Private Stephen Muggeridge

Royal Marine Light Infantry aged 30

The last died on 13 November 1918

Telegraphist Albert Nash

Royal Naval Volunteer Reserve aged 19

The two youngest were aged sixteen

Corporal Robert Majuba Caselton

The Queen's Royal West Surrey Regiment

Died 17 April 1916

Midshipman George Stephenson Wingrove

Royal Navy

Died 1 January 1915

The oldest was aged forty-seven

Brigadier General Archie Stewart Buckle

Royal Artillery

Died 18 August 1916

Fifty-two died on the Western Front

Name **PATERSON A.S.**

Rank **LIEUTENANT**

Service **DUKE OF CORNWALL'S**

LIGHT INFANTRY 8TH BATTALION

Date of death **2/10/1918** Age **29**

ARTHUR STANLEY PATERSON was the son of Arthur, a publisher, and Kate Paterson of Banstead, Surrey. He was born in Hornsey, Middlesex, in 1889 and attended Edward Alleyn's School, an independent boys school in Dulwich. He married Ethel Harris in 1910, in her hometown of Falmouth in Cornwall, then returned to 5 Biggindale Road, Streatham, where they lived with Arthur's parents and four of Arthur's six siblings. By 1911, when both Arthur and Ethel Elizabeth were aged twenty-two, Arthur had become an assistant schoolmaster.

Arthur and Ethel moved back to Cornwall where they had three children, Robert in 1912, Olive in 1913, and Mary in 1915, all born in Truro where Arthur was Assistant Master at the Cathedral School. WWI intervened, and like many masters at the school, Arthur joined the army, serving with the Duke of Cornwall's Light Infantry.

The 8th (Service) Battalion of the Duke of Cornwall's Light Infantry was formed at Bodmin in September 1914, and was attached to 79th Brigade in 26th Division. It moved to Codford and was in billets in Bath in November 1914 before moving to Sutton Veny in Wiltshire in May 1915. In September of that year, it eventually landed at Boulogne then sailed from Marseilles for the port of Salonika in Greece, in November.

The troops were sent to provide military assistance to the Serbs who had recently been attacked by combined German, Austro-Hungarian, and Bulgarian armies. The intervention came too late to save Serbia, and after a brief winter campaign in severe weather conditions on the Serbian frontier, the Anglo-French forces found themselves back at Salonika.

After preparing the port of Salonika for defence, the troops moved up-country. During 1916, further Allied contingents of Serbian, Italian and Russian troops arrived and offensive operations began. These culminated in the fall of Monastir to Franco-Serb forces during November.

There was a second offensive during the spring of 1917, the British part of which was the First Battle of Doiran in April and May. It made little impression on the Bulgarian defences, the front line remaining more or less static until September 1918, when a third offensive was launched. This time, the British attacked at Doiran for a second time and with a breakthrough by Serbian forces west of the river Vardar, the Bulgarian army was forced into a general retreat. The campaign concluded with the surrender of Bulgaria on 30 September 1918.

Lieut A. S. Paterson
D. C. L. I.
Died of Wounds Oct 2ⁿᵈ 1918

It was just two days later that Lieutenant Arthur Stanley Paterson was killed. The Edward Alleyn Club magazine shows that he '. . . *died of wounds at Salonika. He was wounded and taken prisoner by the Bulgars at Doiran. When the Bulgar retreat became a rout, he was abandoned and suffered greatly. His last hours were comforted by the kind attentions and ministrations of another Old Boy, the Rev E C Hudson,* CF *who also had the sad satisfaction of burying him at Karasouli Military Cemetery.'*

Arthur's brother, Thomas, also joined the army and served in the war as a sapper in the Royal Engineers. He survived, and married a local girl, then moved to *Benavista*, Court Road, Banstead. It was probably Thomas who ensured that his brother was commemorated on the Banstead War Memorial.

Arthur's photograph from an album held by the Alleyn's School archives.

In 1922 the Alleyn's School organ was installed as a memorial to the war dead, and the Honours Boards which include the name of Arthur Stanley Paterson, were unveiled in the Great Hall by Lieutenant-Colonel Kirby VC.

The Commonwealth War Graves Commission uses pedestal grave markers at the Karasouli Military Cemetery in Greece. These are better suited than the more usual white headstone, for protection against the elements, including earthquakes, and ease of maintenance and repair, in remote areas. Arthur's plaque bears a message from his wife, children, mother and father:

'Only good-night beloved not farewell.'

Lieutenant
Arthur Stanley Paterson
Karasouli Military Cemetery
Polikastron
Greece
Grave Reference: D. 838

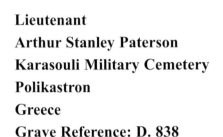

Sources:

Commonwealth War Graves Commission. *Edward Alleyn Magazine* details from www.edwardalleynclub. Salonika Campaign details from The Salonika Campaign Society. Portrait and school hall photographs courtesy of Susannah Schofield of Alleyn's School. Plaque and Cemetery photographs adapted from two supplied by The War Graves Photographic Project.

Fact *file*

World War One statistics – Worldwide

The Great War involved peoples from all over the globe; Russia, France, British Empire, Italy, United States, Japan, Romania, Serbia, Belgium, Greece, Portugal, Montenegro, Germany, Austria-Hungary, Turkey and Bulgaria.

The following figures are generally accepted as the best estimates:

	(millions)
Total Mobilized	65.0
Killed and died	8.5
Wounded	21.2
Prisoners and missing	7.8
Total	37.5

Source : www.spartacus.schoolnet.co.uk

Name SHARMAN C.	
Rank PRIVATE 275240	
Service LONDON REGIMENT	
ROYAL FUSILIERS 3RD BATTALION	
Date of death 15/10/1918 Age 25	

CHARLES SHARMAN was born in Banstead, the son of James and Annie Sharman who had met when James had moved from Suffolk to Banstead. He had lodged in Salisbury Court, next door to Annie Ewins, who was twelve years his junior, and they had married in 1892. James began life in Banstead as a domestic gardener, before becoming the sexton of All Saints Church, gaining responsibility for the maintenance of the church buildings and probably the surrounding graveyard. The couple lived at 2 Salisbury Road where they had nine children. They named their first son James, born in November 1892, and first daughter Annie, born in 1896. Charles was born in between the two on 20 November 1893. The fourth child was Shadrack, born in 1899, followed by Alice in 1900, Nellie in 1901, Gertrude in 1902, Lily in 1904 and finally Winifred born in 1907.

By 1911 Charles was working at a golf club and living at home with his parents and six of his brothers and sisters. His parents and four of his sisters are now buried at All Saints, in the very graveyard once tended by James Sharman.

The family has a large collection of documents from Charles' time in the army and it is clear that he was extremely fond of his sister Annie whom he always called 'Doll'. Throughout his army service from 1914 to 1918 Charlie, as he always signed himself, sent numerous postcards back home to his sister and mother. Doll worked at the post office and grocers known as Tonges, in Banstead High Street, close to The Woolpack Inn and almost opposite the top of Salisbury Road, which, at that time, was a turning off the High Street. Doll and her mother in turn sent letters and parcels to Charlie while he was away on active service.

Charlie and his sister Doll

Many WWI records were destroyed by fire during WWII, and Charles' service history must have been amongst the ones that perished as there are no records for him at the National Archives at Kew. This is unfortunate, as it is clear from other sources that Charles served with at least two different battalions – which have a somewhat complicated relationship – as well as a second regiment.

East Surrey Regiment cap badge

Charles' records show him as:

Private 2765 5th East Surrey Regiment

Private 6847 21st London Regiment (1st Surrey Rifles)

Private 275240 3rd (City of London) Battalion (Royal Fusiliers)

It was not unusual for one man to be transferred from one regiment to another, and since there was no standard army number issued to a man when he joined up, he would be allocated a new number each time he moved to a different unit.

Pre-WWI, territorials signed on to defend the kingdom which meant service in the UK and Ireland only, unless they signed a new contract. The 1/5th East Surreys went off to India, leaving the 2/5th to be used as a recruiting unit as well as home defence. The fractional numbering was used as more men were recruited into the same battalion, i.e. the 5th in this case. The battalion effectively became two battalions, with the first (1/5) going off to fight and the second (2/5), used to accept new recruits. When a unit, not necessarily in the same regiment, needed men, their ranks were increased by drafting replacements from the recruitment units.

One of Charlie's earliest postcards sent from Windsor dated 23 November 1914

'Dear Doll, Many thanks for the handkerchiefs you sent me. I thought you would like this postcard. I wish our dress uniform was going to be like this. I shall not be home this week and so I must dry up, with love from Charlie.'

Charles enlisted at Wimbledon and joined the 2/5th Battalion of the East Surrey Regiment, probably in September 1914, when the battalion was first raised as a home service, second-line unit. In November 1914 the battalion moved to Windsor and became part of 2nd Surrey Brigade, 2nd Home Counties Division. By this time Charles was already sending postcards back home. The fighting in France must have seemed a long way away and the horrors yet to come were far from the mind of the young soldier. Charles, who was in comfortable lodgings with a Mrs Warren-King in Claremont Road, Windsor, wrote, *'We are having a ripping time down here. We went to St George's Chapel, Windsor Castle, yesterday'*. It is no surprise therefore that one of his first postcards was from the *War Cartoons* series. The recruits must have had plenty of time on their hands as the next postcard was dated just three days later. It showed the full history of the East Surrey Regiment, and as usual was addressed to Miss A Sharman, Post Office, Banstead.

In 1915 men who had not volunteered for General Service were transferred to a provisional battalion, leaving the 2/5th composed entirely of General Service men. The battalion moved to Tunbridge Wells in May 1915 and on to billets in Reigate in November of that year.

This photograph, shows Private Sharman (back left) and two colleagues from the East Surrey Regiment

Charles is not wearing an Imperial Service badge and the other two are, which suggests that they went to India with 1/5th Surreys while Charles stayed in England with 2/5th until he was needed in France.

16th Dec 1916

Dear Doll,

Have sent you one of our battalion Christmas cards which I hope you will like. I also thank you for letter and pictorial which I was very pleased to receive, but have not received parcel yet. I hope you are keeping well as I am myself at present. I also hope that you have heard back from Jim [Charles' brother James] *since he has been back. Well Doll, I can find no more to say this time, so I must close.*

Your loving brother

Charlie xxx

Ps I should like another refill please.

Sometime during 1915 Charles joined the 21st Battalion London Regiment (1st Surrey Rifles) as Private 6847 C Sharman. The available records show that Charles must have gone abroad after 1915, as he was not eligible for the 1914-15 Star, or the Territorial Force Medal.

Wherever he was, Charles always remembered his younger sister, and he sent her a special battalion Christmas card that year which incorporated the badge of his new battalion. In July 1916, the battalion transferred to the East Surrey Regiment with the same title. In September that year, another of his postcards shows that Charles was in Le Havre.

A typical example of a WWI silk incorporating flags of Great Britain, Belgium, Swizerland, France, Russia and America. The inclusion of Switzerland is a little strange as that was a neutral country.

Embroidered postcards from WWI are usually referred to as 'Silks'. They were first produced in 1914 and could be found right through the period of the war. They were mostly hand-embroidered on silk mesh and the vast majority were produced by French and Belgian women refugees who worked in their homes and refugee camps. Each strip of silk, often containing as many as twenty-five images, was sent to factories for cutting and mounting on card. Because of their beauty and uniqueness, the WWI Silks were extremely popular with British and American servicemen on duty in France, and for that reason the themes for most of the silks produced were patriotic, often featuring British, French, and American flags, symbols, and greetings.

Most cards could be mailed home at no charge as they were sent using Military Mail pouches. These cards, which were produced in millions, became treasured mementos, and the three examples shown here are only a few of those sent home by Charles.

One of Charles' postcards dated 13 September 1916 from Le Havre shows that he was finally in France. Despite the absence of his records, we can be pretty certain about the time he went into action at the front-line from an extract of the war record of the 21st London Regiment (First Surrey Rifles):

'This was not a time for reflections and our immediate business was to march back to the little village of Millencourt to pick up a draft of three-hundred men from the 2/5th East Surrey Regiment. Refilling and reorganisation proceeded apace and on 27 September [1916] *we marched up to High Wood and bivouacked there in reserve.'*

The name 'High Wood' probably derives from the fact that the wood was at the top of a small hill. The elevation is not that great, but in a relatively flat landscape, height and therefore improved vision, was a tremendous advantage which the Germans, who held the wood in July 1916, were not about to give up easily.

High Wood was the last of the major woods to be captured in the Somme offensive of 1916. The fighting in Mametz Wood and in Delville Wood was hellish, but they were eventually captured as was Trones Wood. And yet, despite a whole series of attacks spanning two months prior to Charles' arrival, High Wood held out until 15 September.

The 21st Londoners were then part of the 47th Division which lost more than 4,500 men before it was relieved by the 1st Division. Just four days after the taking of High Wood, and at one hour's notice, Major-General Barter, commanding the 47th Division, was dismissed by the III Corps Commander, Pulteney, for *'wastage of men'*. The 21st Londoners had gone into battle with nineteen officers and five hundred and fifty men. Only two officers and sixty men now remained, and the draft of three hundred fresh and well trained men from the 2/5th East Surrey Regiment must have been a welcome sight.

Charles soon found himself in the thick of it, as on 7 October, the brigade was ordered back to the front-line, which had advanced some half-a-mile *'since our last show'*. Charles' regiment was expected to capture a position some four hundred yards away but heavy fire and stubborn resistance by the enemy meant that the 21st Londoners had to dig in when only half-way to their objective. The 47th Division, exhausted from heavy fighting and weak from its huge losses, was ordered out of the front-line and by 16 October 1916, it was on its way northwards to the Ypres salient, passing through Boulogne and Calais on the way.

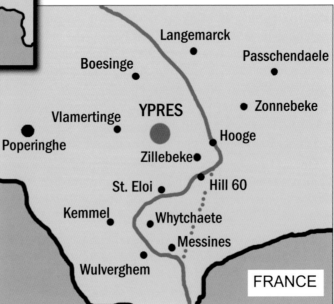

The Ypres salient – a projecting curve in a line of defence – was key to the allies. Ypres was the only major Belgian city not in German hands and had become an important political symbol; if the Germans ever captured Ypres, they would have gained access to the ports on the English Channel, threatening British supply lines.

The solid green line on the map shows the front-line position at midnight on 6 June 1917 and the dotted line indicates the position twenty-four hours later.

The First and Second Battles of Ypres had already taken place in 1914 and 1915, and the 21st Londoners's first encounter with trench warfare in the salient was on 29 October 1916, when they took up their allotted position immediately opposite Hill 60. Fighting was not heavy, and November passed away with little or nothing to vary the dull monotony of trenches or reserve camps. Drainage was a constant problem due to the flat land, and December brought no relief in the depressing weather conditions. New Year's Eve was declared a holiday for the battalion, and feasting on pork, fruits, nuts, and crackers acquired from neighbouring farms and towns such as Poperinghe, was the order of the day.

It was intensely cold and only one water point in the Ypres area remained unfrozen. One soldier even wrote home for his ice skates which arrived in due course!

There was extra training and talk of a 'Spring Offensive'. On the last day of May, the battalion prepared for battle in the knowledge that their next tour on duty would include an attack on a large scale. This engagement was to be the Battle of Messines on 7 June 1917, recognised as one of the most highly organised and successful engagements of WWI.

The battalion war diary records that the men were *'in good spirits and generally in good health'*. Among them was Private Charles Sharman from Banstead.

The men started assembling at 10.00 p.m. on the night of 6 June and had a very early breakfast – at 2.00 a.m. on the 7th. At exactly 3.10 a.m. the battle of Messines and Whytschaete started with the sound of huge explosions, far louder and more destructive than anyone had previously experienced; so huge that they were heard by David Lloyd George, the Prime Minister, in his Downing Street study.

General Plumer had initiated plans to take the Messines Ridge the year before. In preparation for the battle, he had authorised the digging of twenty-two tunnels underneath German lines all along the ridge, his plan being to detonate huge amounts of explosives at zero hour. This was to be followed by infantry attacks to secure the ridge from the surprised and dazed German defenders, the infantry to be heavily supported by artillery bombardments, tanks and the use of gas.

Work on laying the mines began over a year before zero hour on the morning of 7 June 1917. In the face of active German counter-mining, some 8,000 metres of tunnel were constructed under German lines. Occasionally the tunnellers would encounter German counterparts engaged in the same task: underground hand-to-hand fighting would ensue.

When the time came, nineteen of the twenty-two mines were exploded at the same time. The battalion war diary reported, *'Large mines exploded by Hill 60 and St Eloi'*. Records show that the weight of explosives detonated at just these two locations was 123,500 lbs and 95,600 lbs respectively.

That day in June has gone down in history, but Charles had a very personal reason for remembering it well, for it was in action, on that very day, that Private Sharman was shot through the right shoulder. He was treated by the 97th Field Ambulance unit and his injury was recorded as *'gsw shoulder'* – a gunshot wound. Further details were recorded by the Medical Officer as *'T. & T. wd. entering posterior aspect left shoulder and emerging below left clavicle'*. This type of wound, known as a *through-and-through*, indicates that the bullet passed straight through and didn't lodge, so there would be an entry wound and an

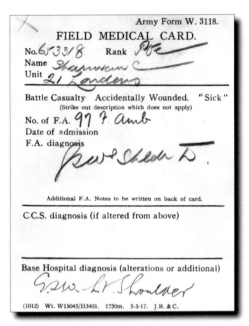

Army Form W. 3118.

FIELD MEDICAL CARD.

No. *6̸5̸3̸3̸1̸8̸*   Rank *Pte*

Name *Sharman C*

Unit *21 Londons*

Battle Casualty   Accidentally Wounded.   "Sick"
(Strike out description which does not apply)

No. of F.A. *97 ¼ amb*

Date of admission

F.A. diagnosis *Gun Shot D.*

Additional F.A. Notes to be written on back of card.

C.C.S. diagnosis (if altered from above)

Base Hospital diagnosis (alterations or additional)
Gsw. Lt. Shoulder

(1012) Wt. W15045/H3401. 1750m. 5-3-17. J.R. & C.

The Field Medical Card recorded the injury sustained by Private Sharman. Intriguingly, the number shown does not match any known service number recorded for Charles.

exit wound and no bullet to extract. The exact circumstances in which Charles was shot are not known, but at times the battalion came under heavy machine-gun fire, and were ordered to withdraw to safer positions. It seems likely, from the nature of the injury, that Charles was retreating at the time he was hit. The Medical Officer would have been more concerned with treating the wound than recording exactly how or where it had happened.

However the injury came about, Charles must have made a good recovery as he was soon back in the field. The 21st Londoners had moved on and it seems that Charles was allocated to the Royal Fusiliers. His time with them was short, as on 26 October 1917 he was captured by the Germans. Charlie recorded a few events in a small notebook, which shows that it only took him three days to get hold of a postcard and send it back home with news of his capture.

He was taken to Dülman Lager Woolf in mid-November, 'lager' being the German word for camp. [Stamm means 'base', hence the abbreviation, Stalag, for base camp, as in Stalag Luft III of the 'Great Escape' fame]. His notebook records that he was able to write a letter home twice a month as well as sending four cards to Banstead in the same period.

He was moved on again, this time to Güstrow in Northern Germany, arriving there on 12 December 1917. Güstrow camp, IX-AK (9th Army Corps area) was situated in pinewoods three miles from the town and was set up as one of the main camps in which prisoners in Germany were registered. Eventually it housed about 10,000 prisoners; French, Belgians, Russians and British. It was guarded by a Landsturm unit from Hessen.

On arrival at a POW camp, soldiers had to strip off and wash, and often never got their own clothes back, especially greatcoats and boots. They were sometimes issued with clogs known as sabots. One soldier, Private Dawson, mentions the sabots in a letter to his mother:

'I can speak of wooden shoes with some authority as I wore them for four months, and I can assure you that to any one who has not been brought up with them, they are an invention of the devil. On frozen ground it is very difficult to keep one's feet and the snow always sticks to the bottom, so that every few yards you must stop and kick it off, on the other hand they are very warm and dry, in fact quite all right if you have not far to walk.'

Thousands of photographs were taken at German POW camps, most sent back home as postcards. Here's one sent by Charles who can be seen seated on the left – notice the footwear.

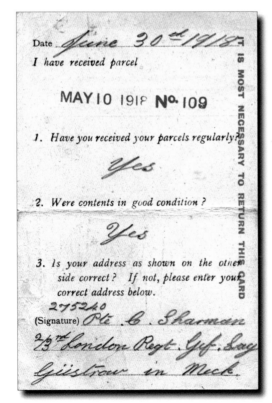

Charles remained at Güstrow for seventeen days before being moved on to Kiel.

It was quite common for photographs to be taken in POW camps, and Charles recorded his photograph being taken in February, and April 1918, having paid *'3 marks 50 phennies'* [phennigs] for the privilege, presumably to the guards. He was able to make such payments as his sister Doll used to send him money orders, for example, one received on 18 January 1918 for 5 marks 79 phennies. He eventually had another source of income, noting that he received his first week's pay on 9 June 1918 at Kiel – *'5 marks 70 phennies'*.

Prisoners received regimental parcels from the Central Prisoners of War Committee at 4 Thurlow Place, London. Each parcel was accompanied by a card which had to be returned to confirm receipt and correct address.

On 4 October 1918 Germany requested a ceasefire. The end of the war was in sight however on 15 October 1918, having been in captivity for nearly a year, Charles died – another victim of WWI to be remembered on the Banstead War Memorial, which was later erected just a couple of hundred yards from the Sharman family home.

Charles had survived four years of war. His mother Annie, and his favourite sister Doll must have been constantly worried about him, and just at the point when there was hope of him returning, his letters and postcards stopped arriving. It is difficult to imagine how distraught they must have felt, knowing that their Charlie had never failed to send them a card, or a letter. They may even have assumed he was on his way back, only to be horribly disappointed when formal notification of Charlie's death was delivered in February 1919.

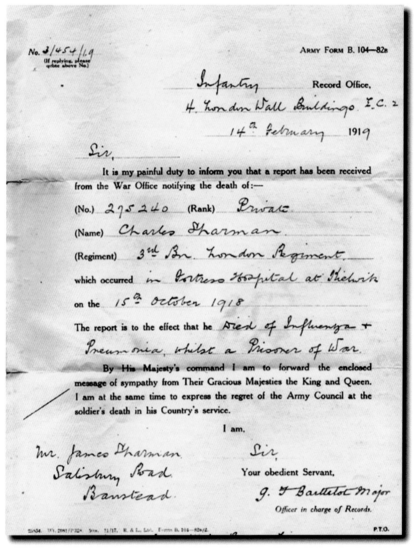

The letter that all parents dreaded, informing Mr and Mrs Sharman of the death of their son.

According to the official notice from the army, Charles died on 15 October 1918 of pneumonia, in the Fortress Hospital at Kiel-wik.

It was to be another fourteen months before the family were advised where Charles had been laid to rest.

The Naval cemetery at Kiel was to be a temporary resting place for Charles, as in 1923, it was decided that the graves of the Commonwealth servicemen who had died across Germany should be brought together into four permanent cemeteries. Hamburg was one of those chosen, and burials were brought into the cemetery from one hundred and twenty burial grounds. The majority of casualties had died as prisoners of war.

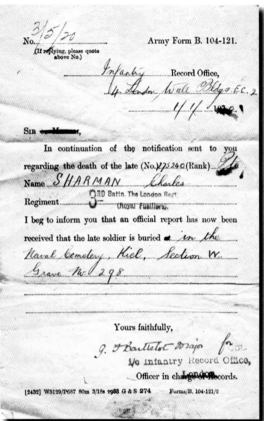

Private 273240 Charles Sharman
Hamburg Cemetery
Germany
Grave Reference: I. E. 12

Charles' headstone incorrectly shows '26th October 1918' as his date of death.

. . THE . .

DAILY ROUTINE

OF A

SOLDIER'S LIFE

TO THE

Titles of Well-known Hymns.

6.30 a.m.	REVEILLE—"*Christians awake.*"	
6.48 a.m.	ROUSE PARADE—"*Art thou weary, art thou languid ?*"	
7.9 a.m.	BREAKFAST—"*Meekly wait and murmur not.*"	
8.15 a.m.	C.O.'S PARADE—"*When he cometh.*"	
11.15 a.m.	SWEDISH DRILL.—"*Here we suffer grief and pain.*"	
1.0 p.m.	DINNER—"*Come, ye thankful people, come.*"	
2.55 p.m.	RIFLE DRILL—"*Go, labour on.*"	
3.15 p.m.	LECTURE BY OFFICER—"*Abide with me.*"	
4.20 p.m.	DISMISS—"*Praise God from whom all blessings flow.*"	
5.0 p.m.	TEA—"*What means this anxious, eager throng ?*"	
6.0 p.m.	FREE FOR THE NIGHT—"*O Lord, how happy we shall be !*"	
6.20 p.m.	OUT OF BOUNDS—"*We may not know, we cannot tell.*"	
10.0 p.m.	LAST POST—"*All are safely gathered in.*"	
10.15 p.m.	LIGHTS OUT—"*Peace, perfect peace.*"	
10.30 p.m.	INSPECTION OF GUARD — "*Sleep on, beloved.*"	

H.W.

One of the documents kept by Doll to remind her of her loving brother Charlie – *"Sleep on Beloved"*

The story of Private Charles Sharman is the last of the WWI stories in this book, but many more men from Banstead took part in the Great War. Some of those who never came back are listed on the Banstead War Memorial or other local memorials, and some are not listed anywhere. Despite that, they should all be remembered. The names of the two young men shown with Charles Sharman in the photograph below are not known, but they are believed to be boyfriends of two of the Sharman sisters. They never came back, and may even be listed on the War Memorial, but we will probably never know.

'Doll', Alice, Nellie and Gertie never married, all losing their pre-war boyfriends over the course of the war. They lived together at De Burgh Park into their old age, and are buried in All Saints Churchyard.

Doll, Annie Elizabeth Sharman, died in January 1981, having kept all of Charlie's documents safe for over sixty years. Thanks to her, and other like-minded relatives of these men of Banstead, their stories can be told, and it is down to each one of us to ensure that their sacrifice on our behalf is never forgotten.

Remember us – we died so young

Sources:

Commonwealth War Graves Commission. Photographs, postcards and documents provided by Jim Sharman, grandson of James, Charles' brother. History of the East Surrey Regiment from Ian E J Chatfield, Curator, Queen's Royal Surrey Regiment Museum, Clandon Park, Guildford. History of WWI 'Silks' from www.ww1-propaganda-cards.com by Paul Hageman and Jerry M. Kosanovich. Details of the 21st Londoners from *A War Record of the 21st London Regiment*.

1939

With the Depression barely a memory and the prospect of two weeks at Butlins's within the reach of the many, 1939 beckons seductively and with much promise. Yet the shadows of Munich are naggingly fresh in many minds. Signs of Civil Defence are everywhere – air raid shelters abound and soon schoolboys are filling sandbags they can barely lift. Many forego those promised holidays as the seemingly relentless march of dictatorships put Europe on trial.

On 1 September Hitler smashes his way into Poland and two days later our fears are confirmed – maybe also our sense of right and wrong. Britain is again at war. Territorials have already left for their units and our Regulars prepare to embark for the mainland of Europe as the British Expeditionary Force. The Royal Navy and the Royal Air Force are poised to expand.

Early action by the RAF showers three million leaflets on the Ruhr, and bombs on the port of Wilhelmshaven. At sea, in September, our aircraft carrier HMS *Courageous* goes down with more than 500 crew; one month later a daring U-boat captain sinks HMS *Royal Oak* in Scapa Flow with the loss of over 800 men. By the end of the year Germany's pocket-battleship, *Admiral Graf Spee*, is heavily damaged by the Royal Navy and is then scuttled outside Montevideo harbour.

As Autumn gives way to winter, British and French patrols cross into Germany's Saar region exchanging sporadic fire with the enemy. Much comfort is felt in reflecting on the huge Maginot Line defences manned by France's great army. At the year's end, what little action there is 'at the front' slows further in heavy snowfalls.

The tank silhouette depicts a Churchill Mk III British tank not available until later in WWII

The peace treaties at the end of WWI resulted in Finland, Estonia, Latvia, Lithuania and Poland gaining independence from Russia. Two new states, Czechoslovakia and Yugoslavia were created largely out of the Austro-Hungarian Empire which was then dissolved, leaving Austria and Hungary as separate countries.

Source: Based on a map from *The Daily Telegraph Illustrated History of the Second World War*

1940

The watch on the Western Front continues amid cold weather and speculation as to the true strength of opposing forces. Many imagine that the troops are to experience what their fathers had suffered in the Great War. U-boat activity is much in evidence and is causing disquiet in Whitehall.

Spring arrives and we immediately learn that the Nazi's plan for Europe has not been put on the shelf. First Denmark and then Norway feel the tread of the German army and it is only a matter of days before WWI's fields of conflict are revisited by the same aggressor. Holland blitzed into submission, Belgium overwhelmed and quick to surrender. The French army, and particularly the BEF, try to stem the irresistible. Three hundred and thirty thousand men are saved from slaughter or captivity by the Royal Navy and the 'little ships', in a mass evacuation from Dunkirk – Operation *Dynamo*.

A new Prime Minister, Winston Churchill reminds the nation, 'Wars are not won by evacuations'; and later, 'Hitler knows he will have to break us in this island or lose the war'. Re-equipping the survivors of the BEF and the biggest ever home defence construction programme are priorities as the UK prepares for a coming invasion.

Now it is the turn of the RAF. In defence of their airfields in South-East England, day-after-day air battles are gallantly fought by 'the few'. A diminishing number of young pilots give 'the Hun a bloody nose' and force a frustrated Luftwaffe to turn its fire on London. Failure to gain control of the skies from the RAF means that Hitler, fearful of an unchallengeable Royal Navy, has to call off his cross-channel plans.

Months of nightly bombing of our towns – The Blitz – brings a momentous year to a close.

Name RICHES L.P. (REVEREND)

Rank CHAPLAIN 4TH CLASS 101549

Service ROYAL ARMY

CHAPLAINS' DEPARTMENT

Date of death 1/6/1940 **Age** 30

LESLIE PHILIP RICHES was the son of Philip and Rosetta Jane Riches née Sturgess. He was born on 27 June 1909 at Northumberland Heath, Erith, and was the oldest of three children. Their mother died in November 1918 when Leslie was just nine years old and their maternal grandparents, James and Sarah Alice Sturgess raised the children.

Theological students dining at Kelham College

At the age of eighteen, Leslie went to Kelham College in Nottinghamshire. This Hall was purchased by the Society of the Sacred Mission in 1903, and was run as a Theological College. Leslie was made a Deacon in 1927 and by 1934 he was ordained as a priest for the Diocese of Sheffield. He became Curate at Mexborough, a town on the outskirts of Doncaster, South Yorkshire, where he was Vicar of St John the Baptist Church, and later Curate of All Saints, Luton, Bedfordshire.

Leslie married Dorothy Evelyn Frances Brown, born in Hertford and just a few months younger than him, at Christ Church, Erith, Kent, on 7 August 1937. At the time of his marriage, Leslie was living in Highfield Road, Luton, and was probably Curate of St Mary's Luton. The couple moved to 39 Sandersfield Road, Banstead, when Leslie became Curate of All Saints Church. He soon became an active member of the Church Institute committee but on 25 October 1939, Leslie joined the Royal Army Chaplains and became Chaplain to the Forces – Territorial Army Reserve of Officers.

SUPPLEMENT TO THE
LONDON GAZETTE,
24 OCTOBER, 1939

25th Oct. 1939:—
Rev. Robert Owen Ailwyn JONES (103401).
Rev. Legh Beauchamp McCARTHY, M.A. (99619).
Rev. Robert MORRIS (101546).
Rev. Cecil MORRISON, M.A. (101168).
Rev. Wilfrid Herbert PARSONS (101547).
Rev. Peter RAWSTHORNE, M.A. (99438).
Rev. Leslie Philip RICHES (101549).

The Reverend Leslie Philip Riches marries Dorothy Evelyn Frances Brown on 7 August 1937

Reverend Riches' new role was the result of an emergency commission which saw him stationed in Portsmouth with Southern Command. The Army Chaplains' Department had been formed some 150 years earlier and received the 'Royal' prefix in February 1919 for its services during World War I when 179 chaplains lost their lives during the war. By that time, chaplains were appointed from various denominations – Anglican, Methodist, Presbyterian, Roman Catholic, as well as Jewish. However, an army chaplain is expected to minister to, and provide pastoral care to any soldier who needs it, no matter their denomination, or faith, or lack of it.

Chaplains are the only British Army officers who do not carry standard officer ranks. They are officially designated Chaplain to the Forces (CF) as in *'The Reverend L P Riches CF'*. They do, however, have grades which equate to the standard ranks, and wear the insignia of the equivalent rank.

Chaplains are usually addressed as 'Padre', never by their nominal military rank:

Chaplain-General (CG) = Major-General

Deputy Chaplain-General (DCG) = Brigadier

Chaplain to the Forces 1st Class (CF1) = Colonel

Chaplain to the Forces 2nd Class (CF2) = Lieutenant-Colonel

Chaplain to the Forces 3rd Class (CF3) = Major

Chaplain to the Forces 4th Class (CF4) = Captain

Leslie Riches was a Captain 4th Class. Despite the army formality, the chaplains are non-combatant, and their work is to sustain, not destroy, hence they carry no arms.

Reverend Riches joined the British Expeditionary Force on 19 January 1940 and was reported *'missing believed drowned'* on casualty list 232, dated 31 May of that year. He was subsequently reported as *'presumed killed in action'* on 1 June 1940. Leslie Riches became one of the ninety-six British army chaplains to die during WWII. His death occured during Operation Dynamo which was the name given to the mass evacuation of British and French soldiers from Dunkirk in France, where they had become cornered. It started on 26 May 1940 and continued through to 4 June. In just this short period, nearly 340,000 British and French soldiers were rescued from the beaches of Dunkirk, by a fleet of hundreds of vessels of every size and shape.

Despite the overall success of the operation, many of the personnel waiting on the beaches, or even in the sea, were killed by low-flying German aircraft strafing the remnants of the British Expeditionary Force. On the beach, over 1,300 nurses dressed the wounded out in the open, and the services of the Royal Army Chaplians must have been stretched to the limit. The BEF lost 68,111 killed, wounded and taken prisoner but 198,229 British and 139,997 French military personnel had been rescued by the fleet of 850 boats.

On the very same day that Reverend Riches died, the New York Times wrote *'So long as the English tongue survives, the word Dunkirk will be spoken with reverence'*.

The Reverend Leslie Philip Riches
Curate of All Saints Banstead
Also remembered on the
Dunkirk Memorial
Column 131.

It takes great courage to go into battle armed only with one's faith and a Bible.

Sources:

Commonwealth War Graves Commission. Personal details and photos from Peter Little, nephew of Reverend Riches. Army Chaplains' history from www.army.mod.uk/chaplains/history. Reverend Riches personal record courtesy of David Blake, curator of the Museum of Army Chaplains. Kelham Theological College photograph adapted from an original by Hans Wild, taken in 1944. Operation Dynamo history and statistics from http://www.historyofwar.org/articles/operation_dynamo.html.

Fact*file*

Banstead War Memorial – World War I – Panel 1 records

NAME	RANK	DATE OF DEATH	CEMETERY/MEMORIAL
MUGGERIDGE Stephen	Private	26/11/1914	Portsmouth England
WINGROVE George Stephenson	Midshipman	01/01/1915	Chatham England
SKELTON Thomas	Lance Corporal	26/01/1915	Menin Gate Belgium
WRIGHT Albert Jessie	Gunner	04/03/1915	Ration Farm France
KNIGHT Stanley Charles	Lieutenant	12/07/1915	Adinkere Belgium
DAVIS Frederick George	Private	02/09/1915	Maroc France
LOW Frederick George	Rifleman	12/09/1915	Loos France
KENNARD Albert Henry	Private	27/09/1915	Loos France
HARDING Harry	Private	01/11/1915	Cambrin France

Name .IVES B.H..

Rank .LEADING SEAMAN P/J 16592............

Service .ROYAL NAVY...............................

.......HM TRAWLER ST ACHILLEUS...........

Date of death ...1/6/1940... Age ....44....

BERTRAM HENRY IVES was the son of Kate Ives, a cook and domestic living at 16 Gloucester Road, Regent's Park. He was born on 23 February 1896 at Queen Charlotte's Hospital in London which was not common, as at that time most births took place at home. Queen Charlotte's was a maternity hospital principally intended for the wives of poor industrious tradesmen, soldiers and sailors, and was unusual as it had been the first hospital to accept single mothers. The father's name is not shown on the birth certificate, and Bertram appears to have simply retained his mother's surname of Ives.

In 1911 Bertram was a wholesale draper's apprentice with J Barker & Co, 63-97 Kensington High Street. This was a vast store selling a huge range of goods, and the owner took every opportunity to acquire the leases and freeholds of adjoining premises. It was destined to become a flagship store for the House of Fraser and only closed as recently as 2005. Back in November 1912 the east section of the main block was devastated by fire

and this incident was probably the cause of a major change of career for Bertram, who at the age of just sixteen joined the navy as a boy entrant. He soon found that the lifestyle suited him well, as two years later, he signed on for a further twelve years.

At the outbreak of WWI Bertram was aboard the HMS *King George V* at Scapa Flow. This ship was built at the Portsmouth Dockyard, and completed two years before the start of the war. In 1915 Bertram was posted to a gunnery school in Portsmouth and later joined the expeditionary force sent to North Russia to assist the White Russians in their struggle against the Bolsheviks during the Russian Civil War. The rather unusual photograph on the left, shows the tallest and shortest seamen in clothing issued for the voyage. Bertram Ives was the tallest, and sent this postcard back home; it is marked March 1919.

Banstead Post Office in 1938 in the same building that still stands there today. Few people will recognise the view down the High Street which would have been very familiar to Bertram Ives prior to WWII.

A year later, Bertram married Evelyn Pope at Kingston and during the following years, he spent much time in the Mediterranean and was away for up to two years at a time. Each time he returned home, he brought back presents as well as bunches of bananas, and oranges. It was a very happy time for his family, as Bertram and Evelyn, living in Kingscroft Road, Banstead, now had four children, Katherine, Felicity, Mavis and Ian.

Bertram retired from the Navy in 1936 and worked as a postman in the village. He and other postmen were called up in 1939, leaving the Post Office with few staff.

Bertram was posted to the Royal Naval Patrol Service aboard an armed Grimsby trawler, the *St Achilleus*. This trawler had been requisitioned for Royal Navy service in August 1939. Trawlers have always had large and clear working decks which were conveniently suitable for depth charge racks, and with the addition of Asdic, and a 4-inch gun up front, they were quickly converted to anti-submarine boats. Asdic, developed through the work

There are no known photographs of HM Trawler St *Achilleus* which was an ASW Trawler similar to the one shown.

of the Anti-submarine Detection Investigation Committee, from which its name is derived, was the main underwater detection device (sonar) used by Allied escorts during the war.

Trawlers were generally used to maintain control of seaward approaches to major harbours. No one knew these waters as well as local fishermen, and the trawler was the ship type these fishermen understood and could operate effectively without further instruction. The Royal Navy maintained a small inventory of trawlers in peacetime, but requisitioned much larger numbers of civilian trawlers in wartime. One trip the *St Achilleus* completed successfully was to Trondheim in Norway, to bring refugees back to England. Inevitably, the trawler was called on to evacuate troops from Dunkirk, and on 31 May 1940, on its third crossing, hit a mine and sank in the Dunkirk area. The reported date of death of Leading Seaman Bertram Ives is the following day.

Edna Touzel, whose father Thomas, took over Bertram Ives' postal round, remembers her dad coming home and saying, *'Ives has gone'*. This news left the post office staff stunned, as he was their first casualty. At that time, it was the custom for postmen to record any monetary gifts given to them at Christmas, and all the postmen agreed that half their collections should go to the family of the postman whose round they had taken over.

One of Bertram's daughters, Felicity, married five years later, in 1945. On her borrowed wedding dress, she added a section of Maltese lace that Bertram had brought back as a souvenir years earlier, from the small island in the middle of the Mediterranean.

Muriel, a young girl who lived around the corner from the Ives family recalled seventy years later how she remembered seeing Bertram Ives for the last time, *'He was on his way to the cinema with his mates, while he was on leave. He was another Banstead man who never came back home'*.

A Maltese lace maker from the period. Bertram liked the delicate hand-made lace from the island of Malta.

Leading Seaman
Bertram Henry Ives
Portsmouth Naval
Memorial
Panel 38, Column 1

Sources:
Commonwealth War Graves Commission. Royal Navy casualty list. Personal details and photographs kindly provided by Mrs Felicity Little, Bertram's daughter. Queen Charlotte's Hospital details from *'A topographical and historical account of the parish of St. Mary-le-Bone'*. Photograph of Portsmouth Naval Memorial panel courtesy of Melissa Channe. Photograph of the Banstead Post Office from the BHRG archives. *St Achilleus* details from the Royal Naval Patrol website. Lace maker image from the collection of Hadrian Wood. Photo of trawler adapted from one on www.uboat.net

Fact*file*

Banstead War Memorial – World War I – Panel 2 records

NAME	RANK	DATE OF DEATH	CEMETERY/MEMORIAL
TONGE Archibald Gervase	Private	20/10/1916	Maroeuil France
WELLER Edwin Albert	Gunner	31/10/1916	Dernancourt France
KING STEVENS Lionel Eustace	Second Lieutenant	20/12/1916	Warlincourt Halte France
SUMNER Stanley S D	Lance Corporal	20/01/1917	Hem Farm France
BALDWIN John Henry	Private	28/02/1917	Niederzwehren Germany
SKELTON Alfred	Private	13/04/1917	St. Sever France
GUEST Allen	Lance Corporal	13/04/1917	Arras France
HARDEN Harry Elbert	Gunner	19/06/1917	Lijssenthoek Belgium
HUNT George	Private	19/02/1916	Cambrin France

Name HOBSON C.A.

Rank PILOT OFFICER 42566

Service ROYAL AIR FORCE

600 SQUADRON

Date of death 3/10/1940   Age 21

COLIN ANTHONY HOBSON was the son of George Colin and May Victoria Hobson née Shuter, of Monxton, Hampshire; he had a sister Olive, and brother Guy. Tony, as he was always called, was educated at Eastbourne College from 1932 through to 1935, and on leaving school worked in a city accountants' office, and subsequently as a clerk in a City stockbrokers' office until 1939. He always enjoyed sports activities especially rugby, rowing and squash.

The family had lived at *Laleham*, Furze Hill, Kingswood, since 1925 but Tony's parents moved to Monxton near Andover, Hampshire, early in the war years. The Hobsons had been in the cutlery business for several generations but neither Tony nor his brother Guy, entered the family firm.

Tony had joined the Territorial Army, enlisting as a gunner in the Royal Horse Artillery, but was discharged in 1939 when he volunteered to join the RAF as aircrew. On 10 May of that year, an RAF Medical Board classified Tony as fit for pilot training, and he was posted to the Civilian Flying School at Redhill in June 1939 for his initial training. In September he moved to No.14 Flying Training School at Kinloss, Scotland, for training on more advanced aircraft, including the twin-engined Airspeed Oxford. By the 3 November he had gained his 'wings'. His course, which he passed with a score of 72 per cent, ended in January 1940 and his final report rated his flying ability 'average'. He had no outstanding faults and *'...he will make a good Officer, with experience'*.

Tony was posted to No.12 Group Pool, at Aston Down, Gloucester, to complete an Operational Training Course. This is where he would have undertaken conversion to the Bristol Blenheim – the aircraft he was to fly operationally once qualified. Following that course, he joined No. 600 'City of London' Fighter Squadron on 3 May at Manston in Kent. The posting to 600 Squadron of the Royal Auxiliary Air Force was more than just chance. The City looked after its own, and the squadron was full of former city workers, financiers, traders, bankers and accountants – so much so that the officers of the squadron were known in the City of London as *'The Gentlemen in Blue'*.

A week after Tony joined the squadron, on 10 May, the Germans invaded France and the Low Countries, and the squadron dispatched six Blenheim Mk1 aircraft to attack Waalhaven Airfield in Rotterdam. Five of the six were shot down by German twin-engined Messerschmitt Bf 110s and seven aircrew killed.

The Hobson family with parents May and Colin, Olive at rear, Guy on mother's knee and Tony with his father.

The raid was ill-conceived and the squadron, which had been working up as a specialist night-fighter squadron since the previous November, was effectively pressed into a daytime ground-attack mission, in which they were required to strafe enemy aircraft on the ground.

It was during the Battle of France that the Bristol Blenheim's weaknesses in the light-bomber role and day-fighter role were revealed. When it entered service before the war, the Blenheim's modern design, in an era when bi-planes were still in service, convinced the Air Staff that it would prove an excellent light bomber, operating in daylight, and surely able to evade enemy fighters. In 1940 the myth was destroyed. Lightly armed and no faster than the latest German fighters, Blenheim losses in that year and into 1941 were disastrous, and the aircraft was soon removed from service in Western Europe.

With France lost, the Royal Air Force prepared to defend the United Kingdom and braced itself for the expected onslaught of the German Luftwaffe.

Although superseded by the Blenheim Mk4 with a redesigned nose, giving more room for the crew and better pilot visibility, 600 Squadron continued to operate both the Mk1 and Mk4. Adaptations for their specialist night-fighting role included the installation of Airborne Interception (AI) radar which although rudimentary, enabled a well-trained crew to find enemy raiders at night. In addition the woefully inadequate armament was supplemented by the installation of an under-fuselage pack of four ·303 (7.7mm) Browning machine-guns. It was using this configuration that Blenheim Mk IFs scored the first AI success against an enemy aircraft on the night of 2-3 July 1940.

On 22 August 600 Squadron moved to Hornchurch, and then on to Redhill on 12 September. By then it was an experienced night-fighter unit, with a reputation as a somewhat elitist and well-connected squadron. This attracted visits by senior RAF officers, all keen to stress the vitally important role that night-fighters were playing in defending the country at night, whilst their colleagues in the day-fighter squadrons, flew their Hurricanes and Spitfires against the Luftwaffe during daylight hours.

In late September 1940, 600 Squadron started to receive Bristol Beaufighters as replacements for its ageing Blenheims. Indeed it was recognised that the Squadron needed to be withdrawn from the South of England to concentrate on training. The move to Catterick in Yorkshire was scheduled for 11 October but in the meantime, patrols continued with both Beaufighters and Blenheims.

Tony Hobson and his crew were never to make the trip north. In the early hours of 3 October 1940, Pilot Officer Hobson and his two crew, Sergeant D A Hughes and AC2 Charles F Cooper, took off from Redhill on an operational patrol, flying Blenheim L4905 (BQ-M). Tony reported to base that one of his engines was experiencing *'irregular running'* but that he intended to continue his patrol. At 0345hrs, at a height of 10,000ft he reported that his engine was unserviceable and that he was returning to Redhill, at the same time, requesting a *'mobile beacon to be switched on'*.

Charles F Cooper

The weather was extremely bad, and in heavy rain, the aircraft ploughed through treetops and crashed on high ground at Broadstone Warren, Forest Row at 0355hrs. All three men were killed, and their Blenheim aircraft was a write-off. As a direct outcome of this accident, the Commanding Officer issued an order that aircraft must not fly below 2000ft until in sight of the airfield.

Pilot Officer Colin Anthony Hobson is included on the Battle of Britain Roll of Honour as he was one of almost 3000 young men – The Few – from Great Britain and overseas,

**This picture shows L8679 BQ-O of 600 Squadron at Redhill in 1940,
a sister aircraft of L4905 BQ-M, the Blenheim that Tony Hobson flew**

pilots and other aircrew, who are officially recognised as having taken part in the Battle of Britain, the qualification being that each flew at least one operational sortie with an eligible unit of the Royal Air Force or Fleet Air Arm during the period 10 July to 31 October 1940.

In the summer of 1940 these men fought and won an historic battle against the German Luftwaffe that is to this day the only battle to have been fought entirely in the air. They came from all walks of life; many were trained and experienced, but most, like Tony, had come from civilian duties to become fighter pilots with RAF Fighter Command. The battle which the Germans thought would be a short prelude before the invasion, lasted almost four months and the dedication, courage and tenacity of those 2,936 men, ensured their eventual success.

Five hundred and forty-four airmen lost their lives during the period of the battle, Colin Anthony Hobson being one of them, the only Battle of Britain pilot listed on the Banstead War Memorial.

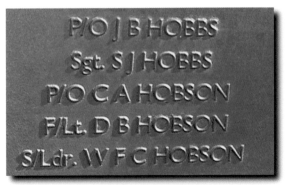

Tony's name on the memorial plaque

The Battle of Britain London Monument on the Victoria Embankment is twenty-five metres long and was unveiled in September 2005. Bronze reliefs, depicting aspects of the battle in the air, and the back-up on the ground, are featured along either side of the sculpture. Bronze plaques listing the names and ranks of the airmen who took part in the Battle, are mounted around

The Battle of Britain London Monument on the Victoria Embankment

the outside of the monument, with the airmen's names grouped under their respective countries. The plaques also incorporate a short description of events, the badges of the RAF squadrons involved, and, facing the RAF Memorial, the Badge of Fighter Command.

The 600 Squadron badge on the Battle of Britain Monument

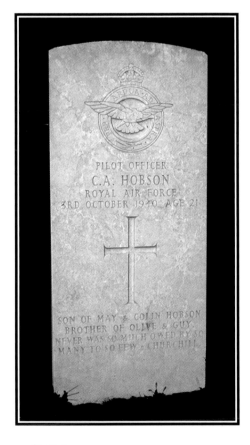

Pilot Officer Colin Anthony Hobson

All Saints Churchyard

Banstead

Grave Reference: west of Church

—— o ——

'NEVER IN THE FIELD OF HUMAN CONFLICT WAS SO MUCH OWED BY SO MANY TO SO FEW.'

Winston Churchill in the House of Commons, 20 August 1940

—— o ——

Note – Tony's inscription is incorrectly shown on the Banstead War Memorial as BA Hobson.

Sources:

Commonwealth War Graves Commission. Roll Of Honour information from RAF Battle of Britain. Crash details from *The Battle of Britain Then and Now* - edited by Winston G Ramsey. Various notes from the Banstead British Legion. Photograph of Pilot Officer Hobson and family photograph courtesy of John Renyard. (John is the son of Olive, Tony's sister). Personal details, service history and memorial photograph supplied by Mike Osborn and his wife, Jennifer, who was Tony's cousin. *Gentlemen in Blue - 600 Squadron* by Hans Onderwater (1997 Leo Cooper). Photograph of 600 Sqn Blenheim from *Camouflage & Markings 2 - For the Battle of Britain (RAF)* - by Paul Lucas, Guideline Publications, Luton, Beds. Details of The Battle of Britain from the Battle of Britain Historical Society. Detail for monument from www.bbm.org.uk.

1941

On the Home Front the blitz continues and clothes rationing is introduced. Before April is out the Germans occupy Bulgaria, Yugoslavia and Greece, and the island of Crete is taken by paratroops. British forces sustain heavy losses.

General Erwin Rommel, is appointed to head Germany's Afrika Korps in support of an ineffective Italian army. They drive British forces out of Libya, North Africa, with the exception of the strategic port of Tobruk which is isolated. Then Rommel is forced back to his 'starting line' and Tobruk is relieved by the year's end.

Hitler, in an order-of-the-day to his troops on 22 June, says 'The battle which is beginning today will decide the fate of the German nation for the next thousand years.' The battle – Operation Barbarossa – is the invasion of Russia. By early December, Leningrad is under siege and German troops are at the gates of Moscow. The all-conquering Wehrmacht expect one more push will see the USSR capitulate, but before the year is out the Russians counter-attack, and the hard winter is not far away.

In spite of our own forces still being short of equipment, we assemble a naval convoy of aid for the Soviets and despatch it via the Arctic Circle to Archangel. Churchill promises Stalin that similar convoys will be sent as regularly as scarce resources will allow.

December brings a turning point in the war as Japan strikes at Pearl Harbor, Hawaii. Within two weeks US President Roosevelt and Churchill reach an historic and far-reaching decision. They agree to pool all military and economic resources to engage in the war – first to defeat Germany, then Japan. Churchill's long-held hope that America would enter the war is fulfilled, though not in a way he could have foretold.

WILLIAM HOBDEN was the son of John and Mary Hobden née Lee, whose marriage was registered in Croydon in the January Quarter of 1913. Mary Lee was the sister of Edward Lee killed on the Western Front in December 1917 during WWI. William who lived in Freedown Lane, Banstead, was one of five children. He attended Sutton County School between 1928 and 1934 and was a very keen member of his House, playing for the football team, acting as captain of the chess team, as well as undertaking the duties of a school prefect. After he left school, William joined the Sutton Branch of Walkers, the jewellers, but left after three years to help his father on the land as a smallholder's assistant. William married Margaret Thomson of Uckfield, Sussex.

In April 1939, with war on the horizon, William joined the Royal Air Force Volunteer Reserve successfully applying for aircrew, and was called up on the outbreak of hostilities. He completed training, receiving his flying brevet in June 1940. He was posted to 37 (Heavy Bomber) Squadron based at RAF Feltwell in Norfolk equipped with the Vickers Wellington Mk1. The squadron had been re-formed three years earlier in April 1937, when 'B' Flight of 214 Squadron was expanded to squadron status, initially equipped with the Handley Page Harrow, but receiving Wellingtons in May 1939.

The Wellington was to prove the mainstay of RAF Bomber Command until the end of 1941 and was considered one of the RAF's most modern types, but its shortcomings in daylight against modern fighter opposition were spectacularly shown early on. Following two abortive anti-shipping strikes, the first being just seven hours after war was declared, 37 Squadron contributed six Wellingtons out of a formation of twenty-two, the others from 9 and 149 Squadrons, to a third raid off the German coast on 18 December 1939. Enemy fighters tore into the formation and their attacks proved devastating. 149 Squadron lost two aircraft, 9 Squadron four aircraft but the loss of no fewer that five of the original six aircraft, resulted in a very subdued Christmas for 37 Squadron.

Wellington attacks off the German coast were banned; the aircraft were retro-fitted with self-sealing fuel tanks and armoured plate, and within months the decision would be made to proceed with the RAF's strategic bomber offensive by night.

The Squadron rapidly gained experience in this new nocturnal role and flew regular missions over north-west Europe; it was during this period that William joined the Squadron. On the night of 20 October 1940, William Hobden flew in one of the seven

Close formation of 37 Squadron Wellingtons over the Middle-East

Wellingtons which attacked the German battleship *Tirpitz* in Wilhelmshaven. On that occasion, no direct hits were reported on the vessel.

In November, 37 Squadron was transferred to the Middle-East. Initial operations were from Malta but by mid-November the squadron was settled in Egypt, based principally at Shallufa.

The Wellington was popular with aircrew due to its ability to absorb considerable damage and yet be able to continue flying, thanks to the design of its framework by Barnes Wallis of Dambuster fame. His geodetic construction, essentially a criss-cross metal structure in the shell of the plane, was immensely strong but light-weight.

The year 1941 was to prove a hard one for the crews of 37 Squadron with the campaign in the Western Desert requiring air support. Long-range missions of ten hours duration were not uncommon, sometimes with two pilots sharing the workload. These often involved the aircraft flying to advanced landing grounds in order to stage their missions. Conditions were basic and very dusty, and deployment to such a base for more than a couple of days resulted in the crews looking distinctly scruffy.

William Hobden was part of an experienced 37 Squadron Wellington bomber crew piloted by Sergeant A T H Gillanders, and was to be heavily involved in operations at the start of 1941. Missions against Hitler's ally, Mussolini, ensured that Italian targets, and targets in North Africa, were the priority in January and February 1941. In particular, Benghazi, which was the centre for the German supply effort within the North African campaign until it was captured on 6 February, and Tobruk. In January 1941, the RAF bombed Naples, and in February attacks on the Italian mainland continued. In the same month Italy invaded Greece, and attacks against Italian targets in occupied Greece now also became part of the RAF's remit in the Mediterranean. On 15 January the squadron attacked Maritza airfield on the island of Rhodes, then moved on to bombing Tobruk in North Africa before returning to Rhodes on the 22 January. Bad weather gave a short respite but in February attacks resumed. The harshness of operating from desert conditions meant that the serviceability of aircraft became a major issue as the abrasive sand played havoc with the engines. Crews were often briefed to fly to their targets over the sea, to avoid the dusty conditions over the land, turning in over the coast at the last possible moment to attack their targets. On 2 February just one aircraft operated against an aerodrome target but had to jettison its bombs after experiencing engine trouble. On 10 February the airfields at Maritza, Calato, Lindos and Kattava were attacked.

Two days later, on 12 February, Sergeant Gillanders' crew left Shallufa for the last time. They were one of six crews which were briefed to fly operations from Greece, based at an airfield at Menidi. A maintenance party of engineers and armourers flew with them in two Bombay transport aircraft. The same night, they attacked airfields at Durrazza and Tirana and on the 14th attacked Rhodes and Scarpanto harbours. The crew of Pilot Officer Wright was lost in Wellington T2821.

Despite the loss of one of the six aircraft the night before, the remaining five aircraft were briefed to attack the airfield at Brindisi on the night of 15 February 1941. Sergeant Gillanders' Wellington T2822-D took off from Menidi with Sergeant William Hobden and the rest of the crew; Sgt W R Green, and Sgt A Flockhart and Sgt McMillan. It is believed to have reached its target where the attack was reported as being successful, but was shot down in the vicinity at about 0455 hours. Three of the crew including William Hobden were killed.

SERVICE AVIATION

MISSING.—Sgt. W. N. Abbott, 903156; Sgt. L. H. Adkins, 755932; Sgt. R. A. Angus, 748062; P/O. E. H. Atkins, 87661; Sgt. T. E. Barnes, A.F.M., 511912; Sgt. D. N. Beal, 745653; Sgt. T. Beckett, 751328; Sgt. A. W. R. Beeden, 552724; Sgt. P. C. Benstead, 800668; Sgt. C. Bourne, 971466; A/C.1 E. Bradbury, 640214; Cpl. F. W. Butler, 529750; Cpl. J. Byrne, 552696; Sgt. H. Cowling, 526616; Sgt. S. Crocombe, 744957; Sgt. G. Crowther, 747813; Sgt. G. Date, 776027; Sgt. J. H. Davies, 565111; A/C.2 J. F. Doublard, 918465; P/O. C. B. Dove, 89060; Cpl. F. J. C. Fife, 330052; Sgt. A. Flockhart, 652082; F/O. R. W. Gair, 36171; Cpl. J. W. Gascoyne, 568753; Sgt. A. T. H. Gillanders, 745285; Sgt. W. A. Griffin, 620429; Sgt. H. T. Hellier, 650067; Sgt. W. Hobden, 745887; P/O. N. Howkins, 86415; Cpl. J. S. Hughes, 540628; Cpl. G. W. Hunt, 567614; Sgt. G. F. Hurworth, 751601; Sgt. E. N. Kelsey, 741557; Act. Flt. Lt. M. J. C. Marks, D.F.C., 72519; P/O. D. A. Maxwell, 84962; Sgt. R. B. Morris, 741251; Sgt. W. D. Morrison, 946356; Cpl. C. J. Murphy, 347359; Sgt. J. Nash, 365515; Sgt. A. H. Paine, 749557; P/O. J. G. Pippet, 86347; Sgt. N. V. Pusey, 580555; Sgt. J. H. Reed, 627136; Cpl. W. R. Salmon, 357144; A/C.2 C. H. Saunter, 918467; Sgt. L. E. Sawyer, 620630; Sgt. H. S. Seward, 902550; Sgt. G. Simpson, 942030; Sqn. Ldr. E. U. G. Solbe, 34090; P/O. D. A. Stanley, 83271; F/O. D. G. A. Stewart, 41624; Sgt. G. C. D. Stowe, 776394; Sgt. D. Strachan, 774065; Sgt. G. Tattersall, 14154; Sgt. H. Teeton, 747731; Sgt. J. Thompson, 526412; Sgt. J. R. H. Webster, 958761; Flt. Sgt. J. J. G. Wells, 4156; P/O. E. T. Wilkinson, 42663; F/O. P. F. Willing, 41090.

Flight Service Aviation newsletter dated 27 March 1941

Royal Air Force Fleet Air Arm news and announcements

This extract shows three of the crew of Vickers Wellington T2822-D reported as missing

Sergeant William Hobden

Sgt (Pilot) Alexander Thomas Holden GILLANDERS - 745285

Sgt (Pilot) William HOBDEN - 745887

Sgt (Wop/Ag) Alfred FLOCKHART - 652082

The other two, Sgt W R Green and Sgt J A McMillan were reported as taken prisoner.

The four surviving crews from the deployment to Menidi returned to Shallufa on the 22nd and were rested from operations for the rest of the month.

Five months to the day after William was killed, his mother, Mary Hobden, wrote to the headmaster of the Sutton County School. She had received a letter from a Wing Commander telling her that it was feared that William had been killed when his aircraft was lost. Mrs Hobden advised the headmaster that she intended to write to the Red Cross in an attempt to get any news from the two captured airmen.

The Suttonian, the magazine of the Sutton County School and the Old Suttonians' Association included Sergeant William Hobden in the Roll of Honour in Issue 114 in December 1941. The piece finishes as follows:

> *'To his widow and baby daughter, to his parents and his family, the Association extends its very sincere sympathy, assuring them that we are all very proud to have known him and to have been associated with one so brave and ready to give all for the sake of his country.'*

It was to be six years later that Mrs Hobden finally learned the location of her husband's last resting place. In a letter dated March 1947, the Casualty Branch of the Air Ministry advised that William and the other two members of the crew had been buried by the Italian Air Force in the cemetery attached to the Brindisi Naval and Air Force Hospital. In order that the graves could be properly cared for, they had been relocated to the Bari Military Cemetery nearby. The three airmen were buried side by side.

William Hobden is listed on the school Roll of Honour which still hangs in the hall as a reminder of the sacrifice made by ex-pupils. He had completed thirty-two missions. Sadly, the name above is that of William's brother, Kenneth Hobden, who was killed in action just nine months later. Their parents, Jack and Mary who had a smallholding at 12 Freedown Lane, off Sutton Lane and alongside Banstead Asylum, ensured that both their sons were remembered on the Banstead War Memorial.

Eventually William's brother Jack married his widow, Margaret. William and Margaret's daughter, Wilma, married another William, by the surname of Ledward, in 1961, and the family still hold the photographs and records from Sergeant Hobden's time in the RAFVR.

Bari Military Cemetery at Carbonara with a view of the Cross of Sacrifice.

Sergeant William Hobden
Bari Military Cemetery
Carbonara
Italy
Collective grave reference:
XI. D. 19-21

William Hobden is one of two Banstead men who flew with 37 Squadron, the other being Peter Denys Parkes.

Sources:

Commonwealth War Graves Commission. *Memories of Wartime Banstead District* a Banstead History Research Group publication. Personal account from Ted Bond, a cousin of the Hobdens. *The Suttonian* magazine from Sutton Grammar School's archives. 37 Squadron background from the BBC's *Peoples War,* RAF website, and *Wise without Eyes (37 Sqn RAF 1939-45)* by Kevin Mears (Hooded Falcon Publications 2005) which also includes the photograph of the Wellington Bombers. Photograph of headstone adapted from one supplied by the War Graves Photographic Project. Extract from the Service Aviation newsletter from the *Flight Global* archive. Service and burial location details supplied by Wilma, daughter of William Hobden.

Fact*file*

Banstead War Memorial – World War I – Panel 3 records

NAME	RANK	DATE OF DEATH	CEMETERY/MEMORIAL
CASELTON Roberts Majuba	Corporal	17/04/1916	Etaples France
EDWARDS George H A	Private	21/04/1916	Dranoutre Belgium
GURNEY Thomas Arthur	Private	07/07/1916	Thiepval France
ARTHUR Henry Bartle Compton	Major	10/08/1916	Gordon Dump France
DANIELS George	Gunner	12/08/1916	Banstead England
BOOBIER Arthur	Private	15/08/1916	St. Sever France
BURBERRY William James	Private	03/09/1916	Thiepval France
STURT Reginald Phillip	Sapper	21/06/1917	Epsom England
WALLIS William Albert	Private	31/07/1917	Ypres Belgium

Name **HOBDEN K.**

Rank **TELEGRAPHIST P/JX 166366**

Service **ROYAL NAVY**

HMS BARHAM

Date of death **25/11/1941**   Age **18**

KENNETH HOBDEN was the son of John and Mary Hobden (née Lee), of 12 Freedown Lane, Banstead. He was the younger brother of William Hobden, also listed on the Banstead War Memorial, and was born in the June quarter of 1923, his birth being registered in Epsom. Kenneth Hobden followed in his brother's footsteps and attended Sutton County School between 1934 and 1939.

In September of 1939 he started his training as a telegraphist with the Royal Navy on the Isle of Man, and did well in his exams, eventually serving on HMS *Queen Elizabeth* in the Middle-East. In 1941, whilst moored in Alexandria Harbour, she was mined by Italian frogmen and grounded in the shallow water. Kenneth then joined the crew of HMS *Barham,* another battleship of the five super-dreadnoughts of the Queen Elizabeth class. The class performed with distinction in WWI but their age was becoming a disadvantage by WWII. HMS *Barham* was also one of the two least-modernized of the class.

HMS BARHAM

William wrote to his mother every week until the 25 November 1941, when HMS *Barham*, having left Sollum, in Egypt, was attacked by a German submarine U-331, commanded by Lieutenant Hans-Dietrich von Tiesenhausen. He evaded the normal defences and fired four torpedoes at the 31,100 ton battleship, from a range of only 750 yards, allowing no time for evasive action. Three torpedoes hit HMS *Barham's* port side causing her to list heavily; fire spread towards the ammunition stores. In under three minutes, the ship rolled over to her port, started to sink quickly, and then suffered a huge explosion leaving two-thirds of those on board dead – over 850 men.

The British Admiralty was immediately notified of the sinking, however it soon became clear that the German High Command did not know that HMS *Barham* had been sunk. The Admiralty took the opportunity to mislead the enemy and to protect British morale, by censoring all news of the incident.

After a delay of several weeks, the Admiralty decided to notify the next of kin, but they added a special request for secrecy. The notification letters included a warning not to discuss the loss of the ship with anyone but close relatives, stating it was most essential that information of the event should not find its way to the enemy until such time as it was announced officially.

By late January 1942, the German High Command had realized HMS *Barham* had been lost and the British Admiralty informed the press on 27 January 1942 explaining the rationale for the news being withheld for so long.

Mrs Hobden wrote to the headmaster at Kenneth's old school and in his reply dated 27 February 1942 he wrote:

'Dear Mrs Hobden,
...I am terribly shocked to have this news.
I have heard bad news of this kind about Old Boys
of the School on so many occasions since the war
began, but I feel particularly sad to hear of Kenneth...'

The instant in which eighteen year old Kenneth Hobden died, was captured in these ten seconds of film.

The Suttonian, the magazine of the Sutton County School and the Old Suttonians' Association, included Kenneth Hobden in the Roll of Honour in Issue 115 in July 1942. The piece finishes as follows:

'We extend our deep sympathy to his parents and family in this, their second bereavement', a reference to Kenneth's brother William, who died in February the same year. Both of Mary Hobden's sons are listed on the school Roll of Honour which still hangs in the school hall as a reminder of the sacrifice made by ex-pupils of the school. Kenneth and William had three other brothers, Jack, Norman and Alfred who had all joined the army but returned home safely.

Brothers William and Kenneth Hobden

Telegraphist Kenneth Hobden
Portsmouth Naval Memorial
Hampshire
Memorial Reference:
Panel 52, Column 3

Sources:

Commonwealth War Graves Commission. *Memories of Wartime Banstead District,* a Banstead History Research Group publication. Personal account from Ted Bond, a cousin of the Hobdens. Photograph of HMS *Barham* courtesy of Mike O'Leary of diving-watch@ntlworld.com. *The Suttonian* magazine and letter to Mrs Hobden from Sutton Grammar School's archives. Sinking details from the HMS Barham Association. The photographs of the sinking of the ship came from the film of one minute and five seconds posted on the internet anonymously, along with the full list of all the men who died, as a tribute to all these victims of war (http://anonymous-generaltopics.blogspot.com/2008/11/hms-barham-04.html). Details of the Admiralty reaction from the website of The sinking of HMS *Barham* by Mike Lynd. Portsmouth Naval Memorial panel courtesy of Melissa Channe.

Fact*file*

Banstead War Memorial – World War I – Panel 4 records

NAME	RANK	DATE OF DEATH	CEMETERY/MEMORIAL
BLUNT George Samuel	Private	03/08/1917	Ypres Belgium
BOWN (incorrectly inscribed as Brown) Victor	Gunner	10/08/1917	Brandhoek Belgium
TAYLOR John William	Private	19/08/1917	White House Belgium
COUCHMAN Charles Edward	Private	26/09/1917	Coxyde Belgium
GATLAND John William	Private	27/10/1917	Artillery Wood Belgium
REYGATE Charles Henry	Private	28/09/1917	Belgian Battery Belgium
PATERSON Arthur Stanley	Lieutenant	02/10/1918	Karasouli Greece
FARLEY William Arthur	Serjeant	13/10/1918	Rocquigny France
NASH George	Private	13/04/1917	Arras France

Name **Excell L. W.**

Rank **Gunner 1799285**

Service **Royal Artillery 433 Battery**
127 Heavy Anti-Aircraft Regiment

Date of death **29/12/1941** Age **19**

LEONARD WILLIAM EXCELL was the son of Albert William and Annie Gertrude née Bowler, who were married in 1918 at Burgh Heath. Albert was a farm worker from Kent until he was injured in an accident and was unable to continue farming. They lived at first in the Maidstone area where Leonard was born, but the growing family moved back to Burgh Heath in the mid-1920s, eventually living at 16 Tattenham Way.

Leonard, or Len as he was known, was the second of five brothers, including Albert, Reginald, Walter George, and Douglas. He was born on 31 December 1921, the same year that the Banstead War Memorial, commemorating the WWI casualties, was unveiled. Prior to joining the Royal Artillery, Len worked as a shop assistant at the Co-op in Rosehill and was engaged to be married.

At the age of nineteen, in August 1941, Len enlisted in Yeovil; his Soldier's Service and Pay Book shows Len as five feet, four and one-half inches tall, weighing one hundred and twenty-six pounds.

He had a fresh complexion with brown hair and brown eyes.

Like most servicemen, Len kept a few small papers in the folder at the back of his service book. One survived and is shown here.

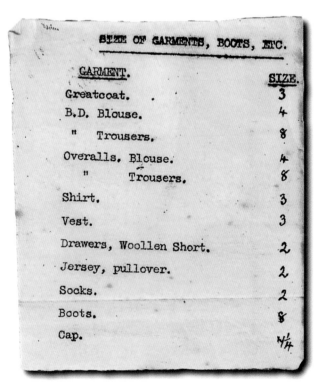

SIZE OF GARMENTS, BOOTS, ETC.	
GARMENT.	**SIZE.**
Greatcoat.	3
B.D. Blouse.	4
" Trousers.	8
Overalls. Blouse.	4
" Trousers.	8
Shirt.	3
Vest.	3
Drawers, Woollen Short.	2
Jersey, pullover.	2
Socks.	2
Boots.	8
Cap.	4½/4

This well-worn piece of paper records the individual items and sizes of Len's clothing issue.

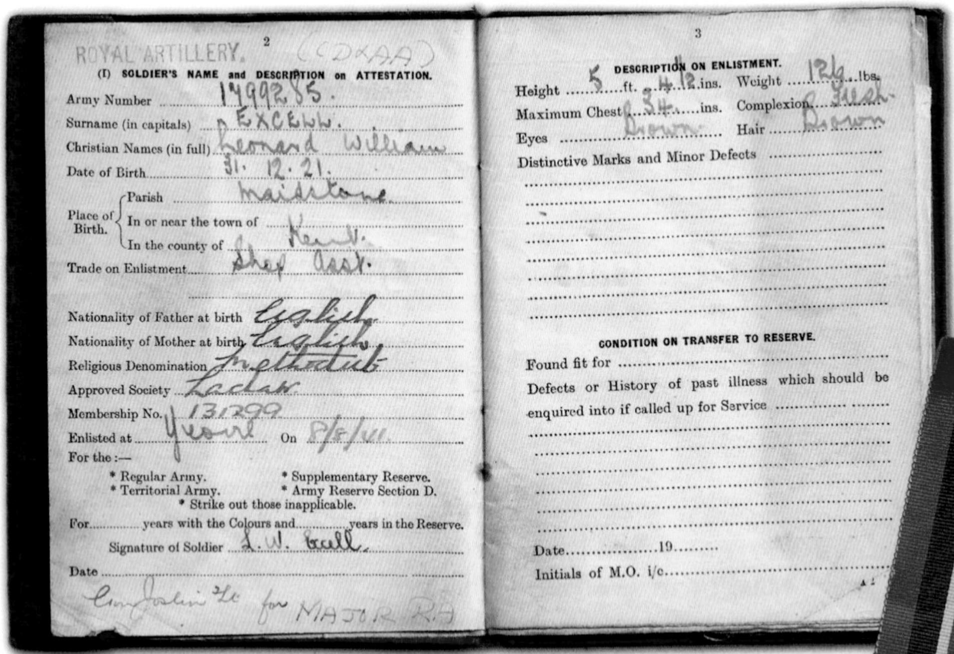

ROYAL ARTILLERY. 2 (CDKAA)

(I) SOLDIER'S NAME and DESCRIPTION on ATTESTATION.

Army Number 1799285.
Surname (in capitals) EXCELL.
Christian Names (in full) Leonard William
Date of Birth 31. 12. 21.
Place of Birth. Parish Maidstone
In or near the town of
In the county of Kent.
Trade on Enlistment Shop Asst.
Nationality of Father at birth English
Nationality of Mother at birth English
Religious Denomination Methodist
Approved Society Ladder
Membership No. 131299
Enlisted at Yeovil On 8/8/41
For the :—
* Regular Army. * Supplementary Reserve.
* Territorial Army. * Army Reserve Section D.
* Strike out those inapplicable.
For .... years with the Colours and .... years in the Reserve.
Signature of Soldier L. W. Excell.
Date ....
for MAJOR R.A.

3

DESCRIPTION ON ENLISTMENT.

Height 5 ft. 4 1/2 ins. Weight 126 lbs.
Maximum Chest 34 ins. Complexion Fresh
Eyes Brown Hair Brown
Distinctive Marks and Minor Defects ....

CONDITION ON TRANSFER TO RESERVE.

Found fit for ....
Defects or History of past illness which should be enquired into if called up for Service ....
Date ....19........
Initials of M.O. i/c........

Len's Soldier's Service and Pay Book

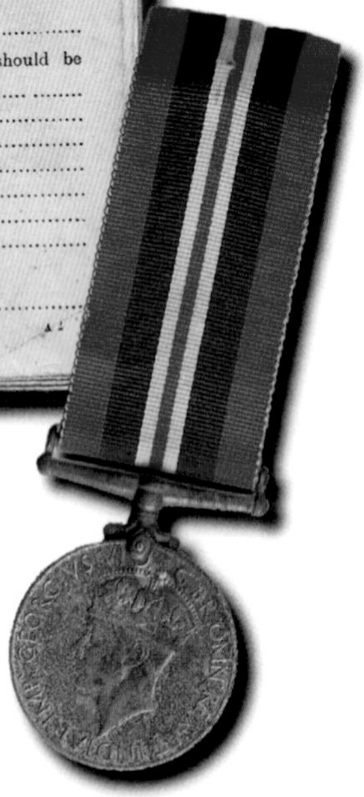

Not long after he joined up, and probably whilst he was still in training, Len contracted spinal meningitis and was admitted to the Billericay isolation hospital. Len was so poorly that an urgent message was sent to Mr Excell via the Metropolitan Police advising that *'...his son, 1799285 Leonard William EXCELL is seriously ill. Would he please attend'*.

Len was eventually discharged and returned home, but the seriousness of his illness caused him to be admitted to Horton Hospital in Epsom, where he died on 29 December 1941, just two days before his 20th birthday.

Len's will, signed in August 1941 on a standard army form designed for *'a soldier desirous of leaving the whole of his Property and Effects to one person,'* shows that Len left everything to his father.

Len's brother, Douglas, has always kept the telegram, bearing the terrible news of his brother's death, along with his medal, and Service and Pay Book, and several other items which remind him of his brother who was lost at such a young age. The family attend the Remembrance Day service at the memorial each year, always remembering the inscription on Len's headstone in Banstead churchyard which reads:

HIS MEMORY IS AS DEAR TO-DAY
AS IN THE HOUR
HE PASSED AWAY

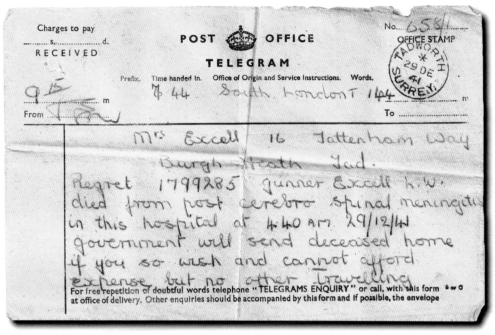

The telegram which brought the news of Len's death

Leonard William Excell
All Saints Churchyard
Banstead
Surrey
Grave location: south of Church
(next to a Yew tree)

Sources:

Commonwealth War Graves Commission. Douglas Excell
(brother) who still lives locally, kindly provided the
photograph, other documents, and medal.

1942

Japanese forces make substantial gains in all regions of the Far East. The Philippines, Dutch East Indies, Bataan, all fall in the early months, including the humiliating surrender of Singapore. Seventy-eight thousand allied prisoners of war in the Philippines are forced on a sixty-five mile 'death march'. The US strike back at Japanese mainland with aircraft-carrier-borne bombers and their navy scores victories in the Coral Sea and at Midway.

In the Mediterranean, the island of Malta is subjected to all-out aerial attack. Attempts to bolster defences with fighter aircraft from Britain end in disaster when almost all are destroyed on landing. Rommel captures Tobruk and drives our army to the outskirts of Cairo and the Suez Canal. General Montgomery is appointed Eighth Army commander and in October it breaks out from El Alamein forcing Rommel to retreat. A combined US and British venture, Operation Torch, lands troops on the North African coast; the Germans there now have to fight on two fronts.

Hitler's reign of terror adds another atrocity when, on the Fuhrer's direct order, the Czechoslovakian village of Lidice is obliterated as a reprisal for the assassination of Reinhard Heydrich, Nazi Deputy Protector of Bohemia and Moravia. All men of the village are shot and the women and children sent to Ravensbruck concentration camp.

A disastrous raid on the French occupied coast at Dieppe causes heavy casualties and shows how difficult a future invasion might be.

Tragic losses in Convoy PQ-17 to Russia add up to 23 merchant ships, 430 tanks, 210 aircraft, 3350 vehicles and 100,000 tons of cargo being sunk. Fighting at Stalingrad reaches a turning point and a German relief attempt fails to reach their trapped 6th Army.

Name .. **BAPLE D. R.** ....

Rank **SECOND LIEUTENANT** ....

Service ...**1ST PUNJAB REGIMENT** ....

...............**6TH BATTALION** ....

Date of death ...**15/2/1942**. Age .....**22**.......

DOUGLAS ROY BAPLE was the son of William and Mary Baple née Cole, of Banstead. Roy, as he was known to his friends and family, was born in late 1919 at St Thomas in Devon. He had a sister, Muriel, and an older brother, Philip Jack – known as Jack. The family came from Torquay and moved to Dorking before settling in Banstead in 1940. William Baple, Roy's father, was the headmaster of Banstead Hall Approved School, pictured below, run by Surrey County Council from 1936. Roy attended St Paul's Church in Nork, every Sunday, together with other local boys who went to his school. He was always a keen sportsman, and after leaving school he worked at a branch of the National Provincial Bank, in London.

Roy served with the Indian 1st Punjab Regiment; during WWII, the Indian Army was the biggest ever raised without conscription and its best troops included well-trained and excellent fighting men. Perhaps surprisingly, most of the men, including many of the higher ranks, did not fully understand what they were fighting for, and it was mostly regimental

Banstead Hall

tradition and affection for the British which saw them triumph on the battlefield on numerous occasions. It was here that British and Indian became comrades like nowhere else.

The 6th Battalion of the 1st Punjab Regiment was raised in Benares in August 1940. In 1942 Roy was with them in Singapore when on 8 February, the Japanese crossed the Johore Straits in strength, landing at the mouth of the Kranji River within two miles of the place where the war cemetery now stands. On the evening of 9 February, they launched an attack between the river and the causeway.

During the next few days fierce fighting ensued, in many cases hand-to-hand, until the greatly superior numbers and air strength of the Japanese necessitated a withdrawal. The 1st Punjab Regiment 6th Battalion was captured by the Japanese on 15 February 1942, the day when the British had little option but to surrender, and it was on this day that Second Lieutenant Douglas Roy Baple was killed. The fall of Singapore to the Japanese army is considered to be one of the greatest defeats in the history of the British Army and probably Britain's worst defeat in WWII. The attack on Singapore demonstrated the way Japan was to fight, using a combination of speed and savagery. As the Japanese attacked through the Peninsula, their troops were ordered to take no prisoners as they would slow up the Japanese advance.

Following the surrender, the Japanese did take about 100,000 men as prisoners. Nine thousand of these men died building the Burma-Thailand railway. The people of Singapore fared worse. Many were of Chinese origin and were slaughtered by the Japanese.

Winston Churchill had stated before the final Japanese attack:

'There must be no thought of sparing the troops or population; commanders and senior officers should die with their troops. The honour of the British Empire and the British Army is at stake.'

Many brave men like Roy Baple died defending this honour.

Roy and his sister Muriel

Roy's name is recorded on the Roll of Honour at St Paul's Church in Nork, as well as the one at Dorking County Grammar School now known as The Ashcombe School.

Roy also has the distinction of being the only WWII casualty inscribed on a WWI panel on the Banstead War Memorial. His name was added years after the rest and, as the memorial gives no indication of which panels relate to which war, the stonemason simply picked the last space on one of the top panels which are all WWI panels.

Second Lieutenant
Douglas Roy Baple
Kranji War Cemetery
Singapore
Grave Reference: 12. A. 18

Sources:

Commonwealth War Graves Commission. Photo of Banstead Hall, personal history and photographs provided by Muriel Baple. Regimental detail from *The First Punjabs - History of the 1st Punjab Regiments 1759 to 1956* by Philip Mason. Events in Singapore from The History learning site. Headstone and Kranji Cemetery photographs adapted from images supplied by the War Graves Photographic Project. Geoffrey Robinson (BHRG) initially explained the inscription discrepancy.

Fact*file*

Banstead War Memorial – World War I – Panel 5 records

NAME	RANK	DATE OF DEATH	CEMETERY/MEMORIAL
BALCHIN Aubrey Alfred William	Rifleman	14/10/1918	Lievin France
BLUNT Percy	Private	17/10/1918	Beirut Lebanese Republic
SHARMAN Charles	Private	15/10/1918	Hamburg Germany
REYGATE Sidney	Private	30/10/1917	Ypres Belgium
LEE Edward	Gunner	29/12/1917	Tincourt France
BAILEY John David	Serjeant	9/01/1918	Banstead England
SOPP Eddie	Private	11/04/1918	Ste. Marie France
CURTIS Arthur	Private	24/04/1917	Arras France
WATERS Albert	Corporal	22/09/1917	Tyne Cot Belgium

ERIC NORMAN GRIMWOOD was the son of Frederick Grimwood and Edith Mary Minton who were married in 1906. During the next sixteen years they had six children. The first was Frederick William born in 1908, then Winifred in 1911, followed by Jessie in 1913, Olive in 1916 and Leonard in 1920. Eric Norman Grimwood was the youngest, and was born in early 1922 at St Olave, Southwark. By the mid-1940s the family had moved to 40 Waterer Gardens, Burgh Heath.

With the outbreak of war, Eric volunteered to join the RAF as aircrew, and as a Volunteer Reservist, signed up for *'the duration of hostilities'*. Eric was selected as a Wireless Operator and Air Gunner, completing his training on 18 September 1941.

On this date Sergeant 1183176 Eric Norman Grimwood was posted from 25 OTU (Operational Training Unit) based at RAF Finningley, South Yorkshire, to 97 Squadron, RAF Bomber Command, based at RAF Coningsby in Lincolnshire.

The squadron was equipped with the Avro Manchester, the twin-engined predecessor to the famous Lancaster. The Manchester was an advanced design, but a notoriously unreliable aircraft, due mainly to the complexities of its Rolls-Royce Vulture engines. The design flaws of the Vulture were never satisfactorily addressed and the operational career of the Manchester was blighted by poor performance and engine failure.

After receiving their Manchesters in February 1941, 97 Squadron, began operations against 'Fortress Europe' in March 1941, in what were the earliest days of the strategic bombing offensive.

It was into this hard-fought and dangerous campaign that Eric would be introduced that September. His role was almost exclusively that of a Wireless Operator, but Eric was also trained as an air-gunner, able to take over either the mid-upper, or tail turret should something happen to one of the specialist gunners.

Eric Grimwood was assigned to fly with the crew of Flight Lieutenant Coton. Other members of the crew included, Pilot Officer Maltby, Pilot Officer Boddington, Sergeants Watkins, Newell and McMahon. The crew regularly flew Manchester, L7489, which had been delivered to 97 Squadron just four days before Eric arrived. The aircraft bore the squadron codes 'OF' and the individual letter 'T', inevitably becoming known as OF-T 'Tommy'.

Sergeant Eric Grimwood flew on many night bombing operations in this aircraft during 1941/2, initially with the same crew, and these were recorded in the squadron Operational Record Book (ORB).

At the end of October 1941 the crew's first target was Kiel, one of the major naval bases and shipbuilding centres of the German Reich and heavily defended with anti-aircraft guns.

Just three nights later, they took T-Tommy to Hamburg. This time the target was the main railway station where they dropped one 4000lb, and two 500lb bombs from 12,000 feet.

An embroidered brevet from a
97 Squadron air gunner

It was Hamburg again a few nights later, with the Blohm and Voss shipyards as the key targets. Although some seventy-five miles from the sea, Hamburg is located at the confluence of two rivers, the Alster and the Elbe. The city's harbour, rivalling London and Rotterdam, is located well inland, yet easily accessible to large shipping, and this would result in the city and its shipyards being visited many times by the RAF during WWII.

Disruption of Germany's industry was a key objective of Bomber Command, and Cologne, an industrial and commercial port in North Rhine-Westphalia, on the banks of the Rhine, was one of the targets in November. On this occasion, the aim was to disable the railway communications. The crew reported a bright moon that night, with thick haze, but occasional gaps, and they released their bombs on the east bank of the river in the region of the target.

Early in 1942, some of the crew members changed, but Eric remained as the Wop/AG with the same aircraft. On 15 January, Eric was back over Hamburg, this time with Pilot Officers Maltby and Kirkwood-Hackett, and Sgts Lancey, Smith, Rouse and Legace. They dropped their bombs on the town, close to another stick of incendiaries.

In February 1942, RAF Woodhall Spa opened as a satellite airfield to RAF Coningsby, and 97 Squadron moved to this new base. At the same time, the squadron began their conversion to the new Avro Lancaster. Often described as the most capable heavy bomber of the war, the Lancaster addressed almost all of the Manchester's failings and two hundred Manchesters, from A V Roe (Manchester), ordered in September 1939, were converted in production to Lancaster I bombers with four Rolls-Royce Merlin engines, and numbered R5482 to R5763. These were delivered between February and July 1942.

Eric's old Manchester, L7489, was transferred to 50 Squadron. On 8/9 April 1942, while over the Danish coast, the bomb doors jammed. The Manchester managed to climb to 4500 feet but was not able to maintain altitude; one engine caught fire and the aircraft crashed, 8 km south-west of Stege, Mon Island, Denmark. Eric had been lucky as he could so easily have been on that aeroplane had the incident occurred a few weeks earlier.

Some of the reports from Eric's later missions seem to have a 'horticultural' theme. On the very same night that Manchester L7489 crashed, Eric and the crew were 'on ops' in their new Avro Lancaster R5495. They were *'gardening in the Rosemary area'* where during an uneventful trip, they *'successfully planted vegetables in the correct position'*. *'Gardening'* was the term used for mine-laying operations which were a key part of the bomber offensive at that time; the RAF laid mines along German shipping routes.

This photograph was taken from a 97 Squadron Lancaster during one of the low-level practice flights undertaken in the build up to the Augsburg raid on 17 April 1942.

Sea supply routes provided a vital lifeline to the United Kingdom via Atlantic convoys, but the German fleet was inflicting very heavy losses on Merchant Navy ships. The Admiralty requested assistance from Bomber Command and raids were planned against the M.A.N. diesel engine works located at Augsburg in southern Germany as part of the plan to disrupt the U-boat campaign.

Two squadrons, newly converted to Lancasters (44 and 97), were selected to carry out a daring low-level raid. Unusually, it was decided that the attack had to be made in daylight, to improve accuracy. The 'Augsburg Raid' took place on 17 April 1942 and at the time was dubbed *'The most daring raid of the war'*. Eric lost several friends that day, as three of the six Lancasters of 97 Squadron were shot down.

On the night of 27/28 April 1942, Eric with the same crew and aircraft, targeted the German Navy's mighty 42,900 ton battleship, *Tirpitz* at Trondheim Fjord. In good visibility, they dropped a 4000lb bomb from 8000 feet. It was seen to burst and the resulting flash lit up the end of the ship but it had exploded harmlessly between the ship and the cliff. The trip in and out had been uneventful and the crew, temporarily based at RAF Lossiemouth in Scotland, repeated the raid on the following night. With German defences strengthened, the flak was much heavier than the previous night, and a heavy smokescreen prevented the crew from observing the result of their efforts. A total of sixty-four RAF airmen were killed between January and April 1942, in the attempts to sink *Tirpitz*. It was finally sunk in November 1944.

In early May, Eric and the crew of Lancaster R5553, coded OF-S 'Sugar', had another lucky escape. Their target that night was an engineering factory in Stuttgart, but on reaching the French coast, the undercarriage lowered of its own accord due to a suspected hit by flak in the hydraulics. The crew abandoned the mission but found that they were unable to jettison their bomb load, as the bomb doors also failed to open. They were forced to land with a full bomb load and without flaps (another hydraulics problem) with the result that the aircraft overshot the runway and crashed. Fortunately, no one was injured but the aircraft was a complete write-off.

Towards the end of June 1942 Bomber Command attacked Bremen with their 'Thousand Force', in reality 960 aircraft, with one of the main targets being the Focke-Wulf aircraft factory. The main objective was to slow or halt production of the Luftwaffe's Fw190 fighter aircraft.

97 Squadron Crew 21. Most of this crew were newly qualified as aircrew but Pilot Officer David Maltby, third from the right in the greatcoat, and next to him, second from the right, Wireless Operator Sgt Eric 'Grim' Grimwood had already flown several operations together. The others are from left to right, Sgt Max Smith (navigator), Sgt Lyle 'Pop' Humphrey (gunner) and Sgt Harold Rouse (bomb aimer). On the far right is Sgt Harvey 'Leg' Legace (gunner) and in the hatch is Sgt George Lancey (2nd pilot). The aircraft they are standing beside was Avro Manchester L7474 in which they flew on just two days, 3 and 8 January 1942.

Five of these seven aircrew survived the war. Maltby and Grimwood, who flew together before the rest of the crew were assembled, both died in the North Sea some 15 months and a few hundred miles apart.

Eric and the crew were assigned to follow up on the initial raid, and made three trips between 27 June and 2 July. On the first of these they encountered three enemy night-fighters and had to take evasive action. Flying one of only twenty-four Lancasters operational that night, their luck held as two other Lancasters were lost.

Bremen records show that two of the large factories hit in the earlier thousand-bomber raid – the Atlas Werke and the Korff refinery – were damaged again, as well as several smaller factories and dockside warehouses. A hospital and an unrecorded number of houses were also hit. Seven people were killed, and eighty injured. Cloud had been a serious problem that night and inevitably impacted on the accuracy of the bombing.

More bombing raids followed in July involving different targets; Wilhelmshaven Docks, Danzig and Duisburg.

RAF Bomber Command losses were very high in 1942 and Eric's luck wasn't to hold. The evening of 26 July 1942 was just like any other. The crew of Lancaster R5487, coded OF-V 'Victor', Flight Officer W McMurchy, Pilot Officer K J Williams, Flight Sergeant J Richardson, and Sergeants J P Doyle, T A Grey, J Barraclough and E Grimwood prepared for their next bombing raid.

They took off from their base at RAF Woodhall Spa just after 2300 hours and headed towards Hamburg, their target for that night. They never returned. How Eric and the rest of

Sergeant Eric Norman Grimwood - Runnymede RAF Memorial - Panel 84

the crew died will never be known. Of twenty-nine main force bombers lost that night, twenty-one can be attributed to Luftwaffe night fighters, but 'V' Victor was not included in this number. Bomber Command recorded the loss with the simple words, *'Presumed lost over the sea.'*

The crew of Lancaster R5487 were all lost. One body, that of Sgt Barraclough, was recovered from the sea, and he was buried in Klovdal Cemetery, Sweden. In 1961, his remains were moved to Kviberg Cemetery. Eric and the others were never found and have no known graves. They are all remembered on the Runnymede Memorial in Surrey.

One of the men who flew with Eric many times, had already moved on, and went on to achieve fame as one of the 'Dambusters' of 617 Squadron who attacked the Ruhr Dams in May 1943. By then he was better known as Squadron Leader David Maltby DSO DFC.

Sources:

Commonwealth War Graves Commission. RAF History of No. 97 Squadron. Family details from Martin Grimwood and Maggie Driver. Manchester L 7489 Crash report from *Air War over Denmark*. Runnymede Memorial and inscription photographs by Laura Wood. Lancaster/Manchester order details from www.sonsofdamien.co.uk. Crew 21 photo originally from Kevin Lancey, kindly supplied by Charles Foster author of *Breaking the Dams*. Embroidered air gunner's brevet belonged to Flight Sergeant Perry of 97 Squadron. Photograph of Lancasters and other background information about the squadron, courtesy of the 97 Squadron Association.

Fact_file_

Banstead War Memorial – World War I – Panel 6 records

NAME	RANK	DATE OF DEATH	CEMETERY/MEMORIAL
NASH Albert	Telegraphist	13/11/1918	Haslar Naval England
BUTLER George	Private	22/10/1917	Tyne Cot Belgium
PIDGEON Alfred Allen	Private	26/10/1917	Tyne Cot Belgium
POWELL George Hillier	Private	21/05/1918	Tannay France
NASH William John	Private	27/05/1918	Soissons France
HILLMAN Jack	Private	14/07/1918	La Clytte Belgium
WIGGLESWORTH Gill Montague	Corporal	22/08/1918	Vis-En-Atrois France
TAYLOR Alfred Frederick Randall	Private	24/09/1918	Tyne Cot Belgium
OLIVER Walter Ernest	Private	17/10/1915	Loos France

Name LAWRENCE S.P.

Rank LIEUTENANT 183825

Service GENERAL LIST

Date of death 4/8/1942 Age 32

STANLEY PERCY LAWRENCE was the son of Percy James Lawrence and Nellie Emily Lawrence née Hefford. He was born on 8 January 1910 and his birth was registered in Kensington where his father had a business making riding breeches.

Sammy aged nine

Stanley, known as Sammy, married Dorothy Violet Lawrence née Clark from Fulham, in 1935. They rented a flat in Ealing, and their daughter Monica was born in April 1938. Four months later, the family moved to *Ambrosia*, Holly Hill Drive in Banstead. Stanley, being by then a Chartered Surveyor with ICI, had a good job and was able to afford the mortgage to buy a lovely house which cost the princely sum of £1,285. The family even had a phone, and Stanley P. Lawrence is listed at the Banstead address in the phone books issued for 1938 to 1943.

Stanley enlisted into the Royal Engineers with the Territorial Army in September 1940. Within a few months he was posted to 'D', and later, 'C' Company. In May 1941, he was discharged, having been appointed to a Commission as Second Lieutenant, The General List. He was immediately appointed Brigade Compensation Officer HQ, 1st Corps.

Sammy and Dorothy on their wedding day in 1935

A note from the Ministry of Defence describes how qualified men who were not suitable for combat still had a part to play in WWII.

'In September 1939, the situation with regard to the supply of officers was different from that which had existed in 1914, mainly in respect of the administrative machinery which now existed for necessary expansion of a wartime officers corps. It was decided that no new permanent commissions would be given after the declaration of war or the outbreak of hostilities, except to persons who had already qualified (by August 1939) for such commissions (through cadet colleges etc). All commissions would therefore be Emergency Commissions in the Land Forces for the duration of the war.

'After the fall of France in 1940, there was a need for a great number of new officers, not unlike the situation which arose in 1914-15. However, all these emergency commissioned officers were not on the still extant General List. It appears that this continued to be used as a home for those men who were commissioned for special duties - for one reason or another these men were not suitable, or qualified for commissions in, say, the combatant arms, or their employment was not appropriate for an ordinary commission - as in the First World War.'

Stanley Lawrence's profession as a chartered surveyor, and his service with the Royal Engineers gave him the skills which the army decided could be more usefully employed in Britain and hence his inclusion in the General List as commissioned for special duties. By mid-May 1941 he was posted to the 9th Surrey Regiment Royal Artillery.

In 1942 he was based in Yorkshire. His battalion would have been spread far and wide, in and around Hull and East Yorks, on various types of ack-ack (from the WWI phonetic alphabet for AA), gun sites. Such battalions were attached to Royal Artillery units to man the guns, with the Royal Engineers more involved with erecting, maintaining and operating searchlights that went with the gun batteries. Stanley would have been in charge of a few companies of men, each manning a particular site or group of sites.

Lieutenant S P Lawrence was stationed at Beverley, a small and pretty market town, about eight miles north of Hull. During this period, Hull was subjected to numerous air raids by the Germans, who frequently dropped their unused bombs over the area prior to heading back to base. The town of Beverley had been largely untouched by bombing raids.

On the bank holiday of 3 August 1942, Stanley Lawrence was off duty and went out for a bike ride cycling through Flemingate which is on the main road approach into the town, just a few hundred yards short of the Minster. A single German plane flew over and dropped four 500kg high explosive bombs on the Flemingate area of the town.

The first bomb damaged a local Tannery while the second exploded in Flemingate, destroying 4 Brentwood Villas. This bomb killed one of the occupants, Mrs Francis Snowden, and badly injured Lieutenant Stanley Lawrence who was cycling past at the time of the explosion. Bomb number three detonated behind Flemingate Methodist Chapel wrecking a medical rest centre, and damaging several cottages in nearby Sparkmill Terrace. The explosion also killed Mr Charles Cross, an off-duty air-raid warden who was sixty-six years old, and who happened to be outside, feeding his rabbits at the time. The fourth bomb failed to detonate.

Lieutenant Lawrence and about fifteen other casualties were quickly ferried to the Beverley Base Hospital. The number of casualties could have been much higher, but on that day the latest *Old Mother Riley* film was showing at the Marble Arch Cinema on Butcher Row and many Flemingate residents had gone to see it.

Stanley Lawrence died from his injuries on the following day, 4 August 1942. He was thirty-two years of age and the cause of death was attributed to 'War Operations'. He is buried in Kensal Green Cemetery in West London which is a private cemetery where families could buy plots for interment. All his family were born and raised in Kensington (or more properly, Notting Hill) and Kensal Green Cemetery seemed the most appropriate place to lay him to rest. All his family are together in the same plot which also has a Commonwealth War Graves Commission headstone.

Ambrosia, Holly Hill Drive

Mrs Lawrence remarried in 1945 and with her husband and daughter continued to live in *Ambrosia*. In 1947 they had another daughter and in 1950 the family moved to another property in Banstead, this time in Colcokes Road. Mrs Lawrence and her husband moved to Cornwall in 1960, after Stanley's daughter Monica, was married at All Saints Church. Thus ended the family's time in Banstead.

Monica still remembers Banstead well, especially the house in Holly Hill Drive. She writes:

'I have very fond memories of Ambrosia. *After my father died, my mother filled the house with people and there was a lot of laughter in spite of it being such a tragic time for her.*

'I wish I'd known my real father. I have no memory of him at all, just images smiling at me out of black-and-white photographs.

'My mother was a war widow and very early on in her bereavement she took me on her knee and showed me his soldiering things, a cane which I still have, and some service medals which she subsequently threw away. "They were only bits of tin, what did I want with those?", she said bitterly, years later.'

Stanley Lawrence

'Another souvenir was a camp bed on which I slept, during the latter half of the war, in the cellar underneath our kitchen. During my school days I used my father's boxed geometry set, a tool of his trade as a chartered surveyor. Not that it helped me like the subject any better, but I somehow felt proud to be using something that his hands had touched.

'When my mother died, among her things were other treasures - a letter written to her by my father when she was pregnant, sepia photos of him as a baby, which I stuck in an album, in some way trying not to lose anything that enabled me to feel a link with him.

'What sort of a father would he have been, I wonder? Would we have had a good relationship? How would he have coped with my truculent teenage years? Would he have been a good mentor? And even - what sort of grandfather would he have been? To me, he will always remain some sort of paragon since I was never able to question anyone about what he had really been like. By the time I was old enough to wonder about these things, my mother had married again and my stepfather never referred to my mother's previous life.

'In some ways I feel robbed of not knowing my father and his family. They all died within four years of each other, thus wiping out almost everything my mother had held dear. No wonder she and I always remained close. I was all she had left of those halcyon days.

'For all my mother's personal tragedy in the war years, my memories of that time are not unhappy. Mainly, they consist of our house full of people and nights spent sleeping in the cellar under the kitchen and a huge spider that visited one evening, a train journey or two which I believe were to see my father when he was stationed in Yorkshire, and being evacuated to the farm cottage of some friends in Berkshire. It is

there that I first encountered geese, barns full of hay, the smell of wood smoke, golden cornfields to play in and always the presence of my mother. I was too young to miss my father, and indeed for the better part of our short time together he had been away working for ICI or in the Forces, anyway.

Sammy with daughter Monica

'I'm sure he had his faults, but I like to think my father would have been a good man and done his best to bring up his strong-willed daughter with firmness, kindness and humour. But then, I suppose that's the ideal all daughters have of a father'.

Living in Holly Hill Drive, the Lawrences were neighbours with the Remané family who also tragically lost the head of the household, Serjeant Clifford Remané. Mrs Lawrence noted that Mrs Remané did not talk about her husband much. She did however feel some affinity with her and she used to say that Mrs Remané was the only other person she knew who had been widowed by war.

Sixty-two years after Stanley's death, Hilda Atkinson recalled the day the German plane bombed Beverley:

'About tea time once, I was going to take a can of tea to my uncle who was a milkman in Flemingate. Because he wasn't in his dairy I knew he would be in the field, milking, so I took it to Mr and Mrs Cross who lived in the bungalow, and left it there for him. On the way back, the plane came over and dropped some bombs hitting houses in Beverley. One bomb hit the bungalow. I am here today to tell the tale, but unfortunately

Mr Cross died. My uncle came back from milking and was disappointed that he couldn't have his tea because the can had been squashed. There were houses in Flemingate bombed. I believe they were called Brentwood Villas'.

Lieutenant Stanley Percy Lawrence
Kensal Green Cemetery
West London
Grave Reference: 47656
Location: Square 9 Row 7

Sources:

Commonwealth War Graves Commission. Photographs and memories provided by Monica Saunders. Photograph of headstone courtesy of Mike Shackel of BHRG. Service record and background information on the General List from a Ministry of Defence letter dated 30 March 1988. Details of the bombing raid from The Beverley Town Council website and Hullwebs History of Hull. Hilda Atkinson's War memories on the BBC Wartime Memories Project – *WW2 People's War* is an online archive of wartime memories contributed by members of the public and gathered by the BBC. The archive can be found at bbc.co.uk/ww2peopleswar.

Fact*file*

Banstead War Memorial – World War I – Panel 7 records

NAME	RANK	DATE OF DEATH	CEMETERY/MEMORIAL
WISCOMBE Frank	Private	08/05/1918	Klein-Vierstraat Belgium
BUCKLE Archie Stewart	Brigadier General	18/08/1916	Heilly France
BUCKLE Cuthbert Charles Corbett	Second Lieutenant	03/07/1916	Serre Road France
BATES Harry	Private	01/07/1916	Thiepval France
CROSS Edward Jasper	Private	08/03/1916	Banstead England
TICHENER George	Private	11/04/1917	Arras France
GARTON Herbert Westlake	Captain	15/09/1916	Thiepval France
GARTON Edward Clive	Second Lieutenant	02/09/1918	Faubourg D'Amiens France
BAPLE (WWII casualty inscribed on WWI Panel) Douglas Roy	Second Lieutenant	15/02/1942	Kranji Singapore

Name	**Needham A.S.**
Rank	**Pilot Officer 117845**
Service	**Royal Air Force**
	Volunteer Reserve 12 Squadron
Date of death	**5/9/1942** Age **32**

ARTHUR SIDNEY NEEDHAM was the son of Arthur Edward and Beatrice Needham, and was always called Sandy. He was born on 17 December 1910 in London, whilst his parents were living in Streatham Hill, in the borough of Wandsworth, where his father was a motor engineers' clerk. The family moved to Banstead sometime after 1928 when Wilmot Way was built.

Sandy was educated at the Archbishop Temple School in Lambeth, where he gained a scholarship to study art; however he was not allowed to take it up, as his elder brother, Thomas, had not obtained one. He did some very credible watercolour paintings, and excelled at drawing although he never followed an art career. Instead he trained in commerce, and gained a place at the Commonwealth Bank of Australia, Old Jewry, London, where he worked in French affairs, being fluent in that language.

In his leisure time Sandy liked to swim, listen to classical music and also work in the garden. As a young man he suffered from asthma and was encouraged by his doctor to go skiing in Switzerland. His condition didn't stop Sandy becoming an accomplished sportsman, and as well as being an active member of the South London Harriers running club, he organised the 2nd Streatham Boy Scouts Group with his colleague, Bill Hogg. It was there that he met Vi, a lady cub-master, who was to become his wife. They married on 16 February 1935, at St. Margaret's, Streatham Hill.

Sandy and Vi on their wedding day in 1935.

[Vi's proper name was Florence but her older sister called her Vi when she was born and the name stuck!]

Their only child, Maggi, was born in 1937 at *Ingleton*, the family home, situated down an unnamed cul-de-sac between 76 and 78 Wilmot Way. The property was immediately behind the end of Sandy's parents' garden, as they lived at 74 Wilmot Way.

With the outbreak of war, Sandy joined the Royal Air Force Volunteer Reserve. Keen to fly, he was assessed by an Air Crew Candidate Selection Board where it was determined that he was suitable for training as an observer, acting as a navigator and air bomber.

Sandy began his initial training in early 1941 in Bude, Cornwall and later in Bournemouth, and at thirty years of age would have been appreciably older than most of his fellow trainees. Many of the letters that he wrote home are treasured by his daughter Maggi to this day, and they give an insight into his time in the RAF.

In July 1941 Sandy was posted to Canada for training under the British and Commonwealth Air Training Plan (BCATP) in common with thousands of trainee aircrew. The peaceful skies over Canada gave the Royal Air Force the opportunity to train and prepare the thousands of young airmen who were ultimately to take the air-war to Germany, as the majority of them would find themselves posted to Bomber Command.

The North American climate presented plenty of challenges for the fledgling fliers and in November 1941 Sandy wrote home, *'Have been kept in a state of uncertainty about flying* [because of the weather] *every evening for a fortnight, sometimes being raked out of bed at 0200 hours and then after hanging about for an hour being told that flying was off, the whole of us were thoroughly browned off, accordingly we all went and got thoroughly "bottled" to a man – oh yes, I was too – but we had a grand time'*. When the proprietor of the bar called the police, because of the general rowdiness, he must have been disappointed to find that they were sympathetic where the young trainees were concerned. Sandy felt that after four months of *'impeccable behaviour'* they were entitled to a momentary lapse, even if the bus driver was not all that pleased with their behaviour on the way home!

Sandy was based at RCAF Goderich, Ontario (31 Air Navigation School) on the shores of Lake Huron, and studied navigation, meteorology and mathematics. He also received training at 31 Bombing and Gunnery School at RAF Picton, east of Goderich in Prince Edward County, a beautiful area of Canada.

His letters home however, reveal the frustration of being away from loved ones and of boredom, even at the training regime, which could mean periods of inactivity interspersed with hectic tuition. Leisure time was difficult to plan for, as notification for periods of leave invariably came at the last minute. He also missed the competitive running which had been so important to him before the war.

Early morning starts, pay-roll mix-ups, extended periods without letters from home and other problems all served to compound the general feelings of homesickness that was natural amongst the trainees, but Canada had its benefits too. Many of Sandy's letters contain references to parcels of 'goodies' sent home to England; stockings for his wife Vi, dresses and handkerchiefs for their daughter Maggi.

Another of Sandy's letters revealed that he grew a moustache – *'what a brute, red and bushy; but I think I shall keep it for a while, chiefly because of the amusement the lads get out of it'*. When told of her father's facial hair, young Maggi apparently made rude remarks

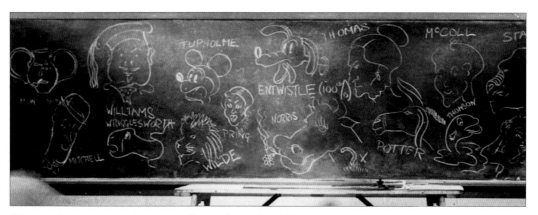

Who was the perpetrator of these amusing chalk drawings? Only one suspect springs to mind – Sandy Needham

about moustaches, and Sandy responded, *'watch out or I'll grow a beard like Father Christmas!'*

While in Canada he stayed with one of the many Canadian families who provided 'foster homes' for the trainees. Sandy was 'adopted' by Charlie 'Screwball' Thomas and his family who lived in a house on a hill overlooking Lake Huron. They took Sandy, who Charlie called 'Red' on account of his hair, to dances and parties and showed him the local area.

Sandy excelled in his training and finished at the top of his course with pass marks for the various disciplines of between eighty-five and one hundred per cent. He would have been extremely proud of his observer's brevet which featured a winged letter 'O'. He liked navigation and meteorology particularly, but upon completion of his training he was identified as a potential candidate for the role of Instructor – Bombing and Gunnery.

He was far from impressed at the thought of a training role, especially in disciplines which didn't particularly interest him and even less at the prospect of an extended period, away from his wife and young daughter. He made his preferences clear but in the meantime discussed Vi and Maggi's possible move out to Canada, in case it became necessary. Unfortunately, as it would turn out, his wishes were realised and he returned to England.

Sandy arrived back in Bournemouth in January 1942 before spending time at Tring (RAF Halton) and then further training at RAF Millom in March, before transiting through RAF West Kirby to RAF Cheddington (also known as RAF Marsworth).

RAF Cheddington in June of 1942, was home to Number 26 OTU (Operational Training Unit). Here, he was crewed with four others to make up the standard crew of the RAF's main twin-engined bomber of the time, the Vickers Wellington.

26 OTU's purpose was specifically to train crews for RAF Bomber Command's night offensive. Here they would fly practice missions and generally get to know their aircraft, their functions, as well as learning to work as a close-knit team. When fully proficient they would be posted to an operational Wellington squadron.

Finally in July 1942, Sandy's crew were posted to 12 Squadron, part of 1 Group RAF Bomber Command based at RAF Binbrook in the Lincolnshire Wolds. Number 12 Squadron's war had already been a busy one. During the Battle of France in 1940 the squadron was equipped with obsolescent single-engined Fairey Battle light bombers, and suffered heavy losses. Afterwards it had been engaged on night attacks against shipping and the German invasion barges being assembled in channel ports.

With the Battle of Britain won and with threat of invasion reduced, the squadron began to re-equip with the Vickers Wellington MK II, powered by Rolls-Royce Merlin engines. The new aircraft were first used in a raid on Emden on the night of 10/11 April 1941, and this marked the beginning of sustained operations against German industrial targets.

By the summer of 1942, Sandy was flying on operations as part of a 12 Squadron Wellington crew, acting as their navigator, and his daughter Maggi recalls that he always had misgivings about bombing areas where there was the risk of civilians being killed or injured. His ethics would have helped him to focus on his task of navigation, since it was his role to get the Wellington to the target area to enable his bomb aimer to drop his bombs accurately. Sandy had even shared his concerns with the family and related how he had to think about *'rats being killed, and not people'*, although he also felt *'that the Germans deserved what they got because they started it and if they stopped then so would we'*.

The squadron continued to play its part in the bomber offensive, and targets included the great capital ships, *Gniesenau*, *Scharnhorst* and *Prinz Eugen*, and even Berlin itself. Its Wellingtons were still in use on night offensives but by September 1942, 12 Squadron was preparing to convert to Avro Lancasters, the next generation of heavy bombers powered by four engines, and with substantially increased bomb loads. Pilot Officer Arthur Sidney Needham was never to see this change.

On the night of 4/5 September 1942, 12 Squadron were briefed to attack the port of Bremen, on the River Weser in north-western Germany. Pilot and captain of Vickers Wellington Mk. II, serial Z8595 that night, was Sergeant T Smith with P/O A S Needham, Sgt F Smith, Sgt R W L Mills RCAF, and Sgt W Anderson making up the rest of the crew, with Sandy, as usual, acting as navigator.

The aircraft took off at 0025 hours from RAF Binbrook, seven miles from Market Rasen and headed east towards Bremen. As they approached the Dutch coast the Wellington suffered engine failure and the pilot made the decision to jettison the bomb load and to return to Binbrook.

Flying on a single Merlin engine the Wellington was unable to maintain height and although the aircraft was just twenty miles from Cromer on the Norfolk Coast, it finally ditched in the sea at 0230 hours. The pilot, Sgt Smith, the sole survivor, was picked up by HMS *Hambleton* after spending three hours in the water. Of the rest of the crew there was no sign; they have no known graves and are commemorated on the Runnymede Memorial.

The raid on Bremen was carried out by 250 aircraft of Bomber Command, of which ninety-eight were Wellingtons. Four were lost, and only one of these – Z8595 – was from 12 Squadron, making it one of the last Wellingtons lost on operations from this squadron.

Mrs Needham never came to terms with the loss of her husband and she emigrated to Australia with Maggi. Nine years after Sandy's death, Vi remarried and lived in Melbourne with her new husband Brad. Even after a very happy second marriage, Maggi recalls that Sandy was never far from her mother's mind:

Pilot Officer
Arthur Sidney Needham
Runnymede RAF Memorial
Englefield Green
Surrey
Memorial Reference: Panel 70

On 25 September 1942 the squadron, newly equipped with Lancasters, moved to RAF Wickenby where it remained for the rest of the war. As a result, the main 12 Squadron memorial is located at Wickenby, and the squadron is not principally associated with Binbrook from where its Wellington operations were flown.

'Sandy was a much-loved man by all who knew him. Very gentle, and I have been told this over and over again. I do remember him and still have his passport photo taken when he was still a young man, five feet ten inches tall, with brown eyes and auburn hair. I also remember the little things, like how he did not like trees being cut down.

'I re-read all his letters recently – Sandy always signed himself John. My mother always liked the name but otherwise I can't remember why she called him that.'

Sources:
Commonwealth War Graves Commission. Free BMD and local telephone directories. 1938 electoral register from The Surrey History Centre at Woking ref CC802/55/3. *Vickers Armstrong Wellington* by Ken Delve. RAF Lossiemouth Memorial website. *Bomber Squadrons of the RAF* by Philip Moyes. www.raf.mod.uk. www.lostbombers.co.uk. RAF Wickenby Museum. Personal information and photographs from Maggi Carver, Sandy's daughter.

Fact*file*

Banstead War Memorial – World War Two – Panel 1 records

NAME	RANK	DATE OF DEATH	CEMETERY/MEMORIAL
Ives			Portsmouth
Bertram Henry	Leading Seaman	01/06/1940	England
Butler			Fleurbaix
Walter William	Private	25/05/1940	France
Locatelli			Tower Hill
Peter Cyril Francis	Cadet	17/01/1941	England
Baker			Halfaya Sollum
Gordon Alfred	Gunner	12/05/1941	Egypt
Riches (Reverend)			Dunkirk
Leslie Philip	Chaplain 4th Class	01/06/1940	France
Hobden			Bari
William	Sergeant	16/02/1941	Italy
Hobden			Portsmouth
Kenneth	Telegraphist	25/11/1941	England
Johnson			Banstead
Alfred William Henry	Private	17/12/1941	England
Biles			Knightsbridge
William Robert Cecil	Second Lieutenant	05/06/1942	Libya
Fletcher (unidentified)			
D J			
Needham			Runnymede
Arthur Sidney	Pilot Officer	05/09/1942	England
Botting			Alamein
Eric Harold	Serjeant	25/10/1942	Egypt
Everett			Minturno
Arthur Henry	Lance Bombadier	19/11/1943	Italy
Cull (incorrectly inscribed as Scull)			Bayeux
Stanley Morris	Trooper	04/08/1944	France
Seal			Runnymede
Leon Harold	Sergeant	20/06/1942	England

Name **YEOMANS S.R.** ....

Rank **CORPORAL 6405490** ....

Service **GLIDER PILOT REGIMENT** ....

.... **2ND ARMY AIR CORPS** ....

Date of death **25/10/1942** Age ......**20**.........

SIDNEY ROY YEOMANS was the son of Sidney and Grace Yeomans of 18 Roundwood Way, Banstead. He was born 3 March 1922 and was always known as Roy.

Roy was seventeen when the war started and, like so many others, he declared his age as eighteen in order to join up. He wanted to join the RAF and train as a pilot, but he failed the medical through being partly colour-blind. He then joined the Royal Sussex Regiment but never gave up his ambition to fly.

An opportunity was presented by Winston Churchill in 1940, when he ordered the Chiefs of Staff to recommend how best to form a new combat arm which was to be delivered to the battlefield by air. The question of recruiting army personnel to train as pilots was a long-standing and contentious issue. Indeed, the Deputy Chief of the Air Staff, Sir Arthur Harris, thought Army flying preposterous. He was quoted as saying;

'The idea that semi-skilled, unpicked personnel – infantry corporals have, I believe, even been suggested – could with a maximum of training be entrusted with the piloting of these troop carriers, is fantastic'.

Harris believed that landing a glider was equivalent to force-landing the largest sized aircraft without engine aid, an operation which has no higher test of piloting skill.

The use of gliders enabled the troops to land together in one place rather than being dispersed, as was the case with parachute assaults. The issue was eventually settled when Germany showed the effectiveness of airborne troops by capturing Crete in May 1941. Churchill called for immediate action, and it was agreed that the Army would supply glider pilots, with the RAF taking responsibility for qualifying them.

Roy must have been delighted to see the following notice posted in messes and NAAFIs:

THE AIRBORNE FORCES OF THE BRITISH ARMY CONSIST OF PARACHUTE
TROOPS AND GLIDER-BORNE TROOPS OF ALL ARMS OF THE SERVICE.
OFFICERS AND MEN IN ANY REGIMENT OR CORPS (EXCEPT RAC), WHO ARE MEDICALLY FIT,
MAY APPLY FOR TRANSFER TO A PARACHUTE OR GLIDER-BORNE UNIT OF THE AIRBORNE
FORCES. A LIMITED NUMBER OF OFFICERS AND OTHER RANKS ARE URGENTLY REQUIRED FOR
TRAINING AS GLIDER PILOTS. APPLICATIONS FOR TRANSFER OR FURTHER INFORMATION
SHOULD BE MADE TO UNIT HEADQUARTERS.

Group photograph of the trainee pilots on Course 6 held at No.21 Elementary Flying Training School at RAF Booker. Roy may be the second from right in the front row.

Shown below, is the coveted brevet issued to the army men who qualified as pilots.

The result of this initiative was the formation in 1942 of the Parachute Battalions and the Glider Pilot Regiment (GPR), whose soldiers wore the distinctive maroon beret and cap badge of the Army Air Corps. Roy applied for a transfer to the Army Air Corps as a glider pilot and this time he was accepted, thus fulfilling his boyhood ambition.

The RAF aircrew selection system was used and all successful candidates were sent to the GPR Depot at Tilshead for six weeks. During this time the recruits were 'put through their paces' in the knowledge that they could be returned to their unit for any reason decided by the Depot staff. Military training was also rigorously upgraded, as all pilots were expected to reach a particular standard as a soldier. The recruits attended Battle Schools where they learned the art of street fighting, and received training on all available weapons. A fully trained Glider Pilot was to be a 'total soldier' able to turn his hand to any situation in the field.

The 2nd Battalion Glider Pilot Regiment, Army Air Corps was created to fly troops, usually an airborne platoon of twenty-eight men, or heavy equipment in large towed gliders, into areas behind the enemy's front-line. Having landed, the glider pilots then fought as infantry or assisted in crewing heavier weapons until withdrawn to fly other missions.

Roy attended No.21 Elementary Flying Training School at RAF Booker, High Wycombe, where after the successful completion of his training course, he would have been awarded his 'wings'. By that time, Roy would have gained experience of flying primary trainers (light aircraft) like the Tiger Moth, and the award of the coveted 'wings' was a recognition of qualification as a pilot, irrespective of what he would subsequently go on to fly. From there Corporal Yeomans would have progressed onto gliding training before being posted to his regiment as an operational glider pilot.

Roy was never to reach this stage. He was killed during his initial training following a mid-air collision, when the tail of his Tiger Moth, DE619, was struck by Tiger Moth DE456, piloted by Corporal L J Crowe. The collision happened at 1030 hours on 25 October 1942, as both pilots were preparing to land, killing Corporal Yeomans and leaving Corporal Crowe seriously injured.

Roy, with his younger brothers, Peter and Michael in the garden at Roundwood Way

A Court of Inquiry concluded that the accident occurred through failure of both pilots to keep an adequate lookout.

This period was early in the history of the regiment, and Corporal Yeomans never had the opportunity to take part in the now famous glider operations of WWII, notably Pegasus Bridge on D-Day, Arnhem, and the Rhine crossing. The many casualties suffered by the Glider Pilot Regiment reflected the hazards of glider operations, but their deeds and achievements were outstanding. It took a lot of courage to fly a glider into enemy territory and land behind enemy lines, knowing that it was a one-way mission.

Roy Yeomans was killed on 25 October 1942, the same day as Serjeant Eric Botting, another Banstead man listed on the War Memorial. Roy is buried in the churchyard, west of All Saints Church in Banstead.

Corporal Sidney Roy Yeomans

All Saints Churchyard

Banstead

Surrey

Location: west of Church

Sources:

Commonwealth War Graves Commission. *The War Memorial, St Paul's Church, Nork, Banstead* by the Banstead History Research Group. Personal details and photographs from Michael Yeomans. Glider Pilot Regiment history from: *The Army Air Corps Association, The Glider Pilot Regiment* website at www.gliderpilotregiment.org.uk and the *89th(Parachute)/317(Airborne) Field Services Security* website – affiliated groups. RAF Booker course photograph and collision details from Steve Wright of *The Glider Pilot Regiment* website. 'Wings' brevet and training information from Mark Stanley.

Fact*file*

Banstead War Memorial – World War Two – Panel 2 records

NAME	RANK	DATE OF DEATH	CEMETERY/MEMORIAL
Durrad			Taukkyan
Ian Stephens	Lieutenant	01/03/1945	Myanmar (Burma)
Grimwood			Runnymede
Eric Norman	Sergeant	26/07/1942	England
Barnes			Portsmouth
Raymond Charles Arthur	A/Sub-Lieutenant	19/08/1942	England
Bissett Johnson (incorrectly inscribed as Johnson			Banstead
Edward Osborne	Serjeant	18/10/1946	England
Baugh (incorrectly inscribed as Bauch)			Banstead
John Hampson	Captain	09/03/1944	England
Cutts			Banstead
Frederick William	Captain	19/11/1946	England
Excell			Banstead
Leonard William	Gunner	29/12/1941	England
White			Banstead
Donald James	Leading Aircraftman	16/04/1941	England
Hobson (incorrectly inscribed as B A Hobson)			Banstead
Colin Anthony	Pilot Officer	03/10/1940	England
Stemp (unidentified)			
A E			
Armstrong			Memorial
Ronald William	Flight Lieutenant	16/03/1942	Singapore
Eason			Chatham
Dennis Bertram	Marine	18/11/1942	England
Sutehall			Runnymede
Peter	Flight Lieutenant	17/01/1945	England
Burr			Belgrade
Jeffery James Kellaway	Flying Officer	08/04/1944	Serbia and Montenegro

Name	BOTTING E.H.
Rank	SERJEANT 6968254
Service	RIFLE BRIGADE 7TH BATTALION
	(1ST BATTALION LONDON RIFLE BRIGADE)
Date of death	25/10/1942 Age 23

ERIC HAROLD BOTTING was the son of Henry Leslie and Primrose Botting, who lived at 125 Nork Way, Banstead. Eric attended Emanuel School, situated just on Wandsworth Common in London, between 1932 and 1937.

Eric's father and grandfather had served with the London Regiment, and from a young age Eric wanted to follow in their footsteps. He joined the Officers' Training Corps as a cadet and his inclusion in the shooting squad suggests he was one of the top marksmen. At that time, Emanuel School had its own shooting range, and the squad would have competed for *The Grundy Cup*, a house competition which had taken place since 1918. The cup was named after two brothers who died in the Battle of the Somme.

In early 1941, Eric married Margaret Snow of Hornchurch, at Romford in Essex. The newly-wed did achieve his ambition of following in his father's and grandfather's footsteps when he also joined the London Rifles. They were formed in 1937 when one battalion left the London Regiment and was designated as The London Rifle Brigade, The Rifle Brigade (Prince Consort's Own). The battalion was divided as 1st and 2nd LRB, in 1939. The 1st became a motorised unit and in 1941 was redesignated as the 7th Battalion, Rifle Brigade. This is the battalion that Eric Botting belonged to.

They arrived in Egypt when things were at a low ebb for the British Eighth Army, following the first battle of El Alamein, in July 1942, where 13,000 lives had been lost. The army had been pushed back to its furthest point. Any further retreat would mean that the Axis forces would gain Egypt. The Axis nations, comprised the countries that were opposed to the Allies during WWII, the three main powers being Germany, Japan and Italy.

The men of the 7th Battalion Rifle Brigade spent a few weeks training in the back areas, mainly to acclimatise them to the conditions of living in the desert; they had a lot to learn. They soon found out that the pictures they had seen in the papers back home, had given them a somewhat false impression of the fit, healthy-looking soldiers, enjoying the sun and open-air life of the desert. In reality swarms of flies pestered them day and night, and they all suffered from desert sores. Their diet consisted of *'corned beef, sand, bread – mostly unfit to eat – and hard tack biscuits'*.

At about the same time, Lieutenant General Bernard Montgomery took command of the British Commonwealth's Eighth Army. He arrived in Egypt and, impressively, managed to visit all divisions and battalions under his command. He made it very clear to the riflemen

This group photograph taken in 1936 shows the Emanuel School shooting squad which included the following: Sgt J W B Armstrong, Cpl D J Warren, Cdt F C Austin, Sgt C Fiducia, Sgt K C Baker, L/Cpl J Pritchard. L/Sgt A S Mann, Capt W Stafford Hipkins, Capt C S Hill, Lieut C E Bond, Sgt E H Dean, L/Cpl B C Smith and Cdt E H Botting (bottom right).

of the 7th Battalion that there was no way that the British would take the offensive, until they had superiority in manpower and firepower. Then followed a lull with little offensives by either side, but it was quite noticeable that both the numbers of men and the amount of materials continued to increase significantly. The unit was given orders that when Rommel attacked they were to carry out an orderly retreat to lure the enemy armour to a point where they had little room to manoeuvre. The ensuing encounter became known as the battle of Alam Halfa, one of the last major attacks by Rommel. The RAF eventually took over and hit the Germans with everything they had, causing them to lose a great deal of armoured strength, something that was to be crucial in the days that followed.

The battalion took part in massive schemes and planned manoeuvres with whole divisions – all a prelude to a major offensive. Their efforts were rewarded with a welcome break, when they were allocated a week's leave, but they were restricted to Cairo. It was a condition that each man had to have five pounds, and some had to borrow money to ensure they could go.

Once back 'on-duty', the unit made its way up to El Alamein secretly, to prevent the enemy noticing. They had reached their starting point for Operation Lightfoot.

The infantry had to attack first. Many of the anti-tank mines would not be tripped by soldiers running over them since they were too light, hence the codename. As the infantry attacked, engineers had to clear a path in the desert sand for the tanks coming up behind.

Another rifleman in the 7th Battalion Rifle Brigade was Thomas Arthur Murray, or Tom, as he was always called. Tom was a year older than Eric Botting, and in later years he recorded the events leading up to the battle which became known as the second battle of El Alamein:

Rifleman Tom Murray

'24 October, 1942

'The night before the battle commenced, the whole battalion was briefed as to roles in the forthcoming battle – what position we were to take, and who was on our flanks.

'The battle commenced with a huge barrage, which for those days was tremendous. The sky was lit up, and fires of burning petrol dumps littered the desert. The engineers, who had moved in first to clear the enemy minefields, had made a path for us to pass through in our trucks. It was such a clear night you could actually see the bombs dropping from a lone Stuka raider, which didn't exactly give us a boost.

'After what seemed years, we reached a position where we had to make our stand. Unfortunately, the ground was rock hard where we were, which made it tough to dig our firing positions.

'I was on a Vickers water-cooled machine-gun and feeling very exposed, firing occasional bursts over the ridge where the fire of a German 88mm gun seemed to come from. Two men had gone back a few yards to dig a hole for us to retreat to, should we be attacked. So we passed the first few hours of our part in the battle.'

The noise can hardly be imagined – there were reports of the gunners' ears bleeding. Nearly nine-hundred field and medium guns fired a barrage which continued for five-and-a-half hours, each gun firing several hundred shells. The enemy gun positions were not a safe place, with tons of shells falling out of the sky all around.

Tom continues:

'Later in the morning we heard the heavy sound of motors, and soon after, we saw tanks coming at us. When 200 yards away, they moved over to the side, stopped and opened up on us. Simultaneously, the heavy guns we were equipped with, opened up, and very quickly, about six of the tanks were burning fiercely. All our trucks were burning and jeeps were being thrown in the air by the fire of these tanks as if a giant hand had tossed them into the air. The flames from these burning tanks were so fierce I could feel the skin being lifted from my face.'

In the ensuing exchange of fire, Tom received a gunshot wound to his left leg and had to be evacuated. Eric survived that first day. The initial thrust had ended by the following day, Sunday the 25th. Both armies had been fighting non-stop for two days. The Allies had advanced through the minefields in the west to make a six-mile wide and five-mile deep inroad. The Axis forces were firmly entrenched in most of their original battle positions and the battle was at a standstill. Serjeant Eric Botting was killed on this day, Sunday 25 October 1942. Eric's Commanding Officer wrote:

'Botting, learning there was a wounded officer some 400 yards out, jumped into his truck and drove towards them. He got almost half-way before being hit by a shell and then machine-gun fire. His death must have been instantaneous - tragic, but a very good show nevertheless, and a great inspiration to his company.'

Cap badge of The Rifle Brigade

Eric and Tom's efforts were not in vain. Eventual success in the battle turned the tide in the North Africa Campaign. Allied victory at El Alamein ended German hopes of occupying Egypt, controlling the Suez Canal, and gaining access to the Middle-Eastern oil fields. Their defeat at El Alamein marked the end of German expansion.

In the end, the Allies' victory was Montgomery's greatest triumph. Winston Churchill famously summed up the battle, on 10 November 1942, with the words:

'Now this is not the end, it is not even the beginning of the end. But it is, perhaps, the end of the beginning.'

Serjeant Eric Botting died trying to save another soldier. Tragically he had just refused a transfer, as he did not want to leave the regiment his father and grandfather also served in – The London Rifle Brigade. Eric left a widow and a young son, after only being married a very short time.

Operational service in North Africa during this period was recognised by the award of The Africa Star, a six–pointed star of yellow copper zinc alloy. The central design is the Royal Cypher of King George VI, surmounted by a crown. The cypher is surrounded by a circlet containing the words 'The Africa Star'.

The ribbon for this medal, along with those of the other Second World War campaign stars, is reputed to have been designed by the King himself. The sand of the desert is represented by pale buff, the Royal Navy (and Merchant Navy), British Army, and Royal Air Force are represented by stripes of dark blue, red, and light blue respectively.

Two riflemen, two different outcomes determined by the events of WWII - Tom Murray received his medal after the war, and Eric Botting is commemorated on the Alamein Memorial and also included on the Roll of Honour in St Paul's Church, Nork.

Serjeant Eric Botting
Nork Roll of Honour and
Alamein Memorial
Egypt
Column 73

Sources:
Commonwealth War Graves Commission. School information and photographs from the Emanuel School archives and the school magazine, *The Portcullis.* Details of the battle at El Alamein, from memories written by Thomas Arthur Murray *Tom's Story,* by kind permission of his daughter Linda, who also photographed his Rifle Brigade Cap badge and his Africa Star. Roll of Honour details from BHRG publication *The War Memorial St Paul's Church Nork Banstead.*

1943

The German 6th Army surrenders at Stalingrad. Over 90,000 German troops are captured and most of those will not see their homeland again. The Russians, after a taste of victory, make extensive progress on several fronts, taking the city of Kharkov. Within a month the Germans retake it and in a few weeks the Russians are pushed back many miles on the south-east front.

Churchill and Roosevelt meet at Casablanca and agree on stepping-up the bombing of Germany and other strategies. 'Uncle Joe' Stalin is too busy to join the two 'supremos'.

In the Far East, Guadalcanal, largest of the Soloman Islands, is taken by the Americans. Britain's Major General Orde Wingate sets up his special forces 'Chindits' on long-range patrols behind Japanese lines in Burma.

By the middle of the year Hamburg's ordeal in a firestorm kills up to 40,000. In Warsaw the Jewish Ghetto population fail in an uprising and those who survive the fighting and destruction are transported to concentration camps. The biggest-ever battle between Russian and German armour ends with Russia expanding the Kursk salient and inflicting one of the most significant defeats of the war in Eastern Europe.

An action-packed Mediterranean theatre of war sees the Germans surrender in North Africa, Allied forces invade Sicily, Rome bombed and Il Duce, Benito Mussolini arrested. The Italian authorities immediately seek a peace settlement but the Germans will have none of it. They pour troops into Italy to wreck any prospect of their ally opting out of the war. One month later the Allies invade the Italian mainland.

As the year enters its fourth quarter the Soviets have more success at Smolensk and Kiev. The Germans experience another Russian winter.

Name **HOSLIN L.C.**

Rank **FLYING OFFICER 120020**

Service **ROYAL AIR FORCE**

VOLUNTEER RESERVE

Date of death **28/4/1943** Age **28**

Louis Charles Hoslin was the son of Charles A Hoslin and Jane Hoslin, who lived at *Santa Maria*, 322 Fir Tree Road, Epsom Downs. Louis spent twenty years of his short life at the family home, close to Banstead.

Louis entered a seminary to train to become a Catholic priest but left before being ordained. His life then took a completely new direction and he joined the Royal Air Force Volunteer Reserve (RAFVR) and successfully completed pilot training in Canada. He returned to Liverpool on the SS *Vancouver Island* on 15 August 1941 with twenty other newly-trained airmen. The ship was the former German merchant ship *Weser* captured off the coast of Mexico by HMCS *Prince Robert* in 1940. It was eventually sunk by a German U-boat in October 1941. All on board perished. Shortly after arriving back in the UK, Charles married Kay Dixon at Westminster.

His service career steered him towards training duties rather than front-line operational squadrons and by April 1943 he was at an RAF base in Scotland.

The Royal Air Force began to use airfields in Dumfries and Galloway for flying training in the late 1930s with several major airfields becoming home to squadrons tasked with the interception of German aircraft attacking Glasgow. Many anti-submarine and air-sea rescue aircraft were based near the port of Stranraer, or further north at the seaplane base in Loch Ryan.

Galloway, and especially Wigtownshire, was a hive of military activity. Airfields sprang up all over the region, along with gunnery and bombing ranges and with the usual support units such as air-sea rescue. The main areas of activity were the seaplane units on Loch Ryan and the Air Observer School at Baldoon, known officially as RAF Wigtown, which is where Louis Hoslin was based.

An old family photo of Louis (on the left) and his brothers and sister.

During the war, the number of flying training crashes involving aircrew was staggering, and the activities at RAF Wigtown were to prove no different. At one stage, so many crews and aircraft were lost during a single month that the authorities even considered closing down the station. On analysis, it was discovered that the majority of crashes were caused by inexperienced and, in some cases, ill-disciplined Czechs and Poles. The solution was to insist on greater discipline and within a short period of time the number of crashes fell to an acceptable level.

Wigtown soon fulfilled the role of a bombing and gunnery school but the base's grass airfield was not fully utilised until 1941, when 1 Air Observation School took up residence.

By 1943 RAF Wigtown (Baldoon) had concrete runways installed and it was here that Louis Hoslin was a staff pilot attached to No.1 (Observers) Advanced Flying Unit. One of his roles was to pilot a target tug, probably one of the least glamorous flying jobs in the RAF, but an invaluable job nonetheless. The tug aircraft towed a drogue – a long sleeve of brightly coloured canvas rather like a huge windsock – that was tethered behind the tug by approximately one hundred and fifty feet of cable. The moving target was then shot at by trainee gunners who could practice deflection shooting on the aerial target.

The drogue was released by an operator and recovered by assessors, and it was quite usual for a first-time gunner to fire hundreds of rounds at the drogue and miss it completely. More worryingly, it was not uncommon for stray bullets to sometimes hit the tug and, for the pilots of these aircraft, it was frustrating, potentially dangerous and dreary work.

By their very nature, the tug aircraft were second-line types relegated from operational duties. To emphasise their training role and make them more visible, the colours of the target towing aircraft were standardised as large black and yellow diagonal stripes on the under surfaces of the aircraft, and later the whole aircraft.

It was fulfilling this vital but tedious work that was to cost Louis Hoslin his life. On 28 April 1943 Flying Officer Hoslin was scheduled to fly a target towing exercise and was allocated Westland Lysander III P9118.

Having completed the exercise, Louis Hoslin descended to release the target drogue for the assessors to retrieve, near Innerwell, seven miles south of the airfield, at 1630 hours. On opening the throttle to climb away, the engine failed, forcing the pilot to make an emergency landing on rough terrain.

A Westland Lysander in target-towing livery

The Lysander landed heavily and turned over, resulting in injuries to both Louis and the drogue operator. Louis, the pilot, was severely injured – intra abdominal injuries, fracture of the right humerus, and severe shock. He was rushed to Galloway House, an emergency hospital set up in the requisitioned home of the Earl of Galloway. His injuries proved fatal and he died that same evening. He was twenty-eight years old.

The drogue operator was not badly injured and was reported as *'making satisfactory progress'*.

Although Louis was a relatively experienced Lysander pilot, with 148 hours flying time on this type of aircraft, the accident investigators thought that the fuel mixture had been set too weak, and that upon opening the throttle suddenly, the engine had choked and stalled. The Air Officer Commanding (AOC), who was keen to give his pilot the benefit of any doubt, asserted that this conclusion was not fully supported by the evidence.

An aeronautical historian who later reviewed the report, considered the original investigation conclusion to be entirely credible, especially as cold weather could exacerbate the effects of the mixture lever set in the 'lean' position.

Louis's wife Kay, was in the early stages of pregnancy when he died and the shock of her husband's tragic death and the resultant stress, caused her to miscarry.

Despite Louis's family living just outside Banstead, in 1951 his father wrote to Banstead Council requesting his son's inclusion on the village war memorial, a request which was willingly accommodated.

Louis lies buried in Epsom Cemetery, not far from his parents' home. He does not have the usual Commonwealth War Graves Commission headstone as he is buried in the family plot, which now includes his father, Charles and his mother Jane.

Flying Officer Louis Charles Hoslin
Epsom Cemetery
Surrey
England
Grave Reference: H 560

Sources:
Commonwealth War Graves Commission. Personal information from Jerry Hoslin. Portrait photo of Louis Hoslin from Andrea Tait. Crash details from aeronautical historian Peter Connon. GC Books (Wigtown) website. *Action Stations 7 (airfields of Scotland)* - David J Smith - 1983. Photograph of Westland Lysander in tug-towing livery courtesy of Doug Fisher – Warbird Depot website. Details of the *Weser* from http://www.airmuseum.ca. Surrey History Centre ref 6128/1/89.

Fact*file*

Banstead War Memorial – World War Two – Panel 3 records

NAME	RANK	DATE OF DEATH	CEMETERY/MEMORIAL
Rees			Berlin
Maurice Owen	Flying Officer	30/01/1944	Germany
Croxall			Floriana
James Frederick	Sergeant	04/07/1943	Malta
Brown (unidentified)			
J			
Peasley			Staglieno
Edward John	Leading Seaman	18/05/1945	Italy
Stanley			Banstead
Leslie Albert	Private	08/05/1947	England
Hart (unidentified)			
R J			
Clark			Bayeux
John Edward	Private	03/08/1944	France
Griffits			Whittlesford
James Olliff	Pilot Officer	28/03/1940	England
Griffits			Memorial
Patrick Gordon	Flight Sergeant	02/10/1944	Singapore
Hoslin			Epsom
Louis Charles	Flying Officer	28/04/1943	England
Best			Chatham
Ronald Stanley	Able Seaman	13/06/1944	England
Bell			Rheinberg
Kenneth Thomas	Flying Officer	02/02/1945	Germany

Name *Lintott J.P.M. DFC*

Rank *Flight Lieutenant (Pilot) 61056*

Service *Royal Air Force*

Volunteer Reserve 85 Squadron

Date of death *9/7/1943* Age *22*

JOHN PETER MARLEY LINTOTT was the only son of Percival and Phyllis Lintott who always called him 'Peter'. His parents were married in Croydon in 1920 and Peter was born on the 22 June 1921 in Beckenham, Kent, his birth being registered in Bromley where his mother's maiden name was recorded as Spence. Peter lived for most of his life at *Romina* 60 Woodmansterne Lane, Banstead, to which his parents moved when he was about three years old.

Peter seems to have been an active sportsman winning a competition in 1938 at Ewell Castle School. The inscription mounted on the cricket ball he kept as a trophy, shows that he threw it seventy-eight and one-half yards to win the competition.

Like many boys who grew up in the 1930s, Peter was aware of, and attracted by, the progress being made in aviation, and living in Banstead, would have seen aircraft in the sky overhead very regularly. He lived a comparatively short distance from Croydon Airport, which at that time was at the centre of world aviation having more international routes than any other airport in the world, the first purpose-built passenger air terminal, as well as the first registered air traffic controller.

Mrs Phyllis Lintott, known in the family as Daisy and later by her granddaughter as 'Granny Phyl', recalled Peter's love of aeroplanes from a very young age. He built and even designed his own model aircraft, photographing them as a record. He was a keen photographer and took his camera to the Hendon air shows of the late 1930s to take pictures of the real aeroplanes.

Peter built numerous models. Shown here is a Gloster Gauntlet, an RAF bi-plane fighter used in the mid-thirties.

Each model was photographed for his album and initially he used cotton wool stuck to a board to simulate clouds in the background. As he progressed, he used perspective to create a far more realistic view, as illustrated here.

Peter as a Cadet in Paignton – 1940

It was not at all surprising then that whilst still a schoolboy, Peter decided that he wanted to become a pilot. After finishing school at Ewell Castle in the early summer of 1939 he applied to join, and was accepted by, the Royal Air Force, being offered a Short Service Commission that August.

The outbreak of war only a month later brought about the cancellation of the Short Service Commission scheme and his acceptance was automatically nullified. Greatly disappointed that this would delay his dream to fly, he immediately applied to join the Royal Air Force Volunteer Reserve.

Reporting to his Aviation Candidate Selection Board on 19 December 1939, the day after his 'official enlistment', Peter was assessed as suitable for aircrew training and at last made the first step along the road to fulfilling his long-held ambitions.

Peter would have to wait a while longer however, as the more pressing needs of fighting a war took precedence over the organisation of the training of new aircrew not already within the 'system'. On 18 June 1940, just a few days before his nineteenth birthday, he was mobilised but it was not until the end of September that Peter was posted to No 5 SFTS (Service Flying Training School) at RAF Ternhill near Market Drayton.

Here Peter learnt to fly, and it was also here that he was assessed as having the aptitude to fly 'single-engined aircraft' which invariably meant 'fighters'. For the young pilots under training, having witnessed the exploits of the men of Fighter Command, who were still in the process of fighting and ultimately winning the Battle of Britain, this must have been welcome news indeed.

Peter passed his SFTS course with a score of 82.8 per cent on 14 February 1941 and was awarded his pilot's 'wings' the following day. Two days later he reported to RAF Grangemouth on Tayside, where he joined the strength of 58 OTU (Operational Training Unit) who were equipped with the Supermarine Spitfire.

On 31 March, newly promoted to Pilot Officer, Peter received his first operational posting to 616 Squadron RAF Fighter Command. Based at RAF Tangmere near Chichester on the Sussex coast, 616 Squadron was one of three fighter squadrons that made up the Tangmere Wing commanded by Wing Commander Douglas Bader, later made famous by the Kenneth More film *Reach For The Sky*, which was about the legless pilot's exploits.

Details of Peter's time with 616 Squadron are few, although on 25 June 1941, his aircraft was apparently shot-up whilst on a sweep over France. He was slightly wounded but made a good landing upon return to base.

Peter as a Spitfire pilot with 616 Squadron.

He wears a standard issue life-jacket known popularly as a 'Mae West' on the basis that it created rather a 'buxom' appearance for the pilots wearing it. Of interest is the personalised 'JPML' design painted on the lifejacket, showing a bit of artistry on Peter's part. His flying helmet with radio leads already plugged in to facilitate a speedy take-off, sits in front of the cockpit's armoured windscreen .

616 Squadron started to re-equip with the Spitfire MkV in July 1941 which helps to date the photograph below as being just before then (spring or early summer) as Peter is standing in front of the older Spitfire MkIIA.

Peter in centre Spitfire with two pupils flying over Romina from HESTON 1941

Peter and Shirley on their wedding day

Peter claimed no aerial victories whilst with 616 Squadron and appears to have been an unremarkable member of the squadron by the standards of the time.

He completed a six-month tour of operations after which he was posted as an instructor on Spitfires to 61 OTU at RAF Heston in Middlesex. After four months, in February 1942 he was posted to 90 Squadron of RAF Bomber Command then equipped with the American built B17 'Flying Fortress' at RAF Colerne in Wiltshire. Why he transferred to 90 Squadron, is unclear, as it was to disband soon after he arrived.

If Peter's service life was temporarily showing a lack of direction (although he was notified of a promotion to Flying Officer in March), his personal life was definitely looking up. In June 1942 Peter married a girl from Croydon whom he had met two years earlier, at the twenty-first birthday party of his cousin Ian Spence. Peter knew that Ian was friendly with two sisters and specifically asked him to invite them to the party. Miss Shirley Winifred Parke, one of the sisters, would eventually become Peter's wife.

Married life would have been a welcome change for Peter, but his wartime career was now to change direction again, and this time, it would lead him into an area of operations in which he would truly excel.

Posted first to 54 OTU in Berwickshire, Peter learned to fly the fast and formidable two-seater, twin-engined Mosquito fighter-bomber, and at the end of the year, he was posted to RAF Hunsdon in Hertfordshire, a satellite airfield of RAF North Weald. He was by this time an experienced pilot with both combat and training tours behind him.

Here he joined the strength of 85 Squadron flying de Havilland Mosquito night-fighters where he was crewed with Sergeant (later Pilot Officer) George Gilling-Lax as his Navigator/Radar Operator. George, who was twelve years older than Peter, had been to school at Marlborough before gaining a first-class degree at King's College, Cambridge. When war broke out, he was a Housemaster at Stowe school. After joining the RAF he trained as a navigator, although on night-fighting Mosquitoes his main responsibility would be the operation of the AI (airborne interception) radar used to locate enemy night-raiders.

No. 85 was one of the RAF's oldest and most distinguished squadrons, with a history going back to the First World War. It was heavily committed in the 1940 Battle of France and Battle of Britain. During the latter, it was based at RAF Croydon (close to Peter's home) under the command of Squadron Leader Peter Townsend, who also oversaw the squadron's conversion to a specialist night-fighting role in the winter of 1940/41. During the Luftwaffe's night offensive, which continued sporadically throughout 1941 and 1942, the squadron experimented with a number of innovations, including the American-built Douglas 'Turbinlite' Havocs, twin-engined medium bombers with a searchlight mounted in the nose to illuminate German bombers, and which would fly with an accompanying Hurricane to shoot them down.

Under their commander, Wing Commander Gordon Raphael, 85 Squadron began to re-equip with Mosquitoes on 15 August 1942, but it would take until October before the squadron saw action with their new charges, when Flt Lt Nigel Bunting damaged a Junkers Ju88 over East Anglia.

It was perhaps appropriate that 85's first Mosquito victory was claimed by their Wing Commander and his navigator, Warrant Officer Nat Addison, when they shot down a Pathfinder Ju88 of I/KG66 on the night of 14 January 1943.

Just days after this victory, Raphael was given a deserved rest from operations and command of the squadron passed to Wing Commander John Cunningham DSO, DFC, who arrived with his navigator Jimmy Rawnsley from 604 Squadron. John Cunningham was one of the most famous RAF night-fighter pilots of the war. He was nick-named 'Cat's Eyes' by the press, on account of his prowess, having already shot down ten enemy aircraft between November 1940 and May 1942. He would destroy several more aircraft whilst on Mosquitoes and ended the war with twenty 'confirmed victories', three 'probables' and seven 'damaged'.

Cunningham was an extremely demanding commander and when he arrived at 85 Squadron he quickly assessed the abilities of the aircrews. Some were posted out of the squadron and several others were brought in. It seems that Peter secured the approval of his new Commanding Officer, and he was promoted to Flight Lieutenant on 17 February.

Under Cunningham's command 85 Squadron was to become a formidable night-fighter squadron. In March they were selected to introduce the high altitude Mosquito NFXV's into service, Flt Lt Nigel Bunting getting one up to 46,000 feet on 10 April. However with the threat of high altitude raids diminishing, these aircraft were withdrawn from service.

In the same month, they also exchanged their Mosquito NFII's for the more advanced NFXII's. These aircraft had the more powerful Merlin 21 or 23 engines and a more advanced AI capability. This new MK VIII radar which operated on a 10cm wavelength required a parabolic reflector to be housed in the nose of the aircraft, giving the Mosquitoes a distinctive 'thimble nose', but making external aerials unnecessary.

The squadron had not seen much action at the end of 1942, but in the spring and summer of 1943 the Luftwaffe embarked on a renewed night offensive, combining the latest generation of it's twin-engined Ju88s and 188s and Dornier 217s, making the less effective Heinkel 111s more or less obsolete.

At 2310 hours on the evening of 24 April 1943, Peter Lintott and George Gilling-Lax took off from Hunsdon to patrol Foulness, before being redirected to North Weald Control. They were then passed over to a Ground Controller (GCI), Sqn Ldr Bickerstaff at East Hill, who vectored the Mosquito crew onto a 'bandit'. The enemy aircraft was closed on from a distance of 14 miles and Lintott and Gilling-Lax eventually spotted the exhaust flames of the enemy bomber.

Closing in still further, they barely made out the silhouette of a Ju88, weaving above an 8/10ths cloud layer. Peter checked once again by flying above and behind the Ju88, before dropping below it, pulling the nose of the Mosquito up and opening fire. His 20mm cannon fire ripped into the fuselage of the Junkers which immediately caught fire. Lintott fired again and the Junkers's starboard engine flashed as it too was hit. The Junkers turned over onto its back and dived vertically into the cloud, disappearing at 0025 hours.

The GCI advised Lintott not to follow due to the poor visibility lower down, but the advice became academic as the crew saw a bright red glow in the cloud, as the enemy aircraft exploded. Lintott and Gilling-Lax resumed their patrol over Foulness, until 0200 hours after which they returned to Hunsdon landing at 0220 hours.

Lintott and Gilling-Lax's first confirmed victory was a Ju88A-14 of 8 Staffel KG6, piloted by Lt A Beyerle who was killed along with two other crew members. Uffz. E Behmer baled out and was captured. The aircraft broke up over Bromley in Kent and wreckage was scattered over a wide area. The largest chunks of wreckage landed on 124-126 Widmore Road, destroying the two large houses. These have since been replaced by a block of flats called Cromarty Court.

A new danger now threatened UK airspace in the form of large numbers of single-engined Fw (Focke Wulf) 190 fighter-bombers which flew intruder missions into UK airspace. A new Schnell Kampfgeschwader, 'Fast' Bomber Group, SKG10 were directed to commence operations against the UK.

It was specifically to address this last threat that after two years at RAF Hunsdon, the squadron were advised on 5 May 1943 (coincidentally the same day that the Squadron was officially presented with its new crest) that they were to move to RAF West Malling in Kent, within the Biggin Hill sector. There remained the question of just how capable the twin-engined Mosquitoes would be against the heavily armed and nimble German single-seat fighters. Any concerns that the squadron might have had in this respect were lost in a display of youthful exuberance, for on 13 May, the day that the squadron left for West Malling, each departing Mosquito crew took it in turns to 'beat up' their old airfield, a display which has gone down in the squadron's history. 'Beating up' their airfield meant that as each aircraft and crew departed, they made a fast low-level pass over the airfield. This was strictly against regulations, although a common enough occurrence amongst the high-spirited young men who flew during the war. The authorities usually turned a blind eye, probably because most base commanders had been pilots themselves!

Any remaining doubts about the capability of the Mosquitoes were soon dispelled as 85 Squadron shot down its first Fw190s on the night of 15/16 May. Two aircraft from 1/SKG 10 sneaking-in at low level across the channel were intercepted by Mosquitoes flown by Sqn Ldr Peter Green and Flt Lt Geoff Howitt. Howitt's victim crashed into the sea south of Hastings whilst Green's crashed near Dover, the first of these single-seat raiders to be brought down on English soil. If this wasn't impressive enough, Flt Officer Bernard Thwaites and his navigator Bill Clemo chased a third Fw190 back across the channel, shooting it into the sea, and then, despite damage caused by the disintegrating enemy plane, also shot down a fourth aircraft. Flt Officer J D Shaw, together with P/O A C Lowton, shot down a fifth Fw190 before the end of the night by braving their own searchlight defences and dispatching their victim over Gravesend, returning to base covered in soot and with a badly damaged rudder; an emphatic demonstration of 85 Squadron's prowess.

Two nights later, on the 18th, Peter Lintott and George Gilling-Lax also enjoyed success against the Fw190s, shooting down an aircraft of 2/SKG 10 over the coast, one of thirteen raiders dispatched from France that night.

Patrolling over Dungeness, Lintott and Gilling-Lax were vectored onto an enemy contact from over forty miles away. Despite clear conditions, the darkness of the sky required skilful guidance by Gilling-Lax using the AI radar. At 21,500 feet over the Thames Estuary, Lintott got a visual of an Fw190 fighter-bomber

George Gilling-Lax

silhouetted against the lighter western horizon. He noted that the Fw190 carried long-range fuel tanks and a bomb under the fuselage. He lost sight of his quarry but closed and picked it up again, noting that the Luftwaffe pilot had just jettisoned his auxiliary fuel tanks. Lintott closed to 180 yards and opened fire from astern, causing flashes and sparks to fly off the enemy aircraft. The Fw190 made a turn to port and Lintott's second burst missed. His third however, resulted in further flashes and sparks through which the Mosquito flew. The Fw190 weaved erratically and disappeared below the nose of the Mosquito. Turning tightly, Lintott and Gilling-Lax saw an explosion beneath them as their victim hit the sea, at 2330 hours, a burning pool of oil and fuel visible for twenty to thirty seconds.

A week later Peter Lintott and George Gilling-Lax would score their third and penultimate 'kill' against a raider from KG66 (Kampfgeschwader - Bomber Group). This was a specialist pathfinder unit established in April 1943 by Oberst Dietrich Peltz, who, at just twenty-nine years old, was the youngest commanding General in the entire Wehrmacht, personally tasked by Hitler to re-galvanise air operations against England. Woefully under-equipped, he stood little chance of success but 1/KG66 started to be re-equipped with the newest and fastest version of the Ju88, the 'S' variant, which used nitrous oxide to boost engine performance.

On the night of 29/30 May 1943, Lintott and Gilling-Lax took off from West Malling in Mosquito NFXII - HK119 coded VY-S. Patrolling above Lewes in Sussex they were vectored onto a 'bandit' seven miles away. They closed in, having to climb progressively, eventually reaching 29,000 feet. The black night sky made identification difficult, and Lintott thought that the enemy bomber was a Dornier 217 instead of the new S-type Ju88s. Having satisfactorily identified the enemy aircraft, Lintott opened fire, damaging the aircraft by setting its starboard engine alight. A second burst achieved the same result on the port engine, causing the crew to bale out. Two or three further bursts resulted in a lazy turn to port and the blazing bomber started to go down. The flames may have caused the raider's nitrous oxide tanks to explode, as the aircraft blew up spectacularly.

The German aircraft was Ju88S-1 (140550) of I/KG66, which broke up in the air and crashed at Isfield, Sussex, at 0150 hours. The three crew, one injured, were taken prisoner. This aeroplane was the first of this new variant to be shot down over England and the first loss for the newly formed KG66.

Lintott and Gilling-Lax were by now seen as rising stars in 85 Squadron with three confirmed 'kills', and with Peter Lintott earning the sobriquet 'killer' in recognition of his exploits.

Mosquito NFXII HK119 - VY-S, airborne from Hunsdon in early May 1943. This aircraft was used by Peter Lintott to shoot down the Ju88S on the night of 29/30 May 1943.

Gilling-Lax had just been commissioned, in time for both himself and his pilot, Peter Lintott, to be recommended for the Distinguished Flying Cross.

DFCs were awarded for *'an act or acts of valour, courage or devotion to duty whilst flying in active operations against the enemy'*. In Lintott and Gilling-Lax's case it was almost certainly for a sustained period of success against the enemy within which skill and courage had been displayed.

In early summer, the squadron was enjoying considerable success against the German intruders, but in July the weather broke. On the afternoon of 9 July, with driving rain and low scudding clouds, two experienced crews from 85 Squadron stood at readiness as an 'all-weather' section. 'B' Flight Commander F/L Geoff Howitt and his radar operator F/O G N Irving were joined by F/L Peter Lintott and P/O Gilling-Lax. They were scrambled in the bad weather to intercept a wave of sneak raiders coming up the Medway under cover of the weather. Twenty minutes after taking off, the sounds of air combat could be heard from the airfield, above the cloud and rain, together with the sounds of anti-aircraft fire. The unmistakable sound of cannon fire from a Mosquito was heard moments before the rising scream of a descending aircraft, cut short by the sound of an ominous thump.

Neither Mosquito returned to West Malling and the frustration and concern on the airfield was considerable. After a short while, the RAF base at Detling just across the Medway Valley reported that a Dornier 217 had crashed close to the airfield. Local anti-aircraft batteries were claiming the kill but it emerged that the local Ground Controller at Wartling had guided Lintott onto this aircraft, and Lintott's Mosquito had been tracking and closing on it for seven minutes before it crashed. The controller had followed both blips on his screen but both had disappeared at the same time at 1727 hours.

A phone call from RAF Bradwell Bay on the other side of the Thames Estuary brought confirmation that Howitt and Irving had landed safely, flying in under the low cloud, having pursued the raiders out to sea. Then finally the news that everyone had been dreading – Lintott's Mosquito was found less than two miles from the wreckage of the Dornier at Boxley near Maidstone, with both crew dead in the cockpit. When it was pointed out to the anti-aircraft gunners that eye-witnesses had described their fire as 'inaccurate', and that if they claimed an enemy bomber shot down, they might as well claim for a Mosquito as well, the gunners withdrew their claim.

The Armament Officer from Fighter Command HQ later inspected the wreckage of the Mosquito and determined that Lintott had indeed fired his guns. Lintott and Gilling-Lax had scored their fourth and final victory (one short of acedom) before they crashed into the ground.

The inspection of the Mosquito revealed that it had partially broken up before it hit the ground. There is the possibility that in his determination to shoot down the Dornier, Lintott may have collided with it. Alternatively, it is also possible that the Mosquito could have been damaged by debris from the disintegrating bomber. It does seem however that the crash was caused by structural failure of the Mosquito due to excessive 'wing loading'. It seems likely therefore that an error of judgement in appalling weather conditions and at a very low level, combined with the distraction of an eagerness to shoot down the intruder, cost Lintott and Gilling-Lax their lives. They were a bitter loss to the squadron.

Lintott's and Gilling-Lax's victim was Dornier 217K-1 (4519) of 6th Staffel KG2, which crashed at Bicknor Court Farm, Detling, Kent. The aircraft disintegrated upon impact and the crew were all killed. They were Oberlt H Zink, Uffz W Bernhardt, Uffz E Freiermuth and Obergftr E Stiermann.

This Dornier 217 was one of ten aircraft dispatched by KG2 on Friday 9 July in appallingly bad weather, and one of these raiders was eventually responsible for the bombing of the Whitehall Cinema in East Grinstead. This was a tragic incident caused by a bomber circling the town before dropping a stick of eight bombs across the Town Centre. It is still unclear what the target was; a convoy of trucks in the High Street or perhaps a train that had pulled into the station. The cost was terrible for so small a town; no fewer than one hundred and eight people were killed, and two hundred and thirty-five injured, requiring a communal burial of some of the victims on the following Wednesday.

It is always perhaps comforting to think that the perpetrators of such an infamous attack failed to escape, and many Banstead villagers believed that this raider was the one shot down by Peter Lintott, but whilst there is a very slim chance that this is so, it seems unlikely. The aircraft had been pursued by Lintott for seven minutes as it looked for targets of opportunity over the Medway area of Kent, and was brought down at Detling in Kent. East Grinstead is in Sussex about thirty miles (as the crow flies) south-west of Detling, which means that had it dropped its bombs on East Grinstead it would have been flying north-eastwards (away from its French base) when Lintott shot it down.

East Grinstead Dornier 217 or not, Lintott and Gilling-Lax's achievements were considerable and were recognised with the award to both men of the DFC, gazetted some two weeks after their deaths. In the short twelve-week period of time that they were together they had accounted for four enemy aircraft destroyed, and were described as *'a brilliant crew and a severe loss to the squadron'.*

Peter's Distinguished Flying Cross and 'wings'

Following Peter's death, his wife Shirley discovered that she was expecting their first child, and early in 1944, she gave birth to a baby girl. The child was called, Jenifer Peta Marley in honour of her late father, and she has always been known as Peta.

Mrs Lintott remarried a Captain Tollington some years later and together, they lived in Germany and later Cyprus. Peta was eventually adopted by Captain Tollington who of course became 'Daddy', although Peta always referred to Peter Lintott, the father she had never known, as 'Daddy Peter'.

Peta has kept several treasured possessions of Peter's, including his photograph albums, cameras, his cricket ball trophy, his DFC, and a purple and white striped silk scarf, matching the DFC ribbon, which she wears every Remembrance Day.

Flight Lieutenant (Pilot)
John Peter Marley Lintott
All Saints Churchyard
Banstead
Surrey
Grave: north-west of main entrance to Church

The poem on the facing page was written by Percy Whichelo in Peter's memory.

Sources:
Commonwealth War Graves Commission. All Saints Church, Banstead. Personal photos, medal and other items courtesy of Mrs Peta Watson. *Night Fighter* by CF Rawnsley 1957. *(85) Fighter Squadron at War* by AJ Brookes 1980. *Fighter Squadrons of the RAF and Their Aircraft* by John Rawlings. 1969. - *The Blitz, Then and Now.* Edited by Winston G Ramsay. (After the Battle). 1990. *Mosquito Aces of WW2* by Andrew Thomas. Osprey. 2005. *Mosquito Fighter/Fighter Bomber Units of WW2* by Martin Bowman. Osprey. 1998. 85 Sqn Association via Paul Abbott. National Archives - 85 Squadron combat reports 'Form F' - J.P.M. Lintott. Poem by Percy Whichelo supplied by Peta Watson.

Peter

"Tall and brave and fair"
A hackneyed phrase;
But one so very true of Peter.
His life so short was mostly
                    in the air.
Flying was his boyhood's thought,
And against slavery everywhere,
Like a bird above the trees,
That is how he fought
For freedom:
Helping to win for England
So much more —
A glory which is hers —and his.

PERCY WHICHELO

In grateful memory

1944

The siege of Leningrad is ended after 872 days by the re-opening of the rail connection with Moscow. By mid-year, for the first time in four years, Russian troops are fighting across other soil than their own.

In the Pacific, the Americans continue to take back islands from the stubbornly resisting Japanese.

On 6 June, a communique tells us 'Under the command of General Eisenhower allied naval forces supported by strong air forces began landing allied armies this morning on the northern coast of France'. D-Day has finally come. Within a 24-hour period a vast armada of 4000 ships has conveyed and landed 160,000 troops and their equipment on Normandy beaches. Resistance from the enemy is stiff but the beachheads are secured despite the Americans taking heavy casualties at Omaha Beach.

Soon the V1 flying bomb appears over southern England and later, V2 rockets. A V1 explodes close by Banstead War Memorial but it survives intact although several properties are severely damaged.

A bomb plot on Hitler's life fails at his field HQ at Rastenburg, East Prussia. General de Gaulle receives rapturous reception in a liberated Paris. The German battleship *Tirpitz* is finally sunk at her Norwegian moorings. British airborne forces make vain attempts to sieze Arnhem Bridge over the Lower Rhine in Holland, in order to outflank the Siegfried Line of German defences.

A week before Christmas the Germans launch a fierce onslaught in the Belgian Ardennes and American troops are forced to retreat. The Battle of the Bulge is one of Hitler's last attempts to prevent the Allies storming into his Third Reich. It ends in a German defeat.

Name ...REEDER R.C.............................

Rank ...SUB-LIEUTENANT (A)..................

Service ...ROYAL NAVAL VOLUNTEER RESERVE....

...FLEET AIR ARM HMS GODWIT (HINSTOCK)....

Date of death ...2/1/1944... Age ...22........

ROBERT CHARLES REEDER was the son of Charles Edward and Clara Reeder, of 4 Wilmot Way, Banstead. Whilst his father was master at the Central Boys School in Picquets Way, Robert attended Sutton County School until 1938. He was very active within the Banstead community being a member of both the Junior Imperial League (Young Conservatives) and the Banstead Downs Lawn Tennis Club, but one of his greatest interests lay in aviation.

Like many local youngsters he was close enough to Croydon Airport to regularly see a wide variety of aircraft in the skies over Banstead, but in Robert's case he also had the example, and possibly the inspiration, of an uncle, Captain R Reeder (also Robert), who flew and was subsequently killed whilst on active service with the Royal Flying Corps in WWI.

Upon leaving school Robert worked for the Civil Service, and when the war started he joined the staff of the Ministry of Economic Warfare (MEW) at Berkeley Square House in

central London. It was here that he met Valerie Sleep, a shorthand-typist, who lived in Highgate, North London, and who would become his fiancée in the summer of 1941. Robert wrote to her every few days throughout his service career, often referring to her as 'Valee'. Over one-hundred letters posted to Valerie by her 'Bobby' have survived in the care of the family, containing much information about Robert's training, his service life, and of course the thoughts and emotions of a young man very much in love, and serving his country in wartime.

The backdrop to the start of Robert's relationship with Valerie was central London at the height of the Battle of Britain and into the Blitz of late autumn and winter 1940.

Robert and Valerie outside the Ministry of Economic Warfare at Berkeley Square House

Like most city workers, duties for Robert weren't confined to his 'day-job' and he did his stint as a fire-watcher high on the roof of the Ministry, boiler-suited and equipped with the ubiquitous tin-hat. This, by all accounts, was a distinctly thankless task, and in a letter posted in the winter of 1940 Robert commiserated with Valerie when she too had to take her turn as a fire-watcher.

Inevitably, active service beckoned, and whilst at the MEW Robert applied to join the Royal Air Force. Failing the selection for aircrew on medical grounds, Robert was determined to find a way to fly and applied instead to join the Fleet Air Arm, the air arm of the Royal Navy. Robert was fortunate to be assisted in his efforts by a Captain Brown, who Robert refers to in one of his letters, as being influential within the Admiralty. Whatever the nature of his medical condition, he was accepted for pilot training.

His active service began on 11 November 1940 when he arrived late in the evening at HMS *St Vincent* at Gosport near Portsmouth, after a five-hour journey from Banstead. Robert seems to have been distinctly unimpressed with initial aspects of life in the Navy. Woken at 0645 hours on his first morning, the entire day was spent queuing for uniform and kit. In the days that followed, his initial training comprised of seamanship, navigation, Morse code, and drill – marching and parading, often in freezing temperatures; as Robert wrote in disgust to Valerie, *'We're not even allowed to wear our greatcoats!'*

If things had started inauspiciously they were about to get worse as Robert was hospitalised for several days after an inoculation was mistakenly injected into a vein rather than muscle. Hospital food didn't help either; on 27 November 1940 Robert wrote to Valerie hoping that her Christmas puddings had turned out okay, adding *'that if you dropped a pound of cement into them I think it would* [still] *make a good show after the food we get here'*.

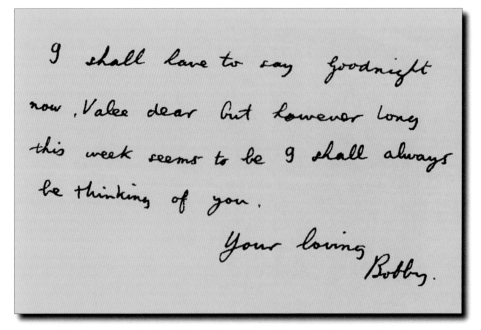

Valerie was never far from Robert's thoughts and he wrote to her every few days

During this period, Robert's letters home mainly concerned how and when he could wangle the odd day of leave in order to get back to London to see Valerie, even if only for an hour or two.

Robert's Christmas at Gosport was largely spent *'swotting'* for his exams, which took place on the 30 December. Worried about the fifty per cent rejection rate and the ignominy of not making the grade, he started to study hard.

Fortunately, Robert passed his initial training exams and in early January was posted to No. 24 EFTS (Elementary Flying Training School) at Luton Aerodrome in Bedfordshire. Although he was now to begin flying training, something that he had been keenly anticipating, he was to discover that the domestic arrangements were not quite what he was expecting. Robert found himself among a group of trainees billeted in a stable block on an estate at Luton Hoo, some three miles from the airfield. They were required to rise at 0630 hours in order to catch the transport to the aerodrome, snatching a hasty breakfast before they left, which meant inevitably arriving hungry with the morning's training ahead of them. 'Improvement' came in the form of a move from the stable block to the Power House – *'dusty, freezing cold and with electricity generators'*.

Service training was not glamorous, and by early February, with snow on the ground and flying out of the question, a demoralised Robert complained to Valerie that it was impossible to keep warm at night *'even with six blankets'* saying that *'I don't care any more if I fly or do ground work'*. Soon after, he caught influenza – another unpleasant experience.

No. 24 EFTS was predominantly equipped with de Havilland Tiger Moth and Miles Magister primary trainers and by late February Robert and the other trainees were soon learning to fly these aeroplanes under an intensive timetable that saw them airborne as early as 0630 hours with flying continuing until dusk. Armament classes, aircraft recognition and navigation were interspersed with flying training.

Robert Reeder under instruction in 1941.

The aircraft is a Miles Magister trainer which was the first monoplane designed specifically as an RAF trainer.

Magister is the Latin word for *'instructor'* or *'teacher'* but the aircraft was more often called *'Maggie'* by many of those who flew it.

On 11 February 1941 there was a fatal crash at Luton and not long after, on 3 March, Robert wrote to Valerie, telling her that whilst taking off, another aircraft had crashed in front of him. The pilot scrambled clear but Robert was shaken up by the accident.

All service pilots at this time were expected to fly solo after ten or so hours of dual instruction. Robert commented in one of his letters that there were several pilots who still hadn't 'soloed' after fourteen hours dual instruction. He flew solo for the first time on 24 March.

During this period Robert was able to get up to London to see Valerie almost weekly. They were keen to get engaged but his letters hint at Valerie's father proving difficult to win round. His daughter's young age and the fact that Robert was going off to war were no doubt factors in his reluctance to agree. Robert completed his basic flying training at the end of April and spent a week with Valerie before returning temporarily to RN barracks at Lee-on-Solent on 5 May. In his letter of the same date he encourages Valerie to *wear your father down'*.

During a few brief weeks at Lee, Robert achieved one ambition when he got to watch an aircraft being launched by catapult. Soon afterwards, in early July, he was posted to 1 SFTS (Service Flying Training School) at RAF Netheravon in Wiltshire, to begin his intermediate training as part of Course Number 22. This would include night-flying, and the new pilots – both Fleet Air Arm and Royal Air Force – would fly more powerful machines including pre-war Hawker bi-planes such as the Audax and Hart.

Robert liked Netheravon. The food was good and he was delighted that the trainees were allocated a batman who made their beds and polished their shoes.

By this time Valerie had agreed to marry Robert and they were in the final stages of persuading Mr Sleep to give his blessing. The 'wearing down' process finally succeeded at the end of July and in a letter dated 30th of that month, Robert was intrigued to know what the reaction of his own family and Valerie's colleagues at MEW had been to the *'engagement bombshell'*.

At Netheravon, Robert grew in confidence and experience as a pilot. He flew solo at night for the first time on 6 July and at the month's end had commenced dive-bombing training. On the last day of the month he was awarded his 'wings', having successfully completed training on the Hawker Hart.

Now living in comfortable quarters, he shared a room with a fellow pilot who had been recovering for five months after a bad training crash. Robert himself would soon experience the dangers of wartime training. On one occasion several of the bracing wires of his Hawker bi-plane broke, and he affected an emergency landing with the top wing of his aeroplane *'wobbling six inches from side to side'*.

In a separate incident, Robert was caught in a storm and had to fly without goggles to improve visibility, with the result that his face and eyes were badly inflamed by the driving rain and hail. He was hospitalised for a week and off flying for much of August.

Confined to ground duties, Robert spent a lot of time training on the Link Trainer, an early flight-simulation trainer, in which trainees learnt the key discipline of relying on their aircraft's instruments.

Towards the end of the course, he graduated onto the Fairey Battle aeroplane and practiced dummy aircraft-carrier deck landings. He wrote that he would have soloed on the light-bomber in record time had his aircraft not been acquired by a senior officer for other duties.

By the end of 1941 Robert had completed his training and as a qualified pilot and Sub-Lieutenant in the Royal Navy Fleet Air Arm, he would have looked towards the final stages of his training before gaining an operational posting, to either a land-based unit, or a carrier-borne combat unit. There are few clues in the surviving correspondence to establish categorically why Robert's service career now took the direction it did, but it seems clear that his underlying 'medical condition' was a factor.

In early 1942 Robert was posted to a communications unit based at a Royal Naval Air Station (RNAS) called HMS *Merlin* at Donibristle in Fife, Scotland. Known colloquially as *Donny-Bee* this was a very busy FAA station as well as a temporary home to many units. Operational units 'worked-up' there prior to deployment or embarkation. Carrier-borne squadrons rotated through *Donny-Bee* between deployments, and Robert met former colleagues from 22 Course passing through the station and onto operational squadrons.

He regularly ferried aircraft around the country and gained experience on several aircraft types, but the spring of 1942 seems to have been an unhappy period for the young pilot.

Separated from his fiancée and unable to see her regularly, his letters reveal how depressed Robert became, even regretting that he had ever joined the FAA and describing a flight in the rear cockpit of a Fairey Swordfish as *'horrible'*. A fatal crash involving a pilot testing a Hurricane fighter in mid-April caused Robert to write that he wanted to avoid test flying altogether and it appears that he relished making himself unpopular with more senior officers by arranging duties for them that would be inconvenient. Perhaps due to this, Robert seems to have drawn the unpopular duty of 'Air Watch Officer' in the airfield's Watch Office (Control Tower) on a very regular basis, and this along with his failure to find suitable 'digs' off the base, or secure a Royal Navy battledress, all seem to have affected his positive outlook.

At one point he wasn't able to fly for six weeks, although he did secure an Instructor's Certificate on the Link Trainer. When he did fly, he was allocated duties such as air-experience flights for young cadets.

It was clear that Valerie was also bored with her own job at MEW and wanted to play a more active role in the war either in the ATS or the WRNSs, the women's branch of the Navy. Robert disapproved, and soon began to hatch a plan to try and get Valerie a secretarial commission in the WRNS, on the base at Donibristle, even asking the previously helpful Captain Brown for his assistance and influence. Robert also felt that with them stationed together and married – once they were both twenty-one – they would easily be able to rent a cottage near the base.

Valerie wears a small pair of Fleet Air Arm 'wings' produced as a brooch. Mothers, sisters, wives, fiancées and sometimes girlfriends, often wore the miniature version in support of their loved ones.

Robert hoped for a conversion course onto twin-engined aircraft that would then mean, together with his limitation to second-line flying duties, that his longer term career would centre on RNAS Donibristle. However, the reality of life in the services during wartime, the unpredictability of postings, duties and dangers, made the couple's plans seem sadly naive, and Robert himself seems to have realised this. In July 1942 a letter to Valerie contains a reference to a medical examination that he hoped would get him passed fit for front-line duties, as well as his suggestion that they suspend their plans until they knew of the outcome.

Despite the boredom, evident frustration, and even depression contained within his letters, there were clearly moments of excitement and even danger, examples including hitting the water with his propeller when flying a low-level photographic sortie over the sea, a live-firing exercise in a fully armed aircraft with air gunner on board, and even escorting four aircraft that were so new that they had not yet been included in any identification manuals.

On 15 July, after a visit to a specialist at Port Edgar, Robert wrote to Valerie telling her that he would not be passed fit for front-line flying and that this conclusion would be communicated to the Royal Navy Medical Board. This decision seems to have been accepted fairly philosophically by Robert, and his priority was now to try and get a posting south, to be closer to Valerie.

In the interim however, he flew as one of twelve ferry pilots, delivering aircraft to maintenance units and squadrons. Although not glamorous work, Robert's flying hours started to build-up and he gained experience on a very wide range of single-engined naval aircraft.

At the end of August 1942, Robert was finally posted south to RNAS Lee-on-Solent at HMS *Daedalas*, where he joined 781 Communications Squadron. Still operating within a communications flight as one of fourteen ferry pilots, he spent periods without flying where boredom and the frustration of being away from home are constant themes in his letters.

Despite being closer to home, his letters reveal that the prospect of marriage seemed to be getting no nearer, although it is unclear whether Valerie's father, or possibly even Valerie herself, was in no rush for the knot to be tied.

One of Robert's letters during this period relays how much he hated Lee-on-Solent, and that if he couldn't get married he'd prefer to be posted onto an aircraft-carrier. Clearly frustrated, his interests extended to making model aircraft and to keeping a pet rabbit. His letters show that he even started calling himself by his new nickname, *'Thumper'*.

By June of 1943 Robert had amassed over 400 hours of flying on single-engined types, including Spitfire (and Seafire), Hurricane, Gladiator, Swordfish, Albacore, Walrus, Fulmar, Barracuda, and more basic types such as the Proctor and Vega Gull. Although he was an experienced pilot, a combination of ill-fortune and carelessness resulted in a number of incidents recorded in his letters, and in his logbook as follows:

Percival Proctor P6071:

Taxiing too fast, ran into van parked on peritrack – 29.4.43 (S/L RC Reeder).

Supermarine Seafire NX963:

Stalled landing, breaking undercarriage – 25.7.43 (S/L Reeder of 781)

Lockheed Vega Gull P5986:

Collided with banking in dispersal bay – 14.8.43 (S/L RC Reeder).

In mid-August Robert suffered a more serious accident, landing very heavily in a Vega Gull and sustaining back injuries. He spent periods in hospital at Haslar and only resumed flying in October.

By the end of 1943, Robert's lengthy spell at Lee-on-Solent was approaching an end, and it was at this time that he undertook an Instrument Flying course which included a test with a Lieutenant-Commander Watson, with whom he was to work again at a later date. Shortly afterwards Robert was posted to RNAS Hinstock in Shropshire, known as HMS *Godwit*.

Hinstock had been commissioned in June 1943, just a few months before Robert's arrival. Previously, it was known as Ollerton, and was used as a Satellite Landing Ground (SLG) by 37 Maintenance Unit at nearby Burtonwood, under the control of the Ministry of Aircraft Production (MAP). The airfield had no all-weather runways and its two grass runways were subject to periods of non-operation in bad weather. In July 1942, when the Royal Navy was looking for an airfield for an Instrument Flying School, the MAP was persuaded to release Ollerton to the Navy. Dominating the airfield was a large three-storey Naval Watch Office, and new hangars and facilities were constructed for the Navy. However, the airfield retained its grass runways.

The resident unit was 758 Squadron, the Naval Advanced Instrument Flying School, equipped with twin-engined Airspeed Oxford and Avro Anson aircraft. The squadron operated at a strength of forty aircraft plus twenty reserve aircraft, although at any given time many of these would be dispersed across other Naval flying schools such as Crail, East Haven, Fearn, and Yeovilton, where Squadron Instructors were sent to provide a short instrument flying course for pupils.

The main skill that pilots learned at HMS *Godwit* was the blind flying 'Beam Approach'. The training involved learning to follow the sound of a radio beam transmitted from the airfield. As their aeroplane followed the beam, the crew would hear a steady note in their headphones and if they strayed to left or right they would hear either dots or dashes depending on which side they had strayed. The small airfield at Hinstock, set within a green, very rural, and sparsely populated Shropshire, was the perfect location for such training.

The Naval Advanced Instrument Flying School was the brainchild of Commander John Pugh, who could see that a new strategy was required to reduce the significant losses suffered by the FAA Combat Air Groups. Despite opposition, Pugh succeeded in convincing the right authorities, and set about looking for the best pilots to act as instructors. One such person known to John Pugh was James 'Jimmy' Watson a gifted pilot and navigator who had taken part in the 1938 air race from Cardiff to London. He and his young son David, were only just beaten into second place by another notable airman – Geoffrey de Havilland. Watson agreed to help Pugh who succeeded in getting his pilot into the Navy without having to complete the usual Naval 'seamanship' training first.

Lieutenant-Commander Watson's role at the flying school was to instruct pilots to use the new Beam Approach which was so critical to Navy pilots who had to land on a moving aircraft-carrier, probably many miles away from their take-off position. Many of the trainees had seen active service and were not impressed by having to return to school, causing instructors to often take them to an area around The Wrekin, a high hill in Shropshire, which was often shrouded by cloud. The trainees quickly realised that they had to pay attention.

The Hinstock aircraft, like all aircraft used for 'beam training', were painted with yellow warning triangles to ensure that other aircraft gave them a wide berth. Naval instructors found that experienced pilots with 300 hours of flying time could master the Beam Approach with as little as eight hours training, providing they did preparatory work beforehand in the Link Trainer.

Perhaps it was his thorough knowledge of the Link Trainer that made Robert Reeder an ideal candidate for instructor at Hinstock. As a Communications/Ferry pilot with no twin-engined experience, he was otherwise not an obvious candidate, although his total flying hours and overall experience obviously contributed to his qualifications for the role.

Robert greeted his posting to Hinstock less than enthusiastically; *'This place is enough to give anyone the willies'*, he wrote. *'I haven't the inclination to visit these one-horse market towns. The Mess itself is pretty deadbeat and it isn't very pleasant flying from the mud patch that the people here call an aerodrome'.* The news that he would have to complete his course (a conversion course onto twin-engined aircraft) before he could expect home leave, which in turn meant that he would not get home for Christmas, proved too much, leading to him refer to his Base Commander as *'that whisky-soaked old fool*!*'*

Having spent Christmas at Hinstock, Robert Reeder's training continued, and although he had flown solo in an Oxford by now, he had to become proficient in all aspects of the Naval Advanced Instrument Flying School's activities before he could instruct others.

On Sunday 2 January 1944, Sub Lt Robert Reeder was allocated Airspeed Oxford MP299 of 758 Squadron for an hour's instruction flight with the senior instructor, Lt Commander Jimmy Watson. They took off from the airfield and climbed away into the gloomy skies.

With their arrival back at Hinstock overdue, and with radio contact also proving impossible, the concern over the missing aircraft caused the alarm to be raised by Hinstock Flying Control. Within hours, the crash site of the Oxford was located and it was clear that both occupants had been killed. Official records report that the aircraft had spun out of low cloud from low level and crashed near The Wrekin.

Lieutenant-Commander James Christian Victor Keiro Watson

The exact crash site seems to have been on a farm at Steeraway just at the end of The Wrekin. Leonard Osborne a local fireman, reported that the aircraft came down inside an area known as Lime Kiln Wood, an event recorded in his diary.

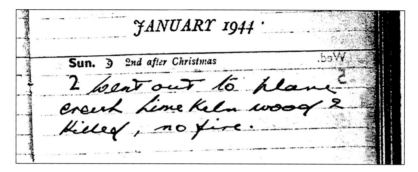

Leonard's young son Arthur, the current keeper of the diary, was just seven years old at the time. He visited the crash site with his brother and several friends to look for souvenirs. He recalled:

'We found the site about thirty to forty feet from the path that runs from Red House, alongside the golf course, to Maddocks Hill quarry. It was just inside Lime Kiln Wood. We found what appeared to be an impact site that was an area of soil and mud heavily impregnated with what I later came to know as hydraulic oil. My brothers commented on the lack of tree damage, suggesting a near vertical crash impact.

'The area had already been cleared so there was not much to find but I caught a glint of a small object in the mud which I picked up. It was a gold cufflink with three initials. The first and the last were definitely J and W. I think the middle initial was a D. JDW in enamel on the oval part of the cufflink. Now, sixty-four years later, I know that one of the pilots killed was James Watson.'

There are no official records of any investigation into the crash, although David Watson, Lt Commander Watson's son, has always known the cause, probably because Base Commander John Pugh was a friend of the family and often visited the Watsons.

John Pugh told the family that the Airspeed Oxfords were dispersed around the airfield as was the normal practice. As such they were exposed to the elements, not generally a problem for training aircraft, regularly checked and maintained.

The problem, discovered some time after the crash, was that wooden pins, components in the rudder of the Oxford, could swell in prolonged periods of damp, and this swelling could result in the rudder jamming in flight. It was not until the same thing happened to a another instructor who somehow managed to free the rudder, that the reason for crashes such as Robert's was fully understood. This probably explains why eyewitness reports record that the aircraft *'spun out of cloud'*.

Pugh wrote a letter of sympathy to Robert's family which his father Charles read out to his class at the school where he taught. One of the pupils, Ted Bond, recalled over sixty years later, *'I will always remember that day as if it were yesterday.'* That letter was dated 8 January 1944 and is shown in full overleaf.

My dear Mr Reeder,

It was with deep regret that I had to inform you by telegram of your son's death. He was at the time receiving flying instruction in order to qualify as a flying instructor and was accompanied by my senior instructor Lt. Commander Watson.

The aircraft was observed to come out of the clouds and almost immediately hit The Wrekin - a high hill in the district. Death could not have been other than instantaneous for both occupants of the aircraft.

Your son was a boy of great promise and his loss to the service will be keenly felt. I wish to express for myself; Officers and ship's Company our deepest sympathy to you and your wife in your great loss.

If there is any service I can render - I am yours to command.

I remain sir

Yours very sincerely

John Pugh Cmdr.

Captain HMS Godwit

Robert's body was brought home to Banstead, where he now lies buried along with other local airmen, just north-west of the entrance to All Saints Church.

Another young man who has never forgotten the tragic incident was Cadet Tim Owen who recalled:

'I was on leave when the crash happened and I did not know either of the two men killed, but I was assigned to guard the body of Lt Commander Watson at Childs Ercall Hall. This was in use as the sick bay at the time and I well remember the two hour-on and two hour-off shifts we did guarding the body of this officer. I was also part of the firing party at his funeral at Hinstock cemetery. It's an experience you don't forget, and last year [2007] I went back to visit his grave.'

Unable to marry her wartime sweetheart, Valerie remained single for another six years, but she remained a friend of the Reeder family throughout her life.

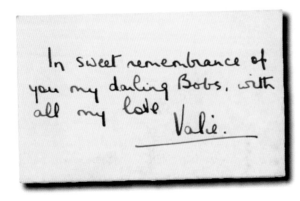

This handwritten little card from Valerie was attached to the wreath which was laid on Robert's grave. Valerie kept it along with all of Robert's letters, and the precious collection is now in the safe keeping of the next generation.

Robert Reeder's story is one of steady service, away from the frontline, yet filled with dangers that ultimately proved fatal. Perhaps uniquely among the men commemorated on the Banstead War Memorial, we have a better idea of Robert's thoughts and emotions during his service because so many of his letters survive. They paint a picture far removed from the perceived glamour of the carefree pilot, and instead reveal the very human perspective of a young man, far from home and loved ones, who has discovered that the romance of flying and military service in wartime are not perhaps as fulfilling as he had anticipated. Like the many thousands who served alongside him, he continued to do his duty until, in the service of his country, it cost him his life.

A postscript to this story comes from Joan Arney, a Banstead resident who was somewhat taken aback to see a photograph of Robert wearing his greatcoat, amongst a compilation presented by the author at a local British Legion meeting. Speaking to the author later in the evening Joan mentioned how she had been a little upset when she saw the photograph earlier. She went on to say that Robert's mother lived to be about 100 years old, since confirmed as 102. Joan was a member of the family that subsequently moved into 4 Wilmot Way, Robert's old address. She recalled how the garden was overgrown and how, when the new family cleared it, they found what was unmistakeably Robert's greatcoat and his flying goggles, along with various Fleet Air Arm memorabilia buried in the earth. Joan also knew that the Reeders had planted a magnolia in memory of Robert. It was only a small shrub when she moved in, in 1961, but is now as tall as a room, and still flowers twice a year. It looks beautiful in spring, surrounded by crocuses, and each year it reminds her of the young man from Banstead Village who died all those years ago. Now, for the first time, she knows what he looked like.

Sub Lieutenant
Robert Charles Reeder
All Saints Churchyard
Banstead
Surrey
north-west of Church

Sources:

Commonwealth War Graves Commission. *The Suttonian* magazine from Sutton Grammar School's archives. Article from the *Herald* (probably the *Sutton Herald* dated around the 15th January 1944). Photographs and letters kindly provided by Bob Payne, Nigel Richardson and Sandie Dixon, all relations of Robert or Valerie. *Casualty Lists of the Royal Navy and Dominion Navies, 1922-Present* researched & compiled by Don Kindell. www.naval-history.net. Details of HMS *Godwit* from Air-Britain's *Squadrons of the Fleet Air Arm*. *Under Five Badges, Memories of Twenty-two Years in Aviation* written by Philip M.Moss. Details about James Watson from Nick Hodson secretary of West Downs. Personal memories following the crash from Tim Owen. Crash site location details from Tom Thorne, air crash investigator. *Shropshire Star* request for information article by Toby Neal. Cause of crash and other information provided by David Watson. Diary entry and memories of crash site courtesy of Arthur Osborne.

Fact*file*

Banstead War Memorial – World War Two – Panel 4 records

NAME	RANK	DATE OF DEATH	CEMETERY/MEMORIAL
Yeomans			Banstead
Sidney Roy	Corporal	25/10/1942	England
Eason (unidentified)			
K W			
Duce			Runnymede
Cyril Cubitt	Sergeant	07/02/1942	England
Plowright			Heliopolis
Reginald Ernest	Leading Aircraftman	25/05/1943	Egypt
Lintott			Banstead
John Peter Marley	Flight Lieutenant	09/07/1943	England
Reeder			Banstead
Robert Charles	Sub-Lieutenant	02/01/1944	England
Barton			Capuccini
Arthur Thomas	Flying Officer	17/04/1944	Malta
Remané (incorrectly inscribed as Remani)			Mainneville
Charles Clifford	Serjeant	29/08/1944	France
Lawrence			Kensal Green
Stanley Percy	Lieutenant	04/08/1942	England
Hayward			Runnymede
Leslie Alec	Flying Officer	12/03/1944	England
Hammond			Ottawa
James Leonard Gordon	Sergeant	01/06/1945	Canada
Roberts (unidentified)			
H W			
Jenkins			Medjez-El-Bab
John Edward	Gunner	16/02/1943	Tunisia
Parkes			Floriana
Peter Denys	Pilot Officer	05/05/1944	Malta

Name HAYWARD L. A. DFM

Rank FLYING OFFICER 124123

Service ROYAL AIR FORCE

VOLUNTEER RESERVE 58 SQUADRON

Date of death 12/3/1944   Age 28

LESLIE ALEC HAYWARD, was the son of Edwin Hayward FSMC FBOA and Edith Mary Hayward née Bray, who were married in 1911. Prior to their marriage, Edwin was a bank clerk and Edith a music teacher. Leslie, or Alec as he was always called, was one of twin boys, he and his brother Antony being born in Wallington, Surrey on 22 April 1915, during the Great War. It was later that the family moved to Banstead where they lived at *Bynebarrow*, 45 Fiddicroft Avenue.

The story of Alec Hayward is inevitably intertwined with that of his brother Antony for the early part of their lives. As twins tend to be, they were not merely brothers but also best friends, and each influenced the other greatly.

Antony always spoke of Alec as the quieter of the twins. He was the scholar of the two and was fascinated by nature – flora and fauna, with a particular interest in butterflies. The summer months would see the two brothers roaming the countryside near their home, catching and identifying butterflies. One day, in his spare time, Alec carved a beautiful figure of a deer out of sandstone, which is treasured by his nephew to this day.

In an ideal world Alec would have liked to have been a botanist, but in Britain in the 1930s the opportunities for a paid career in this field were extremely limited. He needed a 'proper' job, and his great interest would have to remain a hobby. His father was a Fellow of the British Optical Association and Alec joined the profession, training to be an optician. Antony took a job in a city bank as a runner, taking messages from office to office.

This photo was taken in the back garden in Wallington. The lady on the right is the twins' mother Edith, and the one on the left, probably the home help. The young boy is Jack, the older brother. As for the twins – even the family can't tell which one is which!

The non-identical twins with their father. Antony is on the left and Alec on the right. The shorts belie their age as they were in their early twenties at the time this photo was taken.

Alec and Antony were twenty-four when war broke out and although their initial career paths had diverged, they were united in a common desire to serve their country and in their choice of which service to join, as they both volunteered for aircrew duties with the Royal Air Force.

In mid-1940 the brothers attended the Air Crew Candidate Selection Board where they would have been assessed for either pilot or observer training, observers acting as both navigator and air bomber. After initial training and air-experience, the selectors would determine which discipline best suited each candidate. It was determined that Alec would undergo pilot training, whilst Antony was deemed better suited to training as a navigator.

Antony was to become a crew member on multi-engined aircraft, almost certainly bombers, and he would definitely have completed his training before Alec.

Antony passed his training with distinction, being commissioned as a Pilot Officer upon completion. He was posted to 144 Squadron of RAF Bomber Command at RAF North Luffenham sometime around May 1941, where he joined the crew of Sergeant Pilot Don Whiting. Number 144 Squadron flew the Handley Page Hampden bomber which carried a crew of four in cramped conditions. As navigator, Antony would also undertake the duties of bomb aimer.

On 25 August 1941, whilst returning from a raid on the German city of Mannheim, Don Whiting's Hampden was shot down, not far from Brussels. The crew all baled out, but at a very low level, resulting in the deaths of all crew members except Antony Hayward, who sustained leg injuries due to the heavy landing. Even worse, he was captured, and had to face imprisonment for nearly four years. His experiences are a story in themselves and are recorded on the BHRG website on the wartime memories pages. At this point we leave Antony and return to the story of his twin brother.

Alec's more intensive pilot's training meant that it would probably have been completed towards the end of 1941. Further, at some point during this period, he was earmarked for multi-engined training. By this stage in the war, with the Battle of Britain over and with the immediate threat of German invasion subsiding, thoughts had turned to 'hitting back', and increasingly pilots were being directed towards the fast-expanding bomber force. It looked as though Alec would follow his brother into Bomber Command.

Alec converted to twin-engined trainers and was then posted on to an Operational Training Unit. Newly qualified, and now a Flight Sergeant, Alec Hayward's next posting was to 58 Squadron.

At the outbreak of WWII 58 Squadron was based in Yorkshire, flying Armstrong Whitworth Whitley bombers. It first went into action on the night of 3/4 September 1939 when – in conjunction with 51 Squadron – it made a leaflet raid over Germany. This was the first occasion on which RAF aircraft penetrated German airspace during WWII. A few weeks after this operation, 58 Squadron was ordered to an airfield in south-west England for duties with Coastal Command and until late January 1940, was employed on escorting convoys and flying anti-submarine patrols. The squadron returned to RAF Linton-on-Ouse in Yorkshire in February and from April 1940 to March 1942, played a prominent part in the night-bombing offensive as part of 4 Group Bomber Command. Its targets were varied, and ranged from airfields, road and railway communications, marshalling yards and industrial centres, to the Channel ports, oil and petrol installations as well as shipping at sea.

Flight Sergeant Leslie Alec Hayward

It was almost certainly because of its earlier 'loan' to Coastal Command that in April 1942 its transfer to that service was made permanent, and the squadron moved to RAF St Eval in Cornwall at about the same time that Alec joined.

The work of RAF Coastal Command and the theatre of operations in which Alec Hayward was to play no small part, were vital, yet have often been eclipsed by the wartime exploits of Fighter and Bomber Commands. For the greater part of the war, the story of Coastal Command was one of long-range convoy escorts, reconnaissance patrols, anti-shipping and anti-submarine operations. By their very nature, these patrols were long and often very boring, flying over thousands of square miles of ocean searching for targets in the vastness of the Atlantic and far out into the Bay of Biscay. It was here that German U-boats stalked their quarry – the merchant shipping that represented Britain's lifeline for much of the war. Coastal Command's task was a dangerous one with little margin for error, and for aircrew shot down into the sea, the odds for survival were not good.

St Eval was ideally placed for patrols out into the Bay of Biscay, and 58 Squadron was assigned anti-submarine and anti-shipping patrols. The dangers of their work became immediately apparent when, on 19 April 1942, the squadron lost its first Whitley on coastal operations. The following month saw sixty sorties flown, almost all of which were against shipping, although one crew also attacked and probably destroyed a U-boat.

In the early morning of 16 June, at 0335 hours, Alec and his five crew took off in their Whitley, from St Eval and headed west out into the Bay of Biscay on an anti-shipping/submarine patrol. On this occasion the aircraft was carrying bombs rather than depth charges. The crew on that day were F/Sgt Hayward, Sgt Hill, Sgt Young, Sgt Linton, Sgt Walsh and Sgt Wyser.

Far out into their patrol they spotted a German U-boat on the surface, and Alec immediately commenced his attack before the submarine had a chance to complete an emergency dive. This form of attack was inherently dangerous. The Whitley was a heavy bomber and was neither manoeuvrable nor heavily-armed. Its rudimentary bomb load was designed to be dropped from a high level and to explode on impact, either with the target or with the surface of the water. In order to improve the likelihood of a hit, Hayward flew low and 'dived' towards the submarine which was on the surface. The bombs were released at low level, immediately prior to the Whitley pulling up and out of the dive, their momentum propelling them towards the target.

Timing had to be perfect, or the attacking crew risked the detonation of their bombs damaging their own aeroplane. This is exactly what happened, and Alec now found himself in control of a badly damaged aircraft that was not going to make it back to the UK.

Abandoning his attack on the submarine, whose fate remains unknown, Alec asked his navigator to plot a course to Gibraltar. The Whitley lost height rapidly and in an effort to lighten the load, Hayward gave instructions to jettison as much equipment as possible to increase their chances of making landfall. He coaxed the crippled Whitley to within about one hundred and fifty miles of his intended destination before ditching the aircraft in the surf just off the coast of neutral Portugal, at Cape Santa Maria, not far from Faro, in the Gulf of Cadiz. The landing was well-executed and the whole crew scrambled clear of the bomber before realising that they ought to try and destroy it. Failed attempts at destruction were interrupted by the Portuguese 'Fiscal Police' who arrived at the scene and arrested the crew. They were taken to nearby Olhâo and as they departed they saw their Whitley for the last time, almost fully submerged in the rising tide. The Portuguese later made attempts to salvage it.

After brief questioning by the Customs Police, during which the crew gave their name, rank and number, they were handed over to the International Police and taken to Lisbon. The neutral Portuguese were keen not to take sides in the war and Alec's crew enjoyed

Distinguished Flying Medal

friendly treatment throughout. The Portuguese weren't strict about interning combatants either, and upon arriving at Lisbon, the RAF airmen were placed in the charge of Flt Lt Stowe, the British Assistant Air Attaché in Lisbon.

The crew had a brief break in the Portuguese capital before being moved to Caldas Da Rainha, a smaller town just north of the city. They were then transferred to Gibraltar, the location that Alec had been desperately trying to reach, and were repatriated to the UK by ship from there, on 6 July 1942. They arrived at Gourock near Greenock (Port of Glasgow) on 12 July.

As crew captain, Alec Hayward was debriefed the next day by the security services (MI 9) who dealt with 'Escape and Evasion' and who were keen to glean anything that might prove useful to other downed aircrew. With the formalities completed, Alec and his crew returned to their squadron.

Flt Sgt Alec Hayward was awarded the Distinguished Flying Medal for his gallantry in saving the crew of the stricken aeroplane and he also duly secured his membership of *The Goldfish Club,* an exclusive club for airmen who owe their lives to their life jacket or dinghy. It had nine thousand members by the end of WWII. Later in the year Alec received a commission as Pilot Officer.

Goldfish Club badge

Coastal Command continued to be heavily involved in the war over the Atlantic and the Bay of Biscay. The Battle of the Atlantic lasted from the first to the last day of WWII, the only campaign to do so, and was dominated for much of that time by the war against German U-boats. Years of restrictions imposed after WWI had hindered the building of large surface vessels for the German Navy, and battleships that were built, were hunted down and destroyed, or forced to flee to the protection of heavily defended moorings for much of the war. It was Karl Dönitz, head of the U-boat service who persuaded Hitler and the German military hierarchy that his force could wage a more effective war against the allied shipping which was so vital to Britain's ability to continue to fight.

The campaign would be mainly fought in the open Atlantic, in the centre of which was a large expanse of ocean that was out of range of allied air cover. Following the fall of France in 1940, the Germans built several submarine bases along the west coast of occupied France. These bases gave U-boats easier access to the Atlantic although they would have to cross the more dangerous waters of the Bay of Biscay to get there.

A bomber of Coastal Command, attacks with its guns, a disabled U-boat

By the end of 1942, the successes of Dönitz's U-boat crews, now operating together in large 'Wolf Packs', were threatening the very course of the war. In 1939 U-boats had sunk fifty allied ships, and that number increased alarmingly to two hundred and twenty-five in 1940 with the availability of the new bases on the west coast of France. By the end of 1942 U-boats had sunk no fewer than four hundred and fifty-two allied ships and Winston Churchill was later to write that throughout the entire war it was only the U-boat threat that ever really worried him.

It was clear that more resources had to be allocated to deal with the U-boats, and towards the end of 1942 long-range four-engined heavy bombers were made available in greater numbers. American aircraft such as the Fortress and Liberator started to replace the older Sunderland flying boats, and the Handley Page Halifax was selected as the long-range bomber of choice for Coastal Command.

In December 1942, 58 Squadron was re-equipped with the Handley Page Halifax MK II, followed in January 1943 by 502 Squadron, also part of Coastal Command. These two squadrons would now be tasked with developing tactics to counter the U-boats, and they started to receive the latest electronic aids.

Most important were the Air to Surface Vessel (ASV) radar sets fitted to the aircraft. An additional radar aid, code-named 'boozer', detected enemy radar signals and informed the operator that enemy shipping was nearby. But it was the newer ASV MK3 sets that were a formidable asset in the hands of a good operator. Halifax aircraft were now able to detect U-boats on the surface at night as they sailed to intercept the allied merchant convoys.

Alec Hayward was by now an experienced Coastal Command pilot, almost certainly on his second 'tour of operations'. In the Halifax, he was flying one of the most effective anti-submarine 'hunters' of the war and the next twelve months would see 58 Squadron in the front line in the Battle of the Atlantic. Still operating from St Eval, the squadron's efforts were concentrated on the Bay of Biscay – which was to become a dangerous battlefield.

Aware of the intensification of allied air activity, the German Luftwaffe introduced increasing numbers of long-range Junkers Ju88 aircraft as 'heavy fighters' to combat the Coastal Command bombers. In April 1943, a 58 Squadron Halifax was intercepted by no fewer than seven Ju88s, which immediately engaged the bomber, yet in the ensuing fight over the next forty-seven minutes, three of the attackers were damaged before the remainder gave up the chase!

On 7 May 1943, a 58 Squadron Halifax scored the squadron's first U-boat victory, sinking U-663, and four days later U-528 was also sunk by the squadron. The Commanding Officer, Wing Commander W E Oulton, sank the squadron's third U-boat on 15 May and on the next day an Italian submarine was also sent to the bottom of the sea.

The Squadron's aggressive tactics were paying off, but the dangers were ever-present. On 31 May, W/Cmdr Oulton intercepted U-563 on the surface and there ensued a seventy-minute battle in which the submarine's own gunners put up a spirited defence using a cannon mounted aft of the submarine's conning tower. The U-boat was finally finished off by aircraft from other squadrons, but it was clear that a submarine, even damaged and on the surface, was not an easy target.

Halifax II Srs IA (HR744/G) of 58 Squadron, Coastal Command on patrol over the sea

Alec Hayward, by now promoted to the rank of Flying Officer, and his crew routinely flew patrols of eleven hours duration over the Bay of Biscay, hunting submarines as they accessed their home bases in France. The Halifaxes carried six 250lb depth charges for their combined duties of U-boat hunting and convoy patrol work, although these were later supplemented with specially designed 600lb anti-submarine bombs. Following the fights with U-boats on the surface, the noses of the Halifaxes were strengthened and modified to accommodate a larger calibre 0.5 inch Browning machine-gun.

The key to defeating the U-boats and protecting the allied shipping was to optimise the time spent by patrol aircraft in the air, maximising the fuel they could carry and evaluating the pros and cons of fuel versus payload. Tests by 502 Squadron (58's sister squadron at St Eval) resulted in patrols being extended to thirteen hours and one can only imagine the exhaustion that aircrew experienced after such a patrol, looking down on miles of ocean, searching for enemy craft, radar operators constantly scanning their screens. For the pilots like Alec, there was the sheer physical exertion of flying a large heavy-bomber in varying weather conditions for such long stretches, with the ever-present threat of long-range Ju88 interceptors.

Towards the middle of 1943 the U-boats were forced to change tactics. No longer able to cross the Bay of Biscay submerged by day and on the surface at night, the Germans realized that they would have to be prepared to fight allied aircraft on the surface. The U-boats were equipped with twin and quad installations of 20mm cannon in addition to their machine guns, lethal against low-flying aircraft.

On 1 May 1943 Germany's 'Standing War Order 483' was put into effect for the U-boats traversing the Bay of Biscay. This order was to be known as the 'Fight Back' order and it simply meant than when faced with an aircraft attack (and without the time needed to reach a safe depth) the boats would stay on the surface and fight instead of the normal tactic of emergency diving. It was also inspired by the successes of U-333 and U-338 in shooting down a Wellington and a Halifax aircraft respectively in March, and U-191's machine-gun defence that drove off a Liberator in April.

The man who most welcomed this order was Air Marshal Sir John Slessor, Commander of RAF Coastal Command. He wanted to destroy U-boats and if the U-boats stayed on the surface to fight it out, he was more than happy. He was willing to lose an aircraft if that attack also sank the submarine. He reasoned he had more aircraft than Dönitz had U-boats. He could hardly lose this war of attrition.

In December 1943, 58 and 502 Squadrons relocated to the new airfield at St Davids on the Pembrokeshire coast in Wales. Here they were to form a three-squadron Halifax wing, with the third squadron, No. 517, to be based at St Davids satellite airfield at Brawdy, there to act as a meteorological squadron.

In January 1944, 58 Squadron resumed its war against the U-boats. Often operating at night, the Halifaxes carried flares to illuminate the surface when they located a submarine. On 2 January U-445 was attacked and damaged, and three days later U-415 was also damaged.

The dangers associated with this type of operation are demonstrated by the attack on a U-boat on 14 January, by Squadron Leader Grant of 58 Squadron (who was to assume command of the unit in April 1944). Flying at 1,000 feet, Grant's crew picked up a radar contact at a range of twelve miles, losing it, then regaining it when they descended to 600 feet. They dropped their flares at two miles range and immediately spotted a U-boat on the surface. Intermittent radar contact and poor visibility resulted in Grant taking the Halifax down to just 200 feet at which point the German gunners on the submarine opened fire with cannon and machine guns, initially at the flares in an attempt to shoot them out, but then at the Halifax, which had by now descended to 100 feet, from which height the depth charges were released. Grant's crew couldn't confirm what damage had been inflicted, and for the next fourteen minutes the Halifax's turret gunners exchanged intermittent fire with their German counterparts until, despite dropping more flares, contact was lost.

On 7 March 1944 U-311 left its French base at Brest for only its second operational patrol. It was commanded by twenty-seven-year-old Kapitänleutnant Joachim Zander a Berliner from Charlottenburg.

U-311's first patrol, lasting sixty-three days and completed at the end of January, had been unsuccessful, and Zander was determined that his second would be more productive. His submarine was a MK VIIC, completed in Lubeck a year earlier and on this patrol it was scheduled to form a part of 'Wolf Pack Prussia'.

Before leaving Brest, U-311 had received an important modification, one of only two U-boats to be so equipped. The boat had been fitted with a 'navalised' version of the latest Luftwaffe FuG 200 Hohentweil 'Owl' Radar system which was designed to detect approaching aircraft from a range of up to twenty kilometres with a bearing accuracy of one or two degrees. This modification, designated 'FuMO 61' was to play an important role in the events yet to unfold.

A type VIIC U-boat similar in design to U-311

Five days after leaving Brest, U-311 was cruising due west across the northern limit of the Bay of Biscay prior to turning north-west to cross the south-western tip of Ireland and head up into the Atlantic.

Late the previous evening, Alec Hayward and his crew of eight, climbed aboard their Halifax MKII aircraft at RAF St Davids to fly yet another anti-submarine patrol over the Bay of Biscay. Their aircraft, serial number HX225, the last MKII to have been built, carried the individual aircraft letter 'L' on its fuselage. The big four-engined bomber, resplendent in its Coastal camouflage scheme of white with grey upper surfaces, rolled down the main runway of its Pembrokeshire base and Alec guided it south-west towards its patrol area.

Within a couple of hours HX225 was due west of Brest, and shortly after 0100 hours on 12 March 1944, his ASV operator confirmed that he had a contact below. At 0117 hours, receivers in the UK picked up the last radio message from Alec Hayward's radio operator, presumably confirming that they were engaging a submarine.

On board U-311, and using the new 'FuMO 61', the radar operator had detected the approaching Halifax at a distance of eight kilometres. Captain Zander ordered his anti-aircraft gunners to stand by. They swung their weapons aft, pointing their gun barrels in the direction from which they knew an attack was about to come.

Ahead of and below Alec's Halifax, the crew of U-311 suddenly found themselves illuminated by flares. Joachim Zander ordered his gunners, who were ready and waiting, to open fire on the attacking Halifax. Perhaps startled by the swiftness and accuracy of the U-boat's defences, the Halifax dropped its load of depth charges wide and missed U-311. Alec brought the lumbering Halifax around and continued to strafe the U-boat.

In some respects, the contest was now unequal; the U-boat held the advantage, as the Halifax gunners were essentially using rifle-calibre ammunition against the steel-hulled submarine. With Alec's aircraft low over the U-boat, Zander's gunners inflicted fatal hits on the Halifax, as it would have taken only a handful of 20mm cannon rounds in the right areas to bring the bomber down.

At approximately 0120 hours, Halifax HX225 crashed into the sea. There were no survivors and Alec's body was never recovered.

In the immediate aftermath of the attack, U-311 reported back on the effectiveness of the new FuMO 61 radar. *'Radar excellent, aircraft located all the time from 8km to 1km. Without radar, boat would have been surprised from astern'*.

Following this combat episode, Zander and his crew, no doubt celebrating their success, continued their patrol. Four days later, while attacking tanker convoy CU 17, the U-boat was hunted for hours by the surface escorts but managed to penetrate their defences and destroy the large tanker *Seakay*. Zander managed to elude the escorts and get away. However, on 22 April Zander's luck finally ran out when U-311 was sunk by depth charges from the Canadian frigates HMCS *Matane* and HMCS *Swansea* in the North Atlantic south-west of Iceland. The entire crew of fifty-one were killed.

Alec Hayward's war was fought in one of the toughest environments of WWII. In the battle of attrition between aircraft and submarine, there were no real winners, although Coastal Command, later joined by American air forces, ultimately brought about the demise of the U-boat force. The German submariners fought bravely until the end of the war despite suffering grievous losses; as a proportion of their fighting strength, German submariners suffered the highest number of casualties of any body of fighting men, ironically followed by the airmen of RAF Bomber Command.

Alec Hayward's Halifax was one of just four lost by 58 Squadron in 1944, but was one of one hundred and nineteen aircraft positively attributed to the list of aircraft claims made by the U-boat fleet. During the war, Coastal Command destroyed two hundred and twenty German U-boats and sustained losses and write-off's (not all against U-boats) of over seven hundred aircraft.

Flying Officer Leslie 'Alec' Hayward DFM is remembered on the Runnymede Memorial in Surrey, whilst his mortal remains and those of his crew lie with their Halifax bomber in the depths of the North Atlantic ocean.

Alec's twin brother Antony returned home to Banstead after the war and brought up two daughters Liz and Judy, and a son Tim, all of whom have contributed to their uncle Alec's story.

Flying Officer
Leslie Alec Hayward
Runnymede RAF Memorial
Englefield Green
Surrey
Panel 206

The Stone of Remembrance at the Runnymede RAF Memorial. It was designed by Sir Edwin Lutyens to commemorate those of all faiths and none, and can be found in every Commonwealth War Graves Commission cemetery with over 1,000 burials. The words were selected by Rudyard Kipling (1865 to 1936), author and poet. They come from the Holy Bible – King James Version – Ecclesiasticus 44. 9 and a fuller quotation is shown below:

And some there be, which have no memorial...and are become as though they had never been born...

But these were merciful men, whose righteousness hath not been forgotten...

Their seed shall remain for ever, and their glory shall not be blotted out.

Their bodies are buried in peace; but their name liveth for evermore.

Sources:

Commonwealth War Graves Commission. Personal details from Liz Christie and Judy Forth, both daughters of Antony Hayward. June 1942 crash details provided by Carlos Guerreiro author of *Atterem em Portugal. Coastal Support and Special Squadrons of the RAF* by John D Rawlings.1982. *Halifax Squadrons of WW2* by Jon Lake. 1999. *Action Station 3* by David J Smith.1981. *The Handley Page Halifax (Coastal Operations)* by K A Merrick. Aston Publications.1990. Image of 58 Squadron Halifax courtesy of Adrian Perry via Malcolm Barrass of www.rafweb.org. U-boat information from U-boat.net. *Type VII U-boats* by Robert C Stern. Brockhampton Press.1998. U-boat images courtesy of Norman Kraehe creator of www.ww2total.com.

Fact *file*

> ## The memorial was nearly destroyed by a V1 flying bomb

On Tuesday 8 August 1944 a V1 flying bomb (doodlebug) came down at the east end of the High Street killing Donald Horsley, a soldier from the Royal Army Service Corps and causing widespread damage. The forge in the centre of the top photo can be seen on the right hand side in the second image, now completely destroyed.

On the opposite side of the road, the Woolpack Inn was damaged beyond repair. The memorial survived unscathed.

V1 damage in Banstead High Street – August 1944

Name .... PARKES P.D. ....

Rank .... PILOT OFFICER 172073 ....

Service .... ROYAL AIR FORCE ....

.... VOLUNTEER RESERVE 37 SQUADRON ....

Date of death ......5/5/1944..... Age ....20.........

P ETER DENYS PARKES was the son of Major Denys Parkes and Dorothy Parkes of 15 Green Curve, Banstead. Major Parkes, a coffee grower in British East Africa (present-day Kenya), spent time in the Gold Coast and served as an officer in the King's African Rifles in WWI. He then returned to Britain via Guernsey, where he and his brother were tomato growers for a few years, before arriving in Banstead in 1930. He set up a car hire business and he and Dorothy settled down to raise their three sons. Peter was born on 22 September 1923 in St Peter Port, Guernsey and was the oldest of the brothers, John being born in 1925, and the youngest, Martin, in 1928.

Martin, now a member of the Banstead History Research Group, has been able to contribute greatly to Peter's story. *'He was Pete to us, Mother hated it; she always called him Peter'*. Martin's memories are still vivid when he recalls aspects of his eldest brother's life, and he is the safe keeper of Peter's wartime photograph albums which survive in good condition today. Martin's memories also serve to paint a portrait of a Banstead family, during the war, whose members were to play their part in the struggle ahead. Martin was particularly close to his big brother Peter and recalls that he, as the youngest, was *'Mummy's Pet'*, and relied on Peter to look after him. John is described by Martin as *'the rebel'* which probably explains why he went on to spend fifteen years in the Royal Marines.

Peter, John and Martin all attended The Priory, a preparatory school for boys and girls at the western end of Banstead village. After his time there, Peter spent a brief period at the City of London Freemen's School in Ashtead, before his parents settled on Sutton County School, which is where all the brothers eventually went, Peter attending between 1936 and 1940.

The Priory School photographed in 1938

Martin recalls that one of the benefits of their father's occupation was that they often got a lift to school, very unusual in those days. Peter was a good sportsman being a strong swimmer and an accomplished tennis player, and even representing his school at boxing.

Peter's early interest in flying was sparked by visits to Croydon Airport in the mid-1930s. Visits to '*Granny Nichols*', who lived in Wallington, enabled them to better see the aircraft over Croydon, and Martin remembers the family being treated to tea near the Croydon Terminal building from where they could watch the big silver four-engined HP 42 bi-plane airliners of Imperial Airways, as they came in to land. Peter also had a flying model aeroplane – his pride and joy, made by *Frog* and powered by a big rubber band.

The brothers were all members of the 1st Nork Scout Troop. Martin recalls that Peter always kept a lookout for him as he was the youngest and confesses that the Parkes brothers weren't always model scouts; the principal activity during their last Scout Camp to Edenbridge in Kent, in August 1939, seems to have been 'scrumping' apples.

But such games weren't to last as less than a month later Britain was at war with Germany, and their father, Denys Parkes was called up and drafted into the Pioneer Corps, before being posted to Shropshire.

Witnessing the Battle of Britain being fought in the skies over south-east England in the summer of 1940 had an immediate impact, and it was then that Peter decided he wanted to fly. At that time, the three brothers and their mother lived in Green Curve on the Nork Estate in Banstead, from where the boys had clear views of the dogfights and vapour trails overhead. Peter was determined to become a fighter pilot when he got the chance, and two of his friends, Peter Sutehall, a fellow scout who lived at 11 Green Curve, and Basil Silver 'Madman' Jones, an older friend from school – who was already in the RAF by 1940 – both agreed that it was a good choice.

When the Blitz started with a series of night raids in late 1940, an incendiary bomb landed on the road outside the house in Green Curve, causing Dorothy to convince her husband to find them a house in Shropshire. As a result, Dorothy and the three boys moved to Shifnal, close to where their father was stationed. They lived there for about a year and in that time Peter worked as a warehouseman for a chain of grocers – J C Lloyd and Son – courtesy of a friend of their father. By the time they returned to Banstead, in September 1941, Peter was old enough to join up.

He immediately volunteered for aircrew duties with the RAFVR and, with a satisfactory medical examination behind him, was selected for aircrew training, enlisting on 2 October 1941. His induction training took place at the Lord's Cricket Ground ACRC (Air Crew Reception Centre), where he reported on 19 January 1942 and where he was issued with kit, instructed in Physical Education, and where the new recruits were taught how to march.

Peter was posted to an Elementary Flying Training School (EFTS) where he learned to fly. The young airmen were evaluated, and those who failed to meet the required standard as pilots were remustered, often as navigators or air bombers.

It was here that Peter first went solo in a Tiger Moth and, at the end of his course which he passed, he was selected to continue pilot training overseas. Like thousands of trainee aircrew, Peter was sent to Canada for much of his flying training as part of the British and

Commonwealth Air Training Plan. Over 130,000 wartime aircrew would eventually be trained in Canadian skies. Arriving by ship in late 1942, Peter was posted to 71 course 32 EFTS Bowden, Alberta, just north of Calgary. The airfield was equipped with Tiger Moths and the American built Boeing Stearman and Cornell primary trainers.

During his time in Canada, Peter used his Box Brownie camera to good effect, taking photographs of the places he visited or flew over, the men he trained with, and the aircraft he flew. These were all carefully kept in an 'On Active Service' photograph album.

In late 1942 and 1943, the RAF needed bomber pilots and any hopes that Peter may have had to fly fighters were quickly dispelled, although for the young trainees the opportunity to fly any modern service aircraft must have been one they all looked forward to.

Pilot training was a lengthy process, particularly as the fledgling bomber pilots had to learn to fly twin-engined aircraft. At the end of his elementary flying training Peter moved on to 36 SFTS (Service Flying Training School) just north of Bowden in Penhold Alberta. Here he flew Harvard advanced trainers before progressing on to twin-engined aircraft such as the Airspeed Oxford and Avro Anson. Peter took many air-to-air photographs of the school's Oxfords in formation, and of the Oxford's cockpit, or *'office'* as he called it.

THE 'OFFICE' AIRSPEED OXFORD

1585913 LAC. PARKES P.D. ACH/UT PILOT

STEARMAN FJ 911

TIGER MOTH DH 82c No: 5038

One of the photographs taken by Peter - Airspeed Oxfords flying in formation

Peter receiving his Pilot's 'Wings' in Summer 1943

Upon successful completion of his course, Peter was awarded his Pilot's 'Wings' and promoted to the rank of Sergeant Pilot.

Following the end of his training in Canada, Peter returned to the UK in the summer of 1943 to be posted to RAF Lossiemouth in Scotland. Here he joined 20 OTU (Operational Training Unit) which was tasked with the training of night bomber crews. The unit was equipped with Vickers Wellingtons – known as 'Wimpeys', the RAF's principal twin-engined bomber, although by this time starting to be replaced with the newer four-engined 'heavies'.

Peter was crewed with four others to make up the standard crew of the Wellington. They would fly practice missions, navigation exercises and generally get to know their aircraft, their functions, and to work as a close-knit team. When fully proficient they would be posted to an operational Wellington squadron. The whole process usually took about five months and involved about eighty hours of flying in addition to ground instruction.

Upon joining an Operational Training Unit, the most significant event was the 'crewing up process'. The RAF procedure was to herd the assorted aircrew – pilots, air gunners, navigators, bomb aimers and wireless operators – into a hangar, and tell them to sort themselves out into crews. This meant that total strangers had to mingle, and 'interview' each other. The pilot, being the aircraft captain, had to 'propose' to the others, suggesting that they join him to make up a crew.

Peter's brother, Martin, recalls that for some reason, Peter spent a short period in hospital and was not at Lossiemouth on the 'crewing day', but that upon his return a group of four airmen, in a complete reversal of the normal process, had organised themselves into a crew and had decided that Peter was to be their pilot. One of their number, Douglas Margison, a Canadian from Vancouver, was to become a great friend of Peter's in the months that followed. Sadly, as it would transpire, their luck would run out together.

Periodically, the Parkes men would return home on leave. Martin recalls that on one of their last get-togethers, Denys, Peter and John went up to London. They all took part in a shooting competition and John, by this time, a crack shot and a member of the Royal Marines elite 'King's Squad', was disgusted that he was beaten by his father Denys.

Sergeant Peter Parkes and his crew successfully completed their training although not without incident. On one occasion, in freezing wintry conditions, their Wellington's engine carburetor air intakes became blocked with ice. Their aircraft was flying out over the Atlantic and as the engines lost power, it descended towards the icy ocean below. Fortunately, the lower altitude, and possibly the presence of salty air, caused the ice to break up and they returned safely to Lossiemouth.

They were lucky to make it back as losses in training were very high. One of the photographs in Peter's album is a course group photo of fifty trainees on War Course 71, some of whom are marked with a white cross to indicate that they were killed in training accidents. There are ten white crosses on the photograph.

Peter and his crew were to face greater risks when they were deemed ready for combat operations and were posted to 37 Squadron in Italy, on 20 March 1944. The squadron had led a fairly nomadic existence and endured a particularly tough war. Originally part of 3

Group, Bomber Command, based at Feltwell in Norfolk, the squadron had participated in the early night-bombing offensive over occupied Europe. In November 1940 it was transferred to the Middle East as part of 205 Group RAF. Initial operations were from Malta but later the squadron was settled in Egypt, based principally at Shallufa.

37 Squadron Wellingtons at Shallufa.

1941 was to prove a hard year for the crews of 37 Squadron who often flew long-range missions of ten hours duration to support the campaign in the Western Desert. Operations in the Middle East throughout 1942 and 1943 necessitated the squadron moving regularly, through Egypt, Libya, Tunisia and eventually into Italy, using temporary landing grounds with tents and primitive huts as living quarters. Missions were flown over an extensive list of territories including Italy, Albania, Rhodes, Bulgaria, Iraq, Greece, Crete, Syria, Sicily and much of North Africa.

At the end of December 1943, with Axis forces in retreat, the squadron moved to Tortorella, which was one of many airfields on the Foggia plain in Italy, adjacent to the Adriatic Sea and 130 km from Naples. The area had only recently been occupied by the Allies and the airfield, hastily constructed by United States Army Engineers, was now to serve as a main base for their offensive towards the north of Italy.

The airstrip at Tortorella was a single-strip airfield running roughly north-south. It was constructed of well-rolled local soft rock with pierced steel planking on top. This was raised up about nine inches above the surrounding ground to keep the whole runway above water in winter. The airfield was occupied by B-17 Flying Fortresses of the 99th Bombardment Group which was encamped on one side of the strip, and the Wellingtons of 37 and 70 Squadrons of the RAF occupying the other. The Americans operated by day whilst the RAF operated mainly at night.

As a consequence, it was not a particularly peaceful place. USAAF ground crews began their daily inspections at about 0300 hours by starting up all four engines on every B17 aircraft. Eventually, the aircrews came out and did the same thing before they took off. By the time the RAF night bombers had landed and taxied in, it would be about midday and all would be quiet again. Then the Americans would land and taxi in. At dusk, the RAF 205 Group aircraft would warm up and take off and the whole cycle would be repeated. All this activity usually took place in one of two extremes, a thick dust haze, or a boggy marsh; conditions which gave the airfield its local nickname of 'Filthy Foggia'.

After flying the 'clapped out' Wellingtons of the OTUs, Peter was delighted to be asked to ferry a brand new Wellington MkX out to Italy. Powered by the latest Bristol Hercules engines the MkX was the most powerful of the Wellington Series. Martin recalls that his brother reported back to the family, *'The Wellington X is great, everything works!'*

The flight was postponed for a few days, probably due to bad weather, and Peter was able to return home for a day or two's quickly snatched leave. His mother and youngest brother were surprised, but pleased to see him.

Soon he was on his way again saying goodbye to his mother and brother before heading off to Banstead railway station from Green Curve. Martin was never to see him again, and remembers that as a typical teenager, he declined to walk his brother to the station and see him off. He recalls *the last thing I saw of him, literally the last, was the heel of his shoe disappearing behind the front garden hedge.'*

The family received a few letters from Peter when he was in Italy. He visited Naples and reported back that parts of the city had been flattened by bombing and that earth had been piled over rubble still containing the bodies of those killed, to suppress the smell. He also commented on the dreadful state of the accommodation at Tortorella but cheerfully made a reference to his younger days in Banstead, *'under canvas – thank God I was in the Scouts'.*

During the early months of 1944, 37 Squadron was kept busy conducting night bombing raids against the enemy, often in an attempt to disrupt supply lines to the front. This meant that the targets were often shipping or railway marshalling yards. The squadron strength at this time was about twenty-two Wellingtons, of which four aircraft were able to carry the 4,000lb 'cookie' in an internally modified bomb bay.

The 'cookie' was a blast bomb, essentially consisting of a thin-walled steel drum filled with Amatol high explosive. When dropped, it tumbled to earth and detonated upon impact, blasting open roofs and tearing walls apart. It was designed to be used with incendiary bombs, the latter raining down into the exposed roofs to start fires after the main blast had done its damage. The bomb had something of a reputation in Bomber Command and the men who dropped these weapons can perhaps be forgiven for adopting a bit of black humour. Peter was no exception, and in another letter home wrote, *'Dropping cookies, must have killed someone by now!'*

Peter's crew is believed to have flown six or seven missions up to the beginning of May 1944, earning the young flyer promotion to Pilot Officer backdated to January.

The bombing missions continued, and roads, railways, marshalling yards and docks would again be targeted by the squadron. The target on the night of 5 May 1944 was a marshalling yard near Ploesti. This area was a key source of oil for the German war machine and had been targeted many times, particularly by the USAAF, which had already attacked the oil fields in huge numbers earlier that day.

Late that evening, Peter lifted the laden Wellington off from the metallised strip at Tortorella for what was to prove to be the last time, and turned the bomber north-east out over the Adriatic Sea towards the coast of Yugoslavia. Beyond Yugoslavia lay Romania and the huge industrial complex at Ploesti, a round trip of some 1,300 miles, though easily within the range of the Wellington.

The precise details of the fate of Peter and his crew are uncertain. It is known that their Wellington developed engine problems on the outward journey, possibly with one catching fire. Unable to make the target, Peter instructed his crew to ditch the bomb load, after which he attempted to make it back to Italy. The last radio message from the crew confirmed that they were heading back towards Foggia. They never arrived, and with no trace of them found, it is certain that they ditched in the Adriatic, unable to reach the Italian coast. They had survived less than seven weeks on operations.

The full crew of the Wellington, including Peter and his friend Doug Margison, were:

Sergeant Archibald Raymond Mitchell

Flight Sergeant Ronald Cairns

Flying Officer Douglas Millen Margison

Flying Officer Thomas Joseph Pullin

Pilot Officer Peter Denys Parkes

A week or so later, Mrs Dorothy Parkes was at work in an office at the Drift Bridge Garage, between Banstead and Epsom. The garage did 'war work' assembling small components for Fairey Firefly aircraft. She was interrupted there by her neighbour and friend Mrs Hodges who had seen the local telegraph boy delivering a telegram to the Parkes home. One can only imagine the trembling hands opening the envelope, thinking of Peter and John, both on active service abroad, and the anguish that Mrs Parkes must have felt, as she read that Peter was *'missing on a bombing raid'*.

Martin returned from school to hear his mother sobbing upstairs. He called out, and was told the dreadful news.

In some respects, to hear that a loved one was 'missing' was worse than hearing that they'd been killed. Sometimes they were found safe and well, or reported as being prisoners of war, but all too often the news was bad, often made worse by the fact that the circumstances of their loss were unknown. Depending upon the theatre of operations and the nature of the duties being undertaken, it could take a while before a follow-up telegram or letter arrived, carrying the dreaded phrase, *'missing presumed killed'*.

Dorothy wrote to family members and also to Peter's old school headmaster at Sutton County School, saying that *'waiting for news is almost unbearable'*. Days later, John returned home unexpectedly on forty-eight hours leave and strode cheerfully into the house greeting his mother and asking if she'd heard from Pete. Her ashen face stopped him in his tracks; he hadn't got his mum's letter.

Martin remembers that tragic though the loss of Peter was, the experience of their family was far from unusual. After five years of war, people realised that life didn't just stop with the loss of a loved one. Dorothy felt the pain of the loss of her eldest son all her life, but in 1944 she still had to run a house and home, and be a mother to Martin.

Later that summer, in August 1944, Martin was down at Avebury in Wiltshire helping with the harvest. He used to read *Flight Magazine* which in the war years carried RAF casualty lists. Here he saw his brothers name printed; P D Parkes – previously reported missing, now presumed killed.

He telephoned his mother only to find out that she had just received the finality of the news herself. On 16 September 1944, Mrs Parkes wrote to Peter's old headmaster again:

Dear Mr Cockshutt,

You will be sorry to hear that Peter was lost over the Adriatic on May 5th.

I have lately heard from Air Vice-Marshall Baker, a distant cousin of the boys and he says we must give up all hope of Peter's return.

They were already over the sea heading for Italy when they sent out their last message, saying that they hoped to get back on one engine. Had they been picked up by a German ship, which is most unlikely, we would have heard by now.

Peter's commission as Pilot Officer was gazetted on March 28th, and dated back to January 14th. He was pilot of a Wellington.

Please do not write.

Yours sincerely

Dorothy Parkes

Some time later, the family received a letter from the War Ministry advising them that a memorial had been constructed on the island of Malta, upon which aircrew missing in the Middle East operations were to be remembered. It was to be many years before Martin Parkes, was able to visit Malta and see his brother's inscription on the memorial.

Peter's friend and neighbour, Flying Officer Peter Sutehall was mentioned in Despatches for rescuing a crew from a blazing aircraft. He was reported 'lost at sea' on the 17 January 1945 after flying a Beaufighter fighter-bomber on a daylight anti-shipping raid to Den Helder in The Netherlands. Both Peters are listed on the Banstead War Memorial.

Pilot Officer

Peter Denys Parkes

Malta Memorial

Floriana

Malta

Panel 13 Column 2

Sources:
Commonwealth War Graves Commission. Publication - *The War Memorial, St Paul's Church, Nork, Banstead.*
The Suttonian magazine and war letter archives from Sutton Grammar School. Malta Memorial photograph and panel detail courtesy of the Shranz family. Photographs and memories of Peter provided by Martin Parkes, Peter's brother and member of the Banstead History Research Group. Flying Officer Peter Sutehall's information from www.bansteadhistory.com. Photo of 37 Squadron Wellingtons adapted from one in Peter Green's collection.

Fact *file*

Unknown facts – the memorial still holds a few mysteries

THE REDEDICATION CEREMONY AFTER WWII

There can be no doubt that following the end of WWII the casualties from that conflict were added to the memorial, probably in the early 1950s, some thirty years after it was first erected. Inevitably a rededication service would have been held where all the names were read out, prayers said and hymns sung.

Despite the significance, any rededication ceremony remains a complete mystery. Four years of research has so far failed to establish even an approximate date. The British Legion have no record, the church appears to have no record; nothing has been found in Council minutes, school log book or local newspaper archives. Countless people who were around at the time have been asked about it and yet not one single shred of evidence for it taking place has emerged.

THE REMAINING UNIDENTIFIED MEN

Odd as it might seem, it has been more difficult to identify the WWII men than the WWI men who can usually be found in the census data.

J Brown could be any one of several hundred with that initial and surname.

K W Eason – there is a headstone with the same name in Banstead churchyard but the family say he cannot be the person on the memorial.

D J Fletcher may be Dennis Howard Fletcher who lived in Ewell.

R J Hart could be one of four on the CWGC database.

R W Roberts could be one of six possibles.

A E Stemp may be Albert Edward Stemp of Winkworth Cottage but so far there seems to be no connection to the war.

If you have any knowledge of a rededication ceremony or the unidentified men, however small, do please get in touch with the Banstead History Research Group or the Banstead History Centre at the library. Any new information will be added to the BHRG website at www.bansteadhistory.com

Name **CULL S.M.**

Rank **TROOPER 7893618**

Service **23RD HUSSARS**

ROYAL ARMOURED CORPS

Date of death **4/08/1944** Age **22**

STANLEY MORRIS CULL was the son of Maurice Frederick, and Grace Cull née Fish, of Epsom, Surrey. He was born in Bournemouth in early 1922, four years after his parents were married in Brentford, Middlesex. Stanley had one brother, Ronald, and two sisters, and the family home was 23 Tattenham Grove, Epsom.

In later years, every member of the Cull family other than mother Grace, was directly involved in the war effort. Pat Cull recalled: '*My father, Freddie Cull, was in charge of the Home Guard unit, and my younger brother Ronald, was a private until he was called up to serve in the Navy. My elder brother Stanley was in the army (Tank Corps). My sister Dorothy was in the WAAFs doing hush-hush work for radar. As for myself, Pat, I was in the Women's Land Army and later in the WAAFs'.*

Stanley served with the 23rd Hussars 'C' Squadron which was originally a cavalry regiment of the British Army.

The regiment was formed at Penkridge, Staffordshire in December 1940, and there followed months of training, sleeping in tents and Nissen huts throughout the country, until they arrived at Bridlington, Yorkshire, where they finally slept in houses!

The photograph shows Ronald (left) and Stanley (right) at the back. In front are Pat, father Freddie, mother Grace, and Dorothy.

In addition to their training on the Yorkshire Moors, they also trained on the sands of Bridlington. They were happy days; according to some members of the regiment, their happiest days in the Army were spent in Bridlington. The regiment trained hard and acquired the American Sherman tank, and eventually the time arrived when they had to prove themselves and put their training to good use.

The 23rd Hussars was assigned to 29th Armoured Brigade of 11th Armoured Division which landed in France on 'Juno' beach on 13 June 1944, taking heavy casualties as part of the Battle of Normandy. The Division experienced substantial losses during two key operations; Operation Epsom which started towards the end of June, and Operation Goodwood, when the Division lost 200 of its Sherman and Cromwell tanks after just two days of fighting in July. It was immediately withdrawn from the frontline to rest and refit. Trooper Stanley Cull survived the Normandy landings and both these operations.

The original book still held by members of the Cull family

As a result of the significant number of casualties, the 11th Armoured Division had to be reorganized into two Assault Brigade Groups. Stanley Cull's unit were assigned to the 29th Assault Brigade Group where the 23rd Hussars absorbed the remainder of the 24th Lancers (8th brigade), before the Division was once again directed to the west, to take part in Operation Bluecoat.

A detailed description of the fighting that ensued over the next few days is included in *The Story of the 23rd Hussars* which was written and compiled by the members of the regiment in 1946, with a copy going to the next of kin. Included in the book are the events leading to the time of Stanley's death.

During the early stages of Operation Bluecoat, the 11th Armoured Division exploited an opportunity to secure a bridgehead on the Souleuvre river. The following summary is based on the events detailed in the book.

The Division started the attack on 30 July 1944 and progressed quickly towards the south, seizing Martin-Saint-des-Besaces. The intact bridge over the Souleuvre river, enabled it to drive the Germans back, this action later becoming known as the famous 'Charge of the bull'. On 1 August, at first light, the 23rd Hussars renewed their attempts to enter Le Bény Bocage. 'C' Squadron, with the help of a few sappers, cleared some of the mines they had come across and began to push forward. The Third Troop nearly reached the centre of the town, disabling a German Mark IV tank on the way.

TAURUS PURSUANT – The charging bull of the 11th Armoured Division

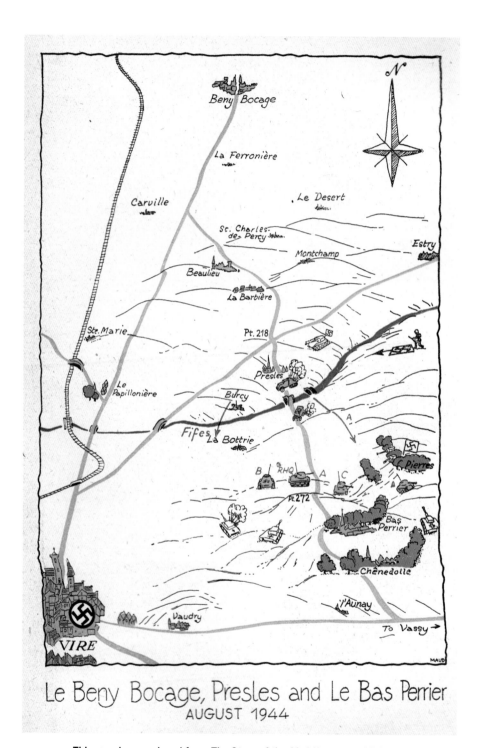

Le Beny Bocage, Presles and Le Bas Perrier
AUGUST 1944

This map is reproduced from *The Story of the 23rd Hussars* published in 1946 by members of the regiment. The book has a detailed account of this and other battles and documents the activities of the regiment during WWII.

The 23rd Hussars moved into the little town on a beautiful sunny afternoon to have a brief rest; it was a charming place, a big village rather than a town. Over the next few days, the regiment moved on south and experienced one of the toughest battles they ever fought.

The road ran south from Le Bény Bocage, through Le Desert, up to Point 218 – a map reference indicating the height above sea level – down the valley through Presles, up again to the high ground of Bas and Haut Perrier, and on to Chênedolle, the objective. 'A' Squadron at the front were ambushed and lost all but four of their tanks. This forced the 23rd Hussars to retreat, and they took up a firm position for the night on a piece of high ground above the little village of Le Bas Perrier.

The morning of 3 August dawned with the prospect of a really hot summer's day. The 23rd Hussars' position was on a hill covered in high hedgerows, banks and cornfields. It was not really big enough for the number of tanks they had, so overcrowding was a bit of a problem. The road from Presles to Chênedolle ran over this hill and it divided 'B' Squadron, who were on the west side, from 'C', Stanley Cull's squadron, who were responsible for the east.

The tanks had been going now for four days with very little respite, and fitters were called in to carry out a few repairs. They set off from Le Bény Bocage, led by Major Whitehill and Captain Sandford in a jeep. Their little column consisted of the three fitters' half-tracks, followed by a Rifle Brigade scout car and an ambulance, which was required by the Medical Officer.

As they began to cross the valley, in the sunshine, a faint noise broke the stillness and aroused the attention of one of the look-outs on the hill. He shouted that there were Germans in the valley and it became clear that the fitters had been ambushed. The men on the hill could see some of the survivors in the valley, their hands raised, standing before their captors.

Major Whitehill and Captain Sandford made it to the hill in their jeep, having run the gauntlet and having had the narrowest of escapes, due to their vehicle being the leading one, and a small target. Half-way across the valley, the leading half-track, which was 'C' Squadron's, received a direct hit from a shell, which killed Sergeant Beresford and half of his crew. Trooper Stanley Cull was killed instantly – another Banstead man had been lost. (Immediately besides the relevant sentence in the Cull's family copy of the 23rd Hussars' book, is a handwritten 'X', indicating that Stanley was killed in this incident). The half-track slewed sideways, preventing the others from getting past, and forced them to a halt. As the crews jumped out, they were surrounded by German infantry and overwhelmed without a chance of fighting, though in the confusion a few men managed to disappear into ditches and crawl back to safety.

The survivors from the 'C' Squadron half-track were all wounded, some more seriously than the others. Lance Corporal Bradley though shaken by blast and burns, pulled Lance-corporal Legg, who was more seriously hurt, to some cover, from which he eventually helped him back to the British lines. On the way he had several skirmishes with the SS infantry and shot two with his pistol and took another prisoner, whom he handed over on arrival. Private Barnett, of the RAMC, who had been in the ambulance, refused to take cover and went to look after a seriously wounded man. He refused to obey the Germans' orders to leave him and, despite the numbers of the enemy troops which surrounded him by this time, he calmly walked past them with his patient, and eventually regained friendly territory. Whenever a German stopped him he pointed to his Red Cross armlet, and on every occasion they let him pass. It was a remarkable display of courage and endurance, for the wounded man could hardly walk, and Barnett knew that the Germans round him were SS men and quite capable of shooting them both.

Cap badge of the
23rd Hussars

Soon the enemy were seen creeping into the village of Presles, and spreading out round it. There was no counter-attack force available and the Germans were now astride the only supply route. The 23rd Hussars were cut off, but had plenty of ammunition, and also food.

It was impossible to launch a counter-attack, as it meant descending from the high ground into the valley. The enemy tanks began to work along the side of the hill above Presles to support their infantry. There were not many of them, but they seemed to be nearly all Tigers and Panthers, using sunken lanes down which they would crawl until they could see a target. Then they would fire a few shots and draw back to cover.

'C' Squadron continued the battle under heavy fire from the enemy's high velocity tank guns. The whistle and crash of the explosions occurred almost simultaneously. As the afternoon wore on, heavier guns were moved up and salvos of shells began to fall around the hill, causing casualties.

As the tanks moved, a heavy high-explosive bombardment began, and a 'C' Squadron petrol lorry exploded with a tremendous roar and flash. Flames rose high in the air and the combined noise was so great that for a moment complete confusion reigned on the hill. Many tanks were thickly covered with branches for camouflage, a precaution which almost certainly saved them from destruction during the next few days.

As visibility decreased, the German fire grew much lighter and the 23rd Hussars had a chance to review their position. If the Germans repeated the exercise on the following day more tanks would be lost, but provided the ammunition did not run out, they would not lose the hill. The most serious worry was the condition and numbers of the wounded. Both Captain Mitchell and Captain Wilcox of the Rifle Brigade were running short of medical stores and there seemed less chance than ever of being able to evacuate the casualties for at least another twelve hours. Both doctors were magnificent in this crisis and inspired the whole force with confidence by their complete and unshakeable calmness. Captain Mitchell worked tirelessly, at times under intense fire and under circumstances which could not have been more trying. Working with the medics was Padre Taylor, displaying a devotion to duty which no one who saw it will ever forget.

A tank of the 23rd Hussars covered in
branches to aid with camouflage

The morning of 5 August found Bas Perrier hill still firmly held. Burnt and blackened vehicles dotted the hedgerows, and beside many of them were a few rough crosses made of two twigs with a beret or a rifleman's steel helmet resting upon each of them. One of these was almost certainly the first resting place of Trooper Stanley Cull.

The tank crews were tired but still full of fight despite the fact that most of them had not spent more than thirty minutes outside their tanks for forty-eight hours. The tanks could not move for fear of giving away their positions, and many in the end had been stationary and camouflaged for five days – a very considerable strain. No one doubted that the Germans meant to take Bas Perrier hill. The regiment sustained and beat back three counter-attacks during the day. That evening of 5 August it was decided to withdraw 'A' and 'B' Squadrons to leave 'C' Squadron to take over the whole regimental position.

Next morning (6th) all was quiet until about midday when the unmistakeable crack of an 'eighty-eight' put everyone on the alert. For the first time the enemy had worked a Tiger up onto a ridge from where is could shell most of the 'C' Squadron tanks. Luckily they were all covered with cut branches, or it might have been serious, for it was quite impossible to see where the Tiger was. It fired at various targets on the hill until a tank in 'C' Squadron began to fire back. This must have worried the Tiger and it eventually withdrew or ceased fire, for no more was heard from him for a while.

By now the Americans were well into Brittany, and the speed and direction of their advance gave most cheering indications of what might be in store for the Germans. On Bas Perrier hill the situation looked quite satisfactory until four o'clock which marked the start of a concentrated bombardment by all the artillery the Germans could muster.

'C' Squadron were beginning to lose tanks. The battle continued unabated, and despite all efforts by 'C' Squadron, and the accompanying infantry (The Warwicks), and the artillery, whose guns were nearly red-hot by now, the enemy began to creep round the left flank. As darkness fell they reached the top of the hill and began to 'bazooka' the tanks. When light failed, the tanks drew back into a close league with the infantry, in order to beat off a night attack.

The Germans did not continue their onslaught after dark and when dawn (7 August) came, the squadron was able to re-occupy most of its positions. 'C' Squadron and the 'B' Squadron troop were relieved at midday, having fought a magnificent battle. For rather less casualties than at Caen, the regiment had inflicted heavy damage on the enemy and had advanced a substantial distance. They had withstood every kind of assault and had given far more than they got. Moreover, everyone felt that the enemy could not withstand such treatment for long and that some day soon the British would advance into France with the Americans, leaving the battered slopes of Bas Perrier ridge many miles behind. Operation Bluecoat drew substantial forces away from the projected German counter-attack at Avranches, and contributed substantially to the later encirclement of the German forces in the Falaise Pocket.

During the week of 1–7 August 1944, the fighting had cost the 23rd Hussars, six officers and forty-seven other ranks wounded, two officers and nineteen other ranks killed. Included in the nineteen other ranks was Trooper Stanley Morris Cull aged twenty-two.

Trooper Ernest Slarks

Another trooper in 'C' Squadron at the time was Ernest Slarks who recalled the details of the battle at the age of 87, some 66 years after the event. *'I was never a military man'* he said. *'I was training to become a Methodist Local Preacher when I got called up in 1942. Stanley and I were both in 'C' Squadron but I never really met him as there would have been about eighty of us.*

'I recall the ambush of the little echelon at Presles as we had a good view from our vantage point. I was the radio operator and my position in the Sherman tank was the farthest away from the hatch opening. In this position I could not normally see much of what was going on outside as I only had a six-inch by two-inch periscope to look through. Wearing a headset also deadens a bit of the sound. I was amazed at the discovery, years later when I read the book of our history, of what critical and terrifying situations we in 'C' Squadron, must have been in, during the battle. My troop commander, Lieutenant Peter Robson, killed on the hill, Sergeant Beresford and Trooper Stanley Cull, along with the other casualties from 'C' Squadron of the 23rd Hussars are listed on our memorial in Bridlington, where we originally did our training.'

Seven days after Stanley was killed, Major Haggar wrote to Mrs Cull:

'Dear Mrs Cull,

I am afraid that I have very sad news for you as your son has been killed in action on August 4th. I felt I must write as soon as possible as I believe that official notification may be slightly delayed.

'No words of mine, or sympathy, can I know help or ease the loss sustained, but I can assure you that I too feel his death very keenly.

'To lose one of my men is like losing one of my family, especially as your son had done so well. I was proud indeed to have men like him under my command.

Stanley and his mother Grace

4.8.44	Sgt	Beresford, C.H.	K.I.A.
	Tpr	Cooper, A.E.T.	K.I.A.
	Tpr	Cull, S.M.	K.I.A.
	Tpr	Sives, R.M.	K.I.A.
6.8.44	Tpr	Beazley, S.	K.I.A.
	Tpr	Danks, C.	K.I.A.
	Tpr	Harrison, A.R.	K.I.A.
	Lt	Robson, P.J.W.	K.I.A.
14.8.44	Tpr	Moore, C.	K.I.A.
	Tpr	Terry, A.E.	K.I.A.
16.8.44	Lt	Treanor, P.M.	K.I.A.
4.9.44	Tpr	Bushnell, J.K.	K.I.A.
	Tpr	Cook, R.	K.I.A.
	Lt	Evans, R.H.	K.I.A.
	Tpr	Watts, A.E.	K.I.A.
9.9.44	Tpr	Sarson, C.T.	K.I.A.
19.10.44	Lt	Turner, F.M.	K.I.A.

A section of the 23rd Hussars' Roll of Honour from the Bridlington Priory Church.

'If it's any consolation to know, he was killed outright and did not suffer. We buried him that evening alongside his fallen comrades. Please accept my heartfelt sympathy, in which I know his friends join me.

Believe me.

Yours Truly

J D Haggar'

It was Major Haggar who presented the Roll of Honour to the Rector of Bridlington Priory Church. It was unveiled in January 1948, and was originally carved by a German craftsman and placed in the Hussars' chapel in Germany, then was erected in its permanent position following the disbanding of the 23rd Hussars.

Like all the other men in this book, Stanley is remembered on the Banstead War Memorial but his name is incorrectly spelt. The inscription shows S.M. Scull instead of S.M. Cull. The error was noticed early on and was put right, presumably using filler of some kind to 'remove' the extra letter S. In a letter dated 24 November 1965, addressed to the Vicar, Reverend F Schofield, the Clerk of the Council writes that Commander Wemyss-Gorman of the British Legion had received a complaint from Mr F Cull regarding the incorrect spelling of his son's name on the War Memorial. The mistake had been put right once but '*repairs are again necessary*'.

Reverend Schofield replied on 26 November, '*The alteration to the name on the War Memorial shall be attended to.*' There is no further correspondence on the matter but forty-five years later, the inscription is still incorrect.

Trooper Stanley Morris Cull
Bayeux War Cemetery
Calvados
France
Grave Reference: XXVI. F. 17

Note: The CWGC date shows 6 August and not 4 August as shown on the Bridlington Memorial and Major Haggar's letter to Mrs Cull.

Sources:
Commonwealth War Graves Commission. Details of Operation Bluecoat and tank photograph from *The Story of the 23rd Hussars* published April 1946. The letter from Mr F. Cull from the archives at the Surrey History Centre ref 6128/1/89. Family photos and documents courtesy of Mr William Newman, son of Patricia Cull. Report on the last reunion of the 23rd Hussars in the *Bridlington Free Press* dated 9 Feb 2006. Photograph of the 23rd Hussars Roll of Honour by courtesy of Colin Hinson of Genuki Yorkshire pages. http://www.genuki.org.uk/big/eng/YKS/. Photograph of headstone adapted from one supplied by the War Graves Photographic Project.

Fact *file*

The Banstead War Memorial was moved in September 1996

The work was carried out by Christian Marshall Ltd., a specialist stone masonry company. The picture below shows the process, which involved erecting a scaffold 'runway' with an overhead track and pulley system.

The Portland stone memorial, which is made up of several separate sections, was dismantled starting with the Celtic cross at the top and followed by the two pieces which make up the column. The lower and heavier parts were lifted off, winched along to the new position and reassembled on the base which was just being prepared when this photograph was taken.

The new position was agreed in order to allow improvement to the junction but usefully, it left the memorial as the focal point at the end of Banstead High Street.

Photograph courtesy of *The Banstead Herald*

Name REMANÉ C.C.

Rank SERJEANT 7928067

Service ROYAL ARMOURED CORPS

3RD ROYAL TANK REGIMENT

Date of death 29/8/1944.   Age 31

C HARLES CLIFFORD REMANÉ was the son of Karl and Emily Remané and was born on 24 January 1913 in Namirembe in the district of Mengo, Kampala, Uganda. His parents, were missionaries in Uganda, where Karl was a doctor. Clifford, as he was always called, and his sister Nora both lived out there for several years. When Emily died, she was buried in Kampala, and Nora and Clifford were sent to England. Karl followed sometime later and subsequently married again, but his new wife and his son did not get on well, and young Clifford eventually went to live with Karl's brother Henry.

In 1901 Clifford's grandfather, Charles Remané, then aged thirty-five and living in Islington, was working as a gold jeweller. Following on in the family business, Karl, and his brother Henry began the Remané Brothers jewellery business, in Hatton Garden in the mid-1920s, a business that still exists today.

Clifford wanted a different career, and at the age of eighteen he enlisted with the Royal Artillery Territorial Army, where he was posted to the 98th Field Brigade. Official records show that he attended the annual camp with his unit every year between 1931 and 1937, and completed his engagement after serving exactly seven years.

On the 2 July 1938, Clifford married Betty Lilian Rees of Purley, Surrey, at St James Church in Purley before moving to Banstead where they lived at *Trenarren* in Holly Hill Drive. This was a brand new property and, as an estate agent based in Banstead, Clifford Remané was well placed to secure it.

War intervened and experienced army men like Clifford were again required to serve their country. In December 1940, at the age of twenty-seven, he re-enlisted, this time with the Royal Armoured Corps. He was immediately posted to the 24th Lancers a 'cavalry' unit of the British army, just formed during that month, mainly from personnel of the 9th Queen's Royal Lancers and the 17th/21st Lancers. It was initially part of the 29th Armoured Brigade of 11th Armoured Division, but later joined the 8th Brigade.

Clifford was appointed Acting Lance Corporal, promoted to Acting Corporal and eventually granted the rank of War Substantive Corporal in April of 1943.

It was during this period that Clifford acquired his nickname, the event being recorded in a book called *None Had Lances - The Story of the 24th Lancers* by Leonard Willis.

'Peculiarities which presented no problem at home seemed rather different in communal living. One man tells how he was subject to sleepwalking and one night woke up to find himself wandering about the barracks, having completely lost his bearings. He called out "Is anyone awake?" A voice answered, a torch was shone and the situation was saved. The torch-owner, Cliff Remané was christened The Lighthouse Keeper.'

Cap badge of the 24th Lancers

Lt Col W A C Anderson, 22 Dragoons, previously with the 24th Lancers, later wrote,

'I have never in my life met a better man or had a better friend. Cliff arrived in 1940 with the 24th Lancers and came to my Squadron. For the first years of his soldiering, he was my tank driver; we had some good moments together and some bad ones. When I was promoted to command the Regiment, I wanted to keep him as my driver but he was far too good a man for that and we had a long discussion about it. I finally persuaded him to take his promotion, and as a Serjeant he served under Major Bourne, one of the finest Squadron Commanders I have ever come across.'

Clifford Remané (second from left) relaxing with three colleagues from the 24th Lancers

On 1 June 1944, Clifford embarked from the United Kingdom with the 8th Armoured Brigade heading for Normandy in France as part of Operation Overlord.

The brigade was ordered to push south and its battalions were soon to come face to face with the enemy. During the night of the 8/9 June, the Sherwood Rangers scouted the terrain around St-Pierre, in lower Normandy, and reported German activity in the area. Accompanying the 24th Lancers on the following day, and riding on top of the Lancers' tanks, were the infantrymen of the 8th Battalion of the Durham Light Infantry (DLI). In the late afternoon the Durhams advanced downhill into the small village of St-Pierre, supported by the 24th Lancers' Sherman tanks.

The German forces rallied, and the Panzer Lehr Division, with the support of panzer-grenadiers pushed into St-Pierre. The town was held by Allied forces overnight, at a cost of heavy casualties on both sides but in the morning the Germans attacked again. Under enormous pressure, the 8th DLI lost its anti-tank weapons and was pushed back towards battalion headquarters. However, following the initial shock, the 8th DLI men fought back. Every available man, including headquarters personnel, joined the defence of a farm on the northern edge of St-Pierre. Sherman tanks from the 24th Lancers moved in to support the Durhams, and blocked any further German armour from moving closer. By lunchtime, the enemy advance had been halted.

This engagement was typical of the type that Clifford Remané would have been involved in, and it was shortly afterwards, on 21 June, that he was promoted to Serjeant. On 3 August, after the 24th Lancers had been disbanded, he was posted to the 3rd Royal Tank Regiment (3RTR).

Another soldier, ex-trooper Eric Clayton, remembers Clifford. *'Cliff Remané was not the stereotyped, raucous, beer-swilling serjeant; rather he was a quiet thinking person with a courteous manner. Although he and I served in the same squadron, conversations were rare and casual, however, through working and moving in the same area, there were many friendly nods or greetings. The decade difference in age between him and an eighteen-year old made him more of a father figure'.*

Cliff Remané was indeed a father, and during his time away he never forgot his family. In one letter addressed to Ann, the eldest of his two young daughters, he says that the rabbit that he and his crew had been keeping had got too big, so he now had a puppy instead, which rode with him in the tank. Unfortunately it was not as well behaved as the family pet back home! Cliff Remané loved animals and was a keen horse rider, an activity still enjoyed by his youngest daughter, Faith and her family.

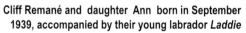

Cliff Remané and daughter Ann born in September 1939, accompanied by their young labrador *Laddie*

On the same day that Serjeant Remané was posted to 3RTR, he was given command of a Mark V Sherman tank. This tank was handed back, presumably faulty, and a second tank, a Sherman 17 pounder, was issued to the Serjeant on 7 August. The Royal Armoured Corps Roll Book records the names of the other three members of his crew as Lance Corporal Oliver, Trooper Butler and Trooper Bernstein. This particular Sherman tank may have been a Firefly which normally carried a crew of four instead of the usual five, as the hull gunner's position was disposed of to make way for extra ammunition. The hull machine-gun was consequently removed and the hole plated over.

Shermans in British service were designated Marks I to V, although the III was uncommon and the IV exceptional, so Marks I, II and V were the most common. The maker is shown as 'Wright', and a Sherman I or II would have the Wright-Continental 9 cylinder radial engine. The Sherman issued to Serjeant Remané in the log book was a Mark I, probably a Sherman Firefly armed with a 17-pounder gun. The machine-gun, if present would have been a Browning, rather than the Besa which was pre-printed in the log.

The roll book was retained by its original writer, Troop Serjeant Harry Dews, long after the war ended. Harry was responsible for keeping the troop roll book which started with the 24th Lancers (3rd Troop 'A' Squadron). When the 24th Lancers were disbanded in late July 1944, Harry continued to keep the roll book up to date, although the complete troop had by then been transferred to 3RTR where it formed 3rd Troop 'C' Squadron to which Serjeant Clifford Remané belonged.

The very last column of the log records the fate of the tank – *Destroyed by enemy action 29/8/44*. By this stage of the war, the Sherman was completely outclassed by the German tanks in a one-to-one situation. The British forces called it 'The Ronson' in reference to an advert for a lighter which included the slogan *'Lights up first time every time'*. This description was based on a design weakness of the Sherman whereby the ammunition store was immediately behind the weakest part of the tank. However the tank had the capability of being mass-produced, and in the end, sheer numbers won the day.

Serjeant Clifford Remané did not live to see that day, as along with one of his crew, he was killed in action near the village of Mainneville in Normandy, only twenty-six days after his posting to the regiment.

Locals recollect that the Germans had been working feverishly and had dug individual holes and trenches on the road from Sancourt to Feularde. At about 1600 hours on 29 August 1944, two Panther tanks, part of the Leibstandarte SS Adolf Hitler, an elite German unit originally set up to be Hitler's bodyguards, took up positions – one at the exit of the village – the other at the side of a small chapel where it had a clear view of both the road and the side of the hill up to the wood where the German infantry was in position.

The War Diary of the 3rd Royal Tank Regiment at Mainneville for 29 August 1944 records that having crossed the Seine at Vernon, 3RTR, part of the 11th Armoured Division, headed north-east towards Gournay on the River Epte. Mainneville is one of a group of villages on the Gournay road which was the centre line of the Divisional advance.

The tank regiment ran into a fair amount of opposition around Mainneville and tried to find routes around it. At approximately 1930 hours, according to the War Diary, 'A' and 'B' Squadrons along with Regimental HQ are across [they don't say across what] and 'B', turning north-west to rejoin the centre line, comes under fire and loses three tanks; meanwhile 'C' Squadron, south of Mainneville, pushes on and also loses three tanks. No casualties are listed but there is no doubt that Serjeant Clifford Remané was in command of one of these three tanks of 'C' Squadron.

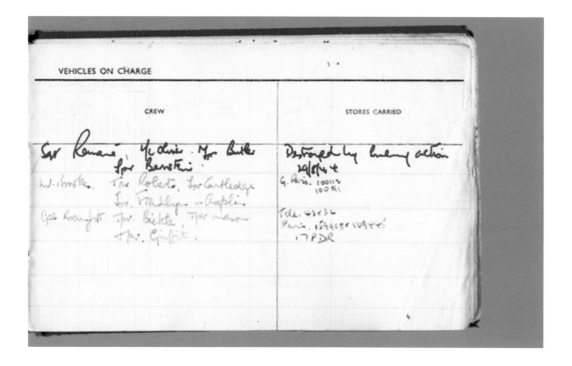

| Enemy tank under cover beside the chapel | Village of Mainneville in the distance | Hidden German infantry in copse | Haystack located in this position |

The photograph above shows the battle scene; 'C' Squadron was assigned to cross the field on the right hand side and draw fire from the German tanks, allowing others to get through safely. Serjeant Remané's Sherman tank was hit by a round fired from beside the chapel, and it was instantly disabled. The only possible cover was a nearby haystack.

Sherman tanks were notoriously difficult to get out of. The turret, where there were two hatches on the roof, for the three crew – commander, gunner and wireless operator/gun loader – was ten feet off the ground. They had the best chance of escaping. The driver had his own small hatch above his seat position in the main tank hull, from where it was impossible to get out if the gun was positioned over the hatch, which it frequently would have been. Shermans, as mentioned, also had a propensity to catch fire, which often meant that the gunner would voluntarily remain in a burning tank, rotating the turret to allow his driver, and usually good friend, to get out, and this often led to great feats of courage and horrendous burn injuries. Fortunately, Clifford's tank did not catch fire and he would have given the order to bale out. No doubt, personal initiative and self-preservation would have played a role in that closely knit group of comrades especially bearing in mind that Clifford may have been injured or dazed and therefore unable to give the order.

Serjeant Remané had two daughters; one, now Mrs Faith Bedford, has conducted a lot of research to establish the exact events that led to her father's death. The family story was that Mrs Remané was told her husband was shot whilst throwing chocolates to the villagers from the top of his tank, although perhaps this is simply what Mrs Remané chose to tell her own two young children.

Faith's determination to uncover the truth led her to two eyewitness accounts of the events on that day in 1944, as well as various letters from Army personnel. The reality of the situation however, with the regiment under heavy fire has, unsurprisingly, led to some conflicting recollections.

One Frenchman, Rene Moulin, aged nine at the time, recounts how the Sherman tank, was hit by a shell from a German tank in an adjoining field. The Sherman did not explode and two of the occupants (presumed to be Bernstein and Butler) escaped from the tank and ran for cover towards a haystack. The boy remembers seeing Serjeant Remané shot and killed, presumably by one of the German infantry known to have been hidden in the wood.

Another account comes from Second Lieutenant J B Millar, who wrote to Mrs Remané on Tuesday 5 September 1944,

'I first knew your husband with the 24th Lancers and he, myself and Sgt Dews formed a happy and united troop. Never have I seen your husband hesitate or lose heart when in the face of danger and he was an example to his crew and those around him by whom he was both admired and respected. His death was instantaneous. The round passed through the turret and caught your husband and L/Cpl Oliver, his ever cheerful operator.' Referring to Bernstein and Butler, he continues *'I saw them jump out of the tank, and am hoping and praying that they are alright.'*

There is little doubt that Lance Corporal William Dan Oliver, aged twenty-six, was killed by the initial strike. There are, however, other accounts of how Serjeant Clifford Remané was finally killed. One possibility, is that dazed from the impact to his tank, he attempted to escape, but was shot while climbing out of the turret, and fell back into the tank. This account supports the local villagers' recollections that two soldiers and their little black dog were later recovered from the tank.

Another version comes from Eric Clayton, a trooper from another tank crew who, along with several others, had managed to scramble across the field to the relative safety of the haystack. Although many decades have since passed, he remembers that day very well. He knew Cliff Remané and recognised him immediately. Eric wrote a vivid description of the events he witnessed on that day.

'Whilst sheltering behind a haystack, I saw a tank approaching less than fifty metres away. Suddenly it stopped and only the commander baled out. He also had difficulty in running and made the decision to flatten himself to the ground and crawl to safety. Masses of little fountains of dust rose continuously around him. As he crawled closer there was a moment of mutual recognition. Then his tense body and facial muscles relaxed as a dozen ragged holes continued to rip into his uniform.'

Trooper Robert William Lawson, from another troop of 3RTR, was also a casualty on that day and it has been suggested that it is his death that Eric has recalled in such detail. However, Eric states that he remembers the events very well.

'When I reached the haystack a tank crew was already there, their commander a Lieutenant. Left still active were the two remaining tanks. The survivors were bunched up behind a person looking out to where the firing was coming from. I think that I probably went to the far side to recce which way to go in anticipation that the enemy infantry would crawl up behind the hedgerow to shoot the survivors. It was at that point I saw the approaching tank and thought it had come to rescue us. The tank stopped and a short time afterwards I saw only one person bale out. The person started to run but after a few yards determined to crawl instead . . .'

There is no doubt that Serjeant Remané's tank was hit by an enemy shell, but did not explode or catch fire. Lance Corporal William Dan Oliver was killed, probably by the first impact, and Clifford Remané was shot shortly afterwards in the act of trying to get to safety. Sixty-six years have since passed, and the exact details are unlikely to ever be known.

This grainy old photo was eventually passed on to Mrs Remané who must have gained some comfort from knowing that her beloved husband had received a proper funeral and lay buried alongside another member of his crew

Lance Serjeant Don Harding of 'C' Squadron 3RTR also wrote to Mrs Remané on 5 September 1944.

'My friends and I found the bodies of your husband and two comrades and we buried them in the cemetery at Mainneville. They were given the best of burials. The French people of the village provided coffins and a Union Jack, and a priest conducted the service. A woman there promised to take photographs for us and if we receive them I will post them on to you.'

The burial took place on 30 August 1944 and the three men were buried in the cemetery on the hill, a little way from the church. Several soldiers attended the funeral. The promised photograph was duly posted to Mrs Remané back in England, along with Clifford's wedding ring.

The temporary crosses shown above were replaced by the more permanent wooden crosses shown here on the right, and these were in turn replaced by the headstones erected by the Commonwealth War Graves Commission. Buried left to right are:

Serjeant Charles Clifford Remané aged 31

Lance Corporal William Dan Oliver aged 26

Trooper Robert William Lawson aged 28

On 21 June 1997 the graves were the focal point of a visit by Captain Stewart Montgomery, who, as a Lieutenant, took part in the battles around Mainneville in 1944. Michel Leve, the local Mayor at the time of the visit, welcomed the Captain *'... to this parcel of earth within the bounds of Normandy which you have, with your companions in arms, liberated, and for which you have suffered along with others who left their young lives here.'*

The Mayor recounted the movements of the 11th British Armoured Division and the 3rd Royal Tank Regiment and described the battle of Mainneville. He finished his speech by thanking the Captain for his visit and by saluting the sacrifice which the Captain and his men had made.

Mainneville is approximately 13 kilometres north-north-west of Gisors in Normandy, France, and the graves are in the cemetery on the hill. Mrs Bedford, who was only eight months old when her father was killed, visits the grave regularly and has high praise for the local villagers who even now, over sixty years later, keep all three graves in immaculate condition. They also hold a small ceremony on Remembrance Day. Unlike many WWII casualties, who are buried in large military cemeteries, these three men are the only soldiers interred in this small village; they could so easily have been forgotten, but the local villagers continue to ensure that this will never happen.

When Mrs Remané received her husband's service medals, her initial reaction was like that of many other women whose husbands and sons had been killed in action; she just wanted to throw them away. Fortunately, this never happened, and they survive to this day to be passed on to the Serjeant's great grandson Alfie.

The family are very keen to ensure that the surname Remané is correctly recorded. It has an acute accent over the 'e' and is pronounced with a long 'a' sound at the end (same as the French sound 'ait'). This probably explains the incorrect spelling of 'Remani' inscribed on the Banstead War Memorial. The stonemasons who refurbished the memorial have confirmed that the error would be easy to correct and this could be arranged at some time in the future.

The decorated graves of the three colleagues from the 3rd Battalion of the Royal Tank Regiment in June 1997

Clifford Remané's World War II medals

1939-45 STAR

Ribbon comprising equal stripes of dark blue, to represent the service of the Royal and Merchant Navies, red, to represent that of the Armies, and light blue to represent that of Air Forces.

FRANCE AND GERMANY STAR NORTHWEST EUROPE (1944-1945)

Ribbon in the colours of the Union Flag, also symbolising those of France and the Netherlands, a central red stripe flanked by white and blue stripes of equal width.

DEFENCE MEDAL (1939-45)

The obverse of the medal (shown here) shows the uncrowned head of King George VI. The reverse bears the Royal Crown resting on an oak tree, flanked by two lions above the words 'The Defence Medal', with the date 1939 top left and 1945 top right. The ribbon is flame coloured in the centre flanked by stripes of green to symbolise enemy attacks on Britain's green and pleasant land, with narrow black stripes to represent the black-out.

WAR MEDAL (1939-45)

The obverse of the medal (shown here) shows the crowned head of King George VI, while the reverse bears a lion standing on a dragon with two heads; above are the dates 1939 and 1945. The ribbon is in the colours of the Union Flag, a narrow central red stripe flanked by narrow white stripes, wider blue stripes, and then red.

Two of several tributes to this family man from Banstead come from Lieutenant Colonel W A C Anderson of the 22nd Dragoons and J B Millar, Second Lieutenant 'C' Squadron. Anderson says, *'I have lost a very great friend and the nation has lost a very fine man. The Lord, for some reason best known to himself, always seems to take away the best.'*

Millar, in a letter dated 5 September 1944, wrote to Mrs Remané. *'Be proud in the fact that your husband gave his life that others might live in freedom. He has now passed to a better world.'*

Serjeant Charles Clifford Remané
Mainneville Communal Cemetery
Eure
France
Ref: Grave 1

Note:
The Banstead War Memorial shows an incorrect spelling of Clifford's surname.

REMANI instead of REMANÉ

Sources:

Commonwealth War Graves Commission. War Diary extracts provided by John Longman of the Regimental HQ of the Royal Tank Regiment. Paragraph from Leonard Willis' book *None Had Lances - The Story of the 24th Lancers* supplied by Pat Gorringe Books. Much of the research and most of the photographs, were provided by Mrs Faith Bedford, daughter of Serjeant Remané, and Naomi Dobson, his granddaughter. Photograph of the serjeant's medals by permission of Alfie Dobson, great grandson. Medal descriptions summarized from details on www.mod.uk. Extracts from *An Ex Trooper Remembers* by Eric Clayton. Scans of the roll book from Harry Dews, and other historical information, provided by Dr Stephen Pannell. Details of the Battle of St-Pierre come from Private R G Goodwin whose memories were recorded as part of the BBC War Memories Project.

1945

The Soviet Army finally enters Warsaw to find total destruction and what remains of a bitter, resentful population. Why did the Russians stand-off when they could have aided the citizen's uprising? The Soviets say they air-dropped food and arms – without parachutes. An oversight or planned cynical act?

General Slim's 'forgotten' 14th Army continue to battle the Japanese, and the Burma terrain, taking Mandalay in late March.

British and American armies are across the Rhine and it seems only a matter of weeks before Germany is occupied from both west and east and 'squeezed' into unconditional surrender. President Roosevelt will not see that day; he dies on 12 April and Harry Truman, succeeding, will now have some weighty decisions to make.

Before April is out the Russians are in Vienna; two allied armies in the west link up at Torgau and resistance in the Ruhr region is over, with 370,000 Germans taken prisoner. The headline on the last day of the month, 'Hitler Dead', seems to provoke little more than numbness in most people – friend or foe.

In quick succession the major elements of German resistance collapse and surrender follows. The end of the war in Europe is marked by VE Day on 8 May. Our eyes turn to the Far East. How many more years of death and destruction before we see Japan defeated?

A general election in the UK gives an overwhelming majority to the Labour Party and Churchill is replaced by a 'new order'.

When the first two atomic bombs fall on Japan the world is stunned by this fearful addition to an armoury of destruction. But now the war must end and a Japanese surrender is inevitable – World War Two is over.

Name *Peasley E.J.*

Rank *Leading Seaman P/JX 166792*

Service *Royal Navy*

HMS Copra

Date of death *18/5/1945* Age *20*

E DWARD JOHN PEASLEY was the son of Albert Edward and Margaret Dorothy Peasley, who lived at Kenneth Road, Banstead. Prior to their marriage, Margaret lived at 1 Salisbury Road, one of the properties that was later to be demolished by the V1 flying bomb that fell on Banstead on the morning of 8 August 1944.

Eddie, as he was always called, had one brother, Robert, and one sister, Grace, and was born in Banstead late in the summer of 1924. As a child he did well at school and was good enough to go on to higher education, and yet he failed the exams which could have earned him a scholarship. His headmaster was furious with him, and asked how this could have happened to which Eddie replied that he did not intend to stay at school as he wanted to join the Navy. When told he was *'very silly'*, as he could have got a commission, the young man was not interested. *'It's not what I want'*, he told his headmaster, *'I'm going in to the Boys Service'*, which is exactly what he did at the age of fifteen. Even at that age Eddie knew what he wanted, and what anyone else said did not matter. It was this attitude that may have cost him his life just five years later.

Eddie was active when he wanted to be and progressed to Patrol Leader in the Woodmansterne Boy Scouts, a role which he enjoyed right up until he joined the Navy. He

was a 'good-looker', a great favourite with the girls, getting many a hiding for being late home from school. Of course, when Eddie chose to be inactive, there was no shifting him. His sister Grace recalls how, while he was waiting for his call-up papers, he used to do a milk round, and the only way his mother could get him out of bed was to tell him that his call-up papers had arrived. Being a quick learner, he soon took no notice, so when his papers did arrive he ignored his mother's call as usual.

Things were about to change. Edward joined the Royal Navy Boys Service where discipline was strict in all aspects; Reveille (the military signal to wake up) was at 0630 hours and lights out at 2100 hours. That was going to take some getting used to, but it was what Edward wanted to do and as always, he did well when he was doing something he liked.

Eddie in the uniform of HMS *Ganges*

Eddie's career in the Navy started at HMS *Ganges,* a shore based training establishment at Shotley, by Harwich Harbour, about eight miles from the county town of Ipswich. By the early 1940s, at about the time the young recruit arrived, those under training numbered about two thousand, with approximately two hundred joining every five weeks.

Early training in the Boys Service involved a constant round of parade ground activities, seamanship and gunnery instruction. Educational subjects and sports were held every afternoon in winter, and each evening in summer. Fitness was key, and school education was alternated with various sporting activities, including football, athletics, boxing and milling – a form of free-fighting using boxing gloves, in the ring.

A key skill was swimming, and boys were taught how, if they could not already swim, with no 'shore leave' allowed until the required level of proficiency in this particular skill was achieved. Later in the course, specialized subjects such as boat work, rowing and sailing would be introduced. The uniforms provided were often too big, which was fortuitous as the array of strenuous activities required a lot of nourishment, and the extra space in the uniform was soon filled!

By December 1940, at the age of sixteen, Edward was in Plymouth on HMS *Emerald* which was in the process of being refitted. It was at this time that he acquired a small diary, and his first entry on 10 December did not bode well. *'Fell down hatch had four stitches carried on work as usual'.* Five days later he was taken into hospital where he stayed for two weeks [he does not say if this was related to the hatch incident].

On 4 January 1941 Eddie received a letter from his girlfriend Evelyn, and on the same day the ship's company was advised by the skipper that they would be *'going away for some considerable time'.* In fact Eddie's first journey must have been one of the shortest on record, as whilst in the process of setting off, the ship's stern hit the jetty, requiring repairs which resulted in a four-day delay. Eventually HMS *Emerald* set off in convoy on its way down the west coast of South Africa. By 23 February the ship had sailed around to Mombasa where Eddie recorded that they picked up the aircraft carrier HMS *Hermes* prior to going on a search for *'raiders'.* Within three days they arrived at the Seychelle Islands

HMS *Emerald*

where there was no sign of the raiders, although it was believed that they were hiding somewhere in the area. The ship moved on again and on 8 March Eddie wrote, *'Went ashore* [at Colombo in Ceylon] *to see Rhythm on the River with Bing Crosby'*. This was the first of many such films that Eddie recorded in his diary.

Over the next month, HMS *Emerald* sailed north off the west coast of India in convoy and *'met'* various ships including HMS *Dauntless* and HMS *Durban,* both cruisers.

Their tour took them to Karachi in British India (now Pakistan) from where, on 10 April, they set off towards Basra – north of the Persian Gulf. On arrival, they *'went up river Euraties* [Euphrates] *to Basra to settle trouble among Arabs started by a Pro-German'*. This was successfully achieved over the following days, after which they painted the ship light-grey and purple for camouflage. Local riots ashore necessitated the landing of a detachment of Royal Marines who joined a group of Ghurkhas to quell the situation.

Eddie continued to write regularly to his parents and to Evelyn and on 13 June 1941 he recorded in his diary that he had also written to *'Granny Peasley'*.

Just two days later HMS *Emerald* was involved in a tragic incident, recorded in Eddie's diary as follows:

15 June – *The 'D' class cruiser Dauntless collided with us port side, killing ten ratings and injuring several others. When Dauntless hit us all the lights went out and it ripped the forward torpedo tubes clean of their base and carried them plus the pinnacle aft wrapping them around the ·5 machine gun and the Captain's boat which caught fire.*

16 June – *Clearing away debris from aft and still bringing out charred bodies from underneath remains of pinnacle etc.*

17 June – *Arrived Singapore at 03.00 went alongside. Ship went down a little in the water and at 17.30 proceeded to floating dock. Still getting out bodies.*

18 June – *Clearing away bodies. 17 dead – 1 dies in hospital and others seriously ill.*

19 June – *Whole ships company went to the F.S.A.* [Fleet Shore Accommodation] *for rest and to leave the ship in the hands of the dockyard men.*

Eddie appears to have taken the incident in his stride and he wrote no more about it though one person he did not forget was his girlfriend. On 24 August, Eddie wrote, *'Exactly one year since day I first met Evelyn'*.

For the next few months through to December, Eddie's ship, HMS *Emerald* continued to conduct patrols and take part in various convoys. Eddie wrote home regularly and continued to receive letters from friends, parents, as well as Evelyn. It is perhaps a surprise then that Eddie arranged a *'date'* with Edna, a girl he met in Durban, South Africa, although he had to cancel it when the ship left for Mombasa at short notice.

By now, America had declared war against the Japanese, and in December 1941 HMS *Emerald* joined the Eastern Fleet as part of the 'Fast Group' which included a battleship, aircraft-carriers as well as cruisers and destroyers. In March 1942 HMS *Emerald* was flagship and in August 1942, by which time, according to Eddie's diaries, it had been painted several times, the ship returned home to Portsmouth for a refit. This presented Eddie with a new opportunity and he decided to join the Royal Navy Commandos.

From this time, entries in Eddie's diary become very few and far between. He had already used the pages in his 1941 diary to record a few entries for 1942, each time adding the new year beside the entry. It seems likely that he did not bother at all with 1943 and 1944, as in the back of his 1945 diary, which is the only other one held by the family, he wrote down many of the places he visited, starting in August 1943. It's an impressive list, including several places in India, Burma, and Egypt, eventually ending up in Italy twelve months later.

On the front cover of his 1945 diary, Eddie, by now a Leading Seaman, had written his unit – 'H' Commando. Each Commando consisted of the following personnel:- 1 Principal Beach Master, 3 Beach Masters, 6 Assistant Beach Masters, 3 Petty Officers, 6 Leading Seamen, 18 Able Seamen, and 39 Ordinary Seamen.

Eddie's unit seems to have trained in jungle warfare at Chittagong in Burma and 'H' party was one of the units involved in the landings on Burma's Arakan coast. These operations commenced with Operation Screwdriver in February 1944 and it was at this time that Eddie was mentioned in Despatches for *'planning and carrying out an operation in the Arakan in close co-operation with the Army'*.

The local newspaper printed the story, and another article a week later records how their reporter had *'unwittingly filled the role of the bearer of good tidings. Mr and Mrs Peasley now of 37 Lambert Road, Banstead, were surprised and delighted to hear that their son, Acting Leading Seaman Edward John Peasley, had been mentioned in Despatches for outstanding services . . . His father claims the Peasley family is the oldest in Woodmansterne.'*

By May 1945 Eddie was based in Genoa at HMS *COPRA* which was an acronym for Combined Operations Personnel Records and Accounts. It was a shore-based establishment set up to process the pay and allowances of personnel serving in Combined Operations.

Eddie's diaries record that he was now writing often to the girl he intended to marry – Molly! Evelyn seems to have been a distant memory by this time. He records several trips to the pictures and only one event of military activity, on 7 April, *'Left Passagrano 07.00 hrs. for eighth army front. Arrived Ravenna 20.00 hrs'*.

Eddie's two surviving diaries

Occasionally he undertook Quarter Master's duties which offered no challenge, and life seems to have been pretty mundane.

By 9 April 1945 the war was coming to an end but the Commanding Officer informed everyone that they would be remaining in Italy until the campaign was entirely over.

Edward wearing his Royal Navy Commando and Combined Operations badge (detail above) on his sleeve

Eddie was involved in one last piece of action on 28 April when he wrote, 'Boarded H.M.S. Marne 05.15 hrs. Proceeded to Genoa. Heavy opposition from shore battery at 13.00 hrs. Arrived Leghorn at 19.30 hrs. Returned to base. Received letter from Mum & Dad'.

Eddie's last entries are shown in full below:

1 May – *Genoa. 3 letters from Molly.*

2 May – *War in Italy finished. Germans unconditional surrender.*

6 May – *Received two letters from Molly. Out sinking mines in the harbour.*

7 May – *Wrote to Molly. Unconditional surrender from Admiral Donitz at 2.41 today. Out sinking mines in the harbour.*

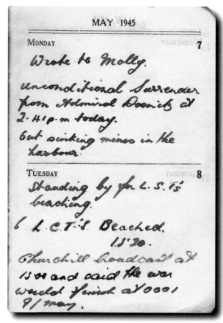

8 May – *Standing by for L.C.T.* [Landing Craft Tank] *beaching. 6 L.C.T.'s beached 13.30. Churchill's broadcast at 15.00 hrs and said the war would finish at 00.01 9th May.*

9 May – *6 L.C.T.'s beached at 12.20 hrs. War finished today. V day. Wrote to Molly.*

10 May – *8 L.C.T.'s beached at 13.30 hrs. Received three letters from Molly and one from Mum.*

12 May – *Churchill spoke at 9.00 pm.*

17 May – *Wrote to Molly. Received photos from shop.*

There are no further entries. Having survived the whole of the war in Europe, to the very end, Eddie was to die on 18 May 1945.

Once again, as he had done at school, Eddie was to ignore advice given to him. Despite warnings not to dive into the sea around the ship, as there was submerged debris, Eddie somehow did exactly that.

Jim Willis, a friend of his from Lambert Road, believes that Eddie was celebrating the end of the war along with mates, and returned to the ship perhaps a bit worse for wear. Whether Eddie consciously dived in, or possibly fell in, is not known, but either way he landed in the water between the ship and the quay. The formal notification from the Navy suggests that Eddie dived in and hit his head on submerged debris. His body was not recovered for two days.

Along with being just a few days away from his twenty-first birthday, Eddie was mere weeks away from marrying his beloved, Molly. She and his parents must have received the devastating news of his death just as everyone in England was celebrating the end of the war in Europe. It is hard to imagine what Molly must have felt when she received the letter he wrote to her just the day before he died, as it would have been received after she knew of his death.

Eddie was buried in Genoa where his grave was marked with a beautifully shaped cross.

Grace, Eddie's sister, got married in 1948, and Molly sent her the lace she was intending to use as a headdress at her and Eddie's wedding. Some two years later, Molly married a Scotsman called Ian McKenzie whom Eddie and his parents had met when they were on holiday at the house of Molly's parents during the war.

By the KING'S Order the name of
A/Leading Seaman Edward John Peasley,

was published in the London Gazette on
4 July, 1944,
as mentioned in a Despatch for distinguished service.
I am charged to record
His Majesty's high appreciation.

First Lord of the Admiralty

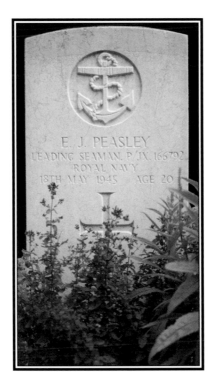

Leading Seaman

Edward John Peasley

Staglieno Cemetery

Genoa

Italy

Grave Reference: I. C. 1

Sources:

Commonwealth War Graves Commission. Royal Navy Commando and COPRA information from Geoff Slee of www.combinedops.com. Photos and personal details and documents kindly provided by Jane Smith. Photograph of HMS *Emerald* in public domain. Headstone photograph courtesy of the War Graves Photographic Project.

Fact*file*

The Banstead War Memorial was restored in October 2005

The inscriptions on all memorials deteriorate over time, and if the names are not to be lost forever, each one has to be painstakingly reinscribed by hand. This requires the work of skilled craftsmen using simple traditional tools.

In 2005, the memorial was thoroughly cleaned to enable, James McGeown, the stonemason, to start the task of recutting almost 1000 letters on the Portland stone panels. The work was completed in time for that year's Remembrance Day.

The photograph below shows the time consuming process. First, horizontal and vertical lines are drawn to ensure that letters can be kept in alignment. Next the area around the words is blackened to provide some contrast, then each small element of every character, that is the same width, is recut using the appropriately sized chisel. In this case the font was also changed to improve readability.

James McGeown at work

Name **HAMMOND J.L.G.**

Rank **SERGEANT 1865865**

Service **AIR BOMBER RAFVR**

NO. 5 OPERATIONAL TRAINING UNIT

Date of death **1/6/1945** Age **20**

JAMES LEONARD GORDON HAMMOND, the son of J L Hammond and Ethel Hammond lived at 32 Winkworth Road, Banstead and attended Sutton County School between 1936 and 1941, where he was known as 'Wally' by his school chums. At home, he was always called Gordon.

Gordon left school when the war was already in its third year, and volunteered for aircrew when he reached the age for active service. Assessed as suitable for aircrew training, his first experience of service life came when he was posted to Babbacombe in Torquay, Devon in November 1943.

Gordon was a keen writer and his letters home give a detailed insight into his brief service career, his training, and his experiences in Britain, and later in Canada. His youthful outlook was reflected in many of his humorous comments and, upon arrival at Babbacombe, his priorities seem to have been the *'good food'*, sea views, and warm weather. He seems to have been less impressed with reveille at 0545 hours!

By August 1944 Gordon was in Canada at MPO (Military Post Office) 304 RCAF (Royal Canadian Air Force) Ottawa. He noted in his letters home that *'they don't know there's a war on here - luxury food, lights at night, and cars'*. His biggest complaint was that this was a *'dry State – no beer'*. Gordon was one of the RAF trainees drafted in to help fight local forest fires. He wrote home on 18 August that this was *'the hardest work I have ever done'*.

In September 1944, Gordon, now training as a bomb aimer, moved on to No.7 Bombing and Gunnery school at Paulson, Manitoba, where he found that dropping bombs was more complicated than he had expected, although he scored a creditable 78 per cent on his first exam. The following month he scored 85 per cent on his last exam, and he wrote to his family that on his latest bombing trip he had an average error of thirty-five yards, which he claimed was *'as good as six direct hits'*. By mid-October he had progressed on to dropping salvos of bombs.

TAYLOR   HAMMOND   JONES   ELEY   MADDOCK   McLACHLAN

OWENS   FELLOWS   TYE   GREEN   JAMES   PRIOR

COURSE 116-9

This photograph is undated however the cedar shingles in the background suggest that Gordon (back row second from left) had started his training at a BCATP facility in Canada, so a reasonable date would be late 1944.

Away from training, Gordon never forgot England or his parents. Three months to the day from arriving in Canada he managed to find four pairs of silk stockings to send home to his mother.

By late November 1944, Gordon had moved on to Number 1 Central Navigation School, in Manitoba. Writing home, he commented that *'the barracks are filthy, overheated by day and like ice boxes at night. The instructors never smile, but the food is not too bad'*. He reported that despite the six feet of snow that was expected, he was now enjoying navigation training. Within a week he was capable of *'landing right on the drome'* [aerodrome] following a 300-mile round trip, no mean feat with the ground covered in snow. He passed his navigation exam scoring 72.8 per cent

With just eight weeks of his training still to complete, Gordon was planning to spend Christmas 1944 on leave in the United States, in Minnesota. Unfortunately the base ran out of US dollars and Gordon was resigned to eating his Christmas dinner in a local café instead.

Winter in Canada got no better and in January 1945 Gordon suffered from frostbite although he soon recovered. In February he qualified, and was shortly expecting a commission.

Gordon then moved to Moncton, New Brunswick and wrote to his parents about the journey. *'On way here met a Negro porter who liked England and Englishmen. Moreover, when he was stationed in England, he was at Banstead of all places. He literally waited on me hand and foot'*.

The training of aircrew in Canada, for Gordon and many of his contemporaries, was the culmination of a well-thought-out strategy. At the start of WWII, Chamberlain's government recognised that airpower was vital to an eventual allied victory and that, in the coming struggle, there would be a need for intensive aircrew training programmes to produce pilots and crews for the Royal Air Force. The peaceful skies above the countries that were then considered part of the British Empire would offer ideal training conditions and Canada was seen as an especially attractive location. Within weeks of the start of hostilities, the Canadian government generously responded to Chamberlain's appeal for help, and quickly became the backbone of what was referred to as the Empire Air Training Scheme (EATS) by the RAF, but was known in Canada as the British Commonwealth Air Training Plan (BCATP).

Jacket crest

At its peak in 1943/4, over 100,000 Canadians were directly employed by the BCATP in 111 units across Canada. Gordon Hammond was just one of nearly 140,000 aircrew who received their training at these facilities.

Gordon's final posting was to 5 OTU (Operational Training Unit) RCAF based at Boundary Bay, British Columbia and administered by Western Air Command at Jericho Beach near Vancouver. From there he faced the real prospect of a posting to an operational squadron.

By early 1944 the BCATP in Canada operated on such a large scale that the needs for aircrew in Europe, seen as the priority for the early war years, were at last being met and even exceeded. It was therefore decided to allocate aircrew to Air Command South-East Asia (ACSEA or SEAC) for operations against the Japanese.

In order to push back the Japanese, the decision was made to use the American B24 Liberator, which was readily available. These aircraft carried a crew of up to eleven, and had a range long enough to operate against the Japanese from bases in India.

The location chosen to train this force was the southern border of Western Canada, with the vast expanse of the Pacific Ocean near at hand. RCAF Boundary Bay, located on the coast just south of Vancouver, was the principal airfield, together with its satellite inland, located a few miles to the east, at Abbotsford.

Location of the RCAF base at Abbotsford

No.5 OTU was formed with twenty-seven B25 Mitchell bombers, and seventeen Liberators at Boundary Bay on 1 April 1944. The twin-engined American B25 Mitchell bombers were used as trainers, allowing the pilots to step up to the big four-engined Liberators in stages, and these were also supplemented with a flight of P40 Kittyhawk fighters, used for fighter affiliation exercises. The initial training was completed at Boundary Bay and the assumption at the time was that the RAF Liberator crews would be flying at night, so the training involved a six-man crew, consisting of two pilots, a navigator, a bomb aimer, a wireless/air gunner, and an air gunner.

A change of plan to enable deployment for daylight operations called for four air gunners and a second wireless/air gunner to make up a ten-man crew. It was at this time that the second base became necessary. From this point on, all Mitchell training was done at Boundary Bay and, once this initial training was complete, all students were sent to the second station at Abbotsford some ten miles east of Boundary Bay. Here they would form the ten-man crews that would eventually be posted overseas.

Abbotsford, with its geographical proximity to both Boundary Bay and the sea, made the location desirable, but limited areas of flat land – necessary for an airfield – meant that there were few location options. As such, Abbotsford had one big disadvantage; it rested at the base of the foothills of the Coast Range Mountains which rose to form an impressively high barrier to the east.

The training regime was extremely comprehensive, including air navigation exercises of up to ten hours duration, formation flying and bombing exercises, air-to-air firing, air-to-ground firing, photographic reconnaissance flights, and night-time cross-country flights.

Liberators at Abbotsford – note the mountain range in the background

Gordon's comments home at this time make interesting reading because, although the OTU represented the final stages of his posting, it was clear that the war was coming to an end and the prospect of operations seemed less likely. He noted, *'The Canadians seem to think the war is over and are demobilising the army and Air Force'*. He also reflected that his pay in Canada was considerably higher than it would be after he returned to the UK – *'I get 60 bucks a fortnight. That's £15 to you. This is the Canadian rate of pay, and when I get back to the RAF, it will go down with a bang'*.

The BCATP plan ended officially on 31 March 1945, but the Royal Canadian Air Force continued to process the crews being trained within the scheme, particularly as the war against Japan continued.

It was in April 1945 that Gordon started gunnery flight firing over the Pacific. *'Tomorrow we start in the Mitchells, flying with our skippers and crew. I've got a nice little compartment in the nose with a lovely view so I shall be quite happy. It's the life for me.'* With the war in Europe nearing its violent end, Gordon speculated that his first operational posting might be to India, a destination that held no great allure for him, commenting that it was no place to celebrate his upcoming twenty-first birthday. He also speculated that the war would probably be over before he was posted, and on the evening of 8 May, wrote to his parents wishing that he could be celebrating victory in Banstead.

He wrote:

'VE Day celebrations here were what I expected - bloody awful! Just cars driving up and down blaring their horns and not a drop of beer in the place.

'This is our last week here, then we go on to another station, then either home or ---!!!? Let's hope it's home. Keep your fingers crossed. In three weeks time it will be a year since I saw you and a year since I had any leave. I'm pretty tired of it all too.'

He had specific messages for both his mother and father:

'You can't drink and fly you know mum. We have to fly so we don't drink. Regarding that permanent commission, dad, the only uniform I ever want to put on again when this war is ended is a civvies - sports coat and flannels. I'm only living for the day I can get out of this and do as I please for a change.

'In about a month from now I shall know whether I am coming home first. It would be just my luck not to.

'That's all, I'll write again soon. Love Gordon xxx'

Gordon's expectation of leaving for another station within a few days, did not materialise, and his letter dated 8 May was to be his last.

On 1 June 1945, nearing the end of their training, Gordon and the rest of the crew were assigned a Liberator (B24J US Serial 44-44312) RCAF Serial KK241 for a navigation exercise, which was to take them to Penticon as a first turning point, then to Revelstoke, and then back to base, a total distance of 509 miles.

It was a very cloudy day, with the cloud base at 3000 feet extending up to 8000 feet. There was higher cloud but nothing unusual, and the crew had clear instructions on when and how they should contact their Abbotsford base. The one difference from their previous flights was that this exercise would be in a fully loaded Liberator.

Liberator KK241 took off at 0906 hours, under the command of Flying Officer William D A Hill. The second pilot was Pilot Officer Gibbons, and the navigator was Sergeant Graham Murray, whilst several other members of the crew were wireless/air gunners. The aircraft climbed to 4000 feet, set course as directed and confirmed their progress back to base. Thirty-four minutes later, the base received a request for a practice fix, i.e. a position. The Liberator's crew were instructed by base, *'Message received. Transmit call sign and dashes'*. This last signal was never acknowledged, despite also being relayed by another aircraft on the same exercise. Repeated efforts were made to contact KK241 but all were without success.

Other aircraft confirmed encountering cloud from 4000 to 8000 feet. KK241 failed to report in at the first turning point, raising further concern, and eventually the time came when it would have been impossible for the aircraft to still be flying, its fuel reserves being insufficient.

Jim Fail, serving with 5 OTU at the time, recalls that when radio contact with the aeroplane was lost and the Liberator failed to return, all rescue services were put on alert, as the fate of the crew could depend on a timely rescue from either the sea to the west, or from the mountainous territory to the east. By this time, the mountain-tops were visible but the valleys were shrouded in clouds.

With the Liberator failing to return to base and with no notification of it having landed elsewhere, KK241 was classified as 'missing', and a telegram, stamped 2 June 1945, was sent to Gordon's family notifying Mr and Mrs Hammond that their son, James Leonard Gordon Hammond, was reported missing, as a result of air operations.

The following days can only have been an anxious and dreadful time for the family.

Back in Canada, a vast area was searched by air immediately, but the weather remained unfavourable for the first two weeks of the month. Notwithstanding the poor weather, a large ground search was quickly organised and this went on day and night from 1 to 16 June. During this period, every available aircraft combed the region, each being allocated areas of ocean or land. In all, nearly two hundred men were used on the ground search, and over fifty aeroplanes flew 372 sorties, collectively flying some 700,000 miles over the mountains, in their desperate search for KK241.

Gordon Hammond 'reported missing'

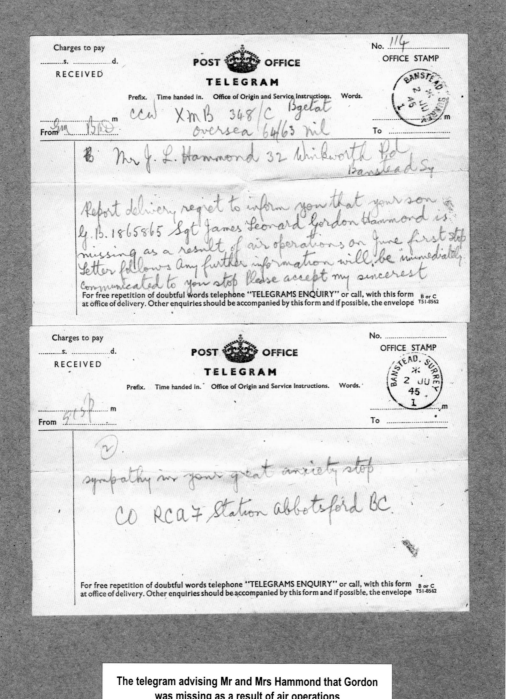

The telegram advising Mr and Mrs Hammond that Gordon
was missing as a result of air operations

It was impossible for bomber crews to fly in and out of the Chilliwack Mountains in their search for their lost colleagues, so smaller aircraft had to be used for this task. Late on 16 June, the clouds lifted above the peaks of the Cheam range and the wreckage of KK241 was spotted by an RCAF pilot, Flying Officer Roy C Archer of Saskatoon. He was flying a single-engined Noorduyn Norseman communications aircraft out of Sea Island, the military section of Vancouver Airport, and finally found what everyone had been dreading. The wreckage of the Liberator was sighted on the rocky slopes of Mount Welch. The bomber was thirty-six miles off-course, although just a few minutes flying time east of Abbotsford, and had crashed less than 100 feet below the mountain's 7730-foot summit.

The aircraft had completely disintegrated and there was no possibility of survivors. The incident is regarded as the worst of 5 OTU's history, although there were other crashes and numerous fatalities.

Early on 17 June, a small party of experienced mountain climbers, led by Command Search Rescue Officer, Squadron Leader Lee, started off in an attempt to reach the wreckage. The trip was made over difficult trails using truck, jeep, Bren-gun carrier and packhorse, to an advance camp some eight miles from the base of Mount Welch. From there all supplies had to be carried by the party. A day's climbing followed and on the second night, camp was made at about 3000 feet below the site of the crash.

It was not until Wednesday 20 June that Squadron Leader Lee and one other group member reached the crash site, having already confirmed, via wreckage strewn down the mountainside, that this was indeed the final resting place of Liberator KK241.

On Monday 25 June the same group returned with Flight Lieutenant Gilbert, an Anglican padre. All the remains were buried and a rock grave erected in the saddle between Mount Welch and Mount Still, topped by an RAF white cross. The cairn was beautified with wild mountain flowers which the group had gathered and made into a wreath, and F/L Gilbert conducted a simple but dignified service. A salute to the comrades who had perished on the mountain was fired, and several photographs taken to record the event.

On 27 June 1945, in Banstead, another letter was delivered to Mr and Mrs Hammond, sent by the Padre on his return from the expedition.

'It would be impossible for me to over emphasize the inaccessibility of the location ... the steep mountain grades, the tangled underbrush, the avalanche snow and the fording of numerous creeks made it impossible for us to bring out the bodies of the eleven Royal Air Force lads. Even the burial party of six persons all of whom were experienced mountaineers, except myself, required nine days to complete the work entailed in the mountain burial . . . the grave site is indeed a most beautiful spot; it seems literally on top of the world. All the lads were buried together side by side, comrades in death as they had been in life as members of the crew of the fateful Liberator.'

Wing Commander D J Williams, Officer Commanding, RCAF Abbotsford, wrote to the Hammonds on 12 July 1945. He explained that the Liberator had crashed into the side of Mt. Welch, at a height of 7000 feet and had exploded on impact, with only part of the tail section remaining in situ. The explosion loosened tons of rock and snow which came down the mountainside together with considerable wreckage from the aeroplane.

Previous page:

TOP – The search for Liberator KK241 covered an extensive mountainous area of the Chilliwack Mountains

BOTTOM – The expedition team and pack horses on their way to the crash site

This page:

ABOVE – Flight Lieutenant Gilbert the Anglican padre makes his final salute at the stone cairn

 LEFT – The RAF cross bearing the names of the twelve aircrew who were killed. The flag is the ensign of the Royal Canadian Air Force

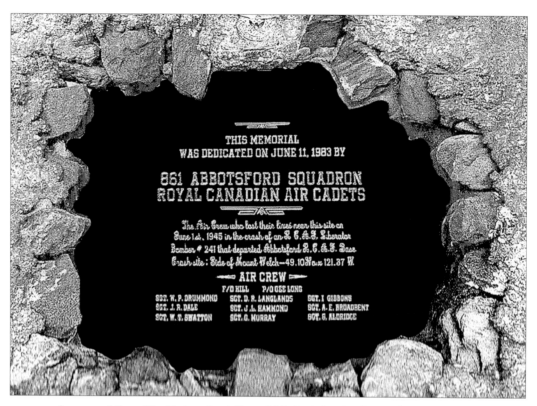

THIS MEMORIAL
WAS DEDICATED ON JUNE 11, 1983 BY

**861 ABBOTSFORD SQUADRON
ROYAL CANADIAN AIR CADETS**

*The Air Crew who lost their lives near this site on
June 1st, 1945 in the crash of an R.C.A.F. Liberator
Bomber # 241 that departed Abbotsford R.C.A.F. Base
Crash site: Side of Mount Welch—49.10 Nox 121.37 W.*

AIR CREW
F/O HILL   P/O GEE LONG
SGT. W. P. DRUMMOND   SGT. D. R. LANGLANDS   SGT. I GIBBONS
SGT. J. R. DALE   SGT. J L. HAMMOND   SGT. A. E. BROADBENT
SGT. W. T. SWATTON   SGT. G. MURRAY   SGT. G. ALDRIDGE

A representation of the Airplane Creek Memorial dedicated to the aircrew of Liberator KK241

Gordon Hammond lost his life just ten weeks before the war finally ended. He never had to bomb the Japanese, and his mortal remains lay high in the mountains of British Columbia to this day. In 1982, Chris Weicht, the Commanding Officer of the Air Cadet Squadron at Abbotsford, hiked into the mountains in search of the grave, but could find no sign of it. Numerous landslides over the previous thirty-seven years had removed any evidence of the location, and had even brought many pieces of the aircraft down as far as the base camp. Chris decided to construct a new monument to the deceased airmen, a feat that was accomplished on 11 June 1983. It was constructed on an island in Airplane Creek near the location of the Squadron Leader's camp of 1945. The monument included a complete engine from the aircraft, mounted in a vertical position, with its base encased in 200 pounds of concrete which had been carried to the site by the cadets. Local stone and other wreckage was placed around the monument. A stainless steel plaque was mounted at the base, listing the airmen's names, and details of the tragedy.

Of all the men commemorated on the Banstead War Memorial, Sergeant James Leonard Gordon Hammond has the highest and the most remote of final resting places of any of his Banstead contemporaries. He and the rest of the aircrew of KK241 have never been forgotten by the Canadians, who have erected several memorials to this crew and other casualties from RCAF. The most recent is the cenotaph at Boundary Bay, erected in July 2005, whilst perhaps the most poignant is the Hydrangea Memorial at Chilliwack Middle School, which was rededicated as recently as May 2009. The living memorial was started in 1941 by mothers and wives of Chilliwack district airforce personnel, who planted a blue hydrangea for each airman lost, and one in memory of the crew of Liberator KK241, forty-nine in all. The fallen airmen continue to be remembered by the children at the school where a memorial ceremony is held each May.

Six weeks after the Japanese surrender, 5 OTU was disbanded. Its remaining Liberators were sold as scrap in 1946.

ABOVE – The rededication ceremony at the Living Memorial of Blue Hydrangeas at Chilliwack Middle School in British Columbia, Canada, held on 6 May 2009. Mr Reg Daws, Regional Vice-President (Lower Mainland) Pacific Group of the Air Force Association of Canada (on the left) accompanied by Major Angus Haggarty of the Salvation Army.

LEFT – The plaque on the cenotaph at Boundary Bay unveiled on 5 July 2005 and dedicated, amongst others, to the memory of those who served with # 5 Operational Training Unit

The image above shows a section of one of Gordon's first letters to his parents. In many of them he mentions presents, and home, and how he longed to be back in Banstead. Gordon never saw Banstead again, and is one of a number of Banstead men who were killed in accidents during WWII, and are now remembered on the War Memorial.

Sources:

The main source of information comes from documents and photographs retained by the family and, at the time of writing, held by Mrs Ann Edwards (known as Gwen), sister to Gordon Hammond. These include twenty-four letters from Gordon as well as correspondence from Canada following the crash. The fate of KK241 is also recorded in the Chilliwack Archives which hold a copy of an article written by Chris Weicht, Commanding Officer of the Air Cadet Squadron at Abbotsford, as published in the *BC Aviator* Vol. 3 No 2 Oct/Nov.1993. The article is titled '*Liberator VY KK241 - Lest We Forget*'. Some of the information detailed in the article has since been updated following further detailed research by Michael DesMazes who also provided the photograph of the Liberators at Abbotsford (courtesy of Wing Commander MacKay). Michael provided additional information on the aircraft used by 5 OTU as well as identifying the pilot of the Norseman from an article in the *Vancouver Sun* dated 18 June 1945.

Okanagan Researcher, Vol. 16 (4), June 2000 (*Mountaintop Memorials* by Gayle Jesperson). *The memoirs of JEH Fail (Jim) - 5 OTU, Boundary Bay 1944/5*. The Chilliwack Archive - Chris Weicht, Commanding office of the Air Cadet Squadron at Abbotsford. The SEAC aviation/Liberator history site at www.rquirk.com. *Aircrew Unlimited*, John Golley - PSL 1993. Captain Jason White, Regional Cadet Air Operations (Pacific) photographed the cenotaph and provided an article from the Ex-Air Gunner's magazine – *Short Bursts* on the ceremony at the cenotaph. The *Suttonian* magazine from Sutton Grammar School's archives. RCAF ensign from www.rcaf.com ensign. Chilliwack Museum kindly provided a report and photos of the Living Memorial at Chilliwack Middle School. Bob Young, Principal at Chilliwack Middle School, photographed the service in May 2009.

1946

First meeting of the United Nations General Assembly of fifty-one member nations takes place in London. Will this be a lasting legacy of the war years or will it fail? Another League of Nations? Or a palpable reconciling of the world?

Bread is added to the list of rationed items. A measure that the U-boats failed to bring about is now deemed a necessity. Austerity Britain is a fact of life for a country verging on bankruptcy. The National Health Service is enacted by a socially committed Labour Government. They make mistakes but their intentions seem honourable and they set down a more equitable future for the country.

Arabs riot at the prospect of a Jewish state in Palestine. Chinese communists go to war against the Nationalists.

The Marshal Plan is a propositional saviour for war-ravaged Europe and perhaps we are learning from the past that there may be benefits to mankind in the way we treat our former enemies.

Ah! Yes! The news we have all been waiting for! The first in a never-ending line of Kalashnikov AK automatic rifles is born – what a boon to a shattered world!

A year to reflect – on the price of peace; on the dead, the injured and the missing; on the death-camps; on the de-humanised; on the displaced. Six years of war. What was it all about? Why did it happen? Where do we go from here?

More questions than answers, and surely yet more questions to come.

Name **BISSETT JOHNSON E.O.**

Rank **SERJEANT 6665016**

Service **GORDON HIGHLANDERS**

1ST BATTALION LONDON SCOTTISH

Date of death **18/10/1946**   Age **44**

EDWARD OSBORNE BISSETT JOHNSON was the son of Edward Henry and Jeannie Isabella Johnson. Eddie was born in Solihull in 1902 and had one brother Henry, and one sister Nancy who kept an old family photograph album which included many pictures of Edward. All three siblings also retained their mother's maiden name, 'Bissett', which was combined with 'Johnson' as the new family name. Eddie was a very private individual and very little is known about him.

An entry in a 1926 copy of *The Journal of Mental Science* records that Edward had gained a nursing qualification at Banstead in Surrey. The following year, in 1927, he married his first wife Katherina Dunkeld; his second marriage, to Dorothy Robson in 1939 is captured in the photograph below. Edward and Dorothy both psychiatric nurses who first met at Banstead Asylum, lived at 18a Buff Parade, Banstead. They had one son, Alastair,

in May 1941. Dorothy always referred to her husband as 'Johnnie', and both were active members of their local British Legion, whilst Edward was also a highly skilled water-colourist.

When war intervened Edward enlisted with The London Scottish Regiment which was part of the Gordon Highlanders. For the first two years of the war the three battalions within the regiment were engaged in training and defence duties at home.

Edward was with the 1st Battalion which went overseas in August 1942, as part of 56th (London) Division and joined the Persia and Iraq Force in the area of Kirkuk. The

**Badge of
The London Scottish Regiment**

battalion, as part of 168 Brigade, joined the 50th (Northumbrian) Division for the invasion of Sicily and remained with them throughout this campaign. After the invasion of Italy, the battalion rejoined 56th Division and served with them in both the 5th (American) and 8th Armies during the Italian campaign.

The battalion fought in all the major battles, from the River Volturno to the crossing of the River Garigliano, the Anzio Bridgehead, the breaking of the Gothic Line and the subsequent fighting on the banks of the River Po. After crossing the Po, they formed part of the force which chased the remnants of the German army to Trieste where the battalion became part of the Army of Occupation.

The exact circumstances of Edward's death are not clear. He survived to see the end of the war but died from peritonitis following surgery to remove a section of his stomach due to an ulcer. An untreated ulcer can burn through the wall of the stomach or other areas of the intestine, allowing digestive juices and food to leak into the abdominal cavity. This type of ulcer is most often caused by bacteria, but can also be the result of a penetrating injury to the lower chest or abdomen such as a knife wound, or a blunt abdominal trauma to the stomach, both consistent with a war injury.

Edward died on 18 October 1946.

Edward's son Alastair went on to become a well-known and very well-respected Professor of Private Law, whose dedication to his students was matched only by the dedication to his subject. Many women who find themselves going through a divorce now share in their partner's pension and see some recompense for their forfeit of earnings while bringing up children. They have Alastair Bissett-Johnson to thank.

Serjeant Edward Osborne Bissett Johnson was buried in the churchyard at All Saints Banstead and is recognised as a casualty of war by his Commonwealth War Graves Commission headstone. The words still clearly visible at the bottom of the stone read

IN MEMORY

OF MY BELOVED "JOHNNIE"

THE FLOWERS OF THE FOREST

ARE A 'WEDE AWA'

The quotation comes from a poem called *Flowers of the Forest,* an ancient Scottish lament for the defeat at Flodden in 1513 when Scotland lost thousands of her men, many of her nobles, and her king James IV, during the battle with the English in Northumberland. Several versions of the lyrics exist, notably Jean Elliot's, written in 1756. Most renditions are played on the Great Highland Bagpipe and due to the content of the lyrics and the reverence for the tune, it is one of the few tunes that many pipers will only perform at funerals or memorial services, and only practice it in private or to instruct other pipers.

This section is just four lines:

Dool and wae for the order sent oor lads tae the Border!

The English for ance, by guile wan the day,

The Flooers o' the Forest, that fought aye the foremost,

The pride o' oor land lie cauld in the clay.

A fine tribute to a Gordon Highlander.

Serjeant
Edward Osborne Bissett Johnson
All Saints Churchyard
Banstead
Surrey
Grave: south-east of Church

Sources:
Commonwealth War Graves Commission. Regimental history from http://www.londonscottishregt.org. Photographs and personal information courtesy of David Bissett-Powell, Ann Bissett-Johnson and other family members. Obituary of Alastair Bissett-Johnson by Shona Main of HeraldScotland (website). Article on perforated gastric ulcers www.emedicine.medscape.com. *Flowers of the Forest* information from www.folkmusic.net.

Fact*file*

The one hundred and eighteen men listed on the memorial never returned home, ultimately giving their lives for their country, and every November, rain or shine, the people of Banstead, alongside relations and descendants of those lost, gather to honour their memory. Following a service held at All Saints Church, where all the men's names are read out, people from many local groups and organisations form a long procession, and led by the clergy of several faiths, make their way along the High Street to the memorial. Here, large crowds gather for the Remembrance Day Service, where each organisation is called on to lay a wreath of poppies.

Prayers are said, hymns sung, and The Last Post is played by a lone trumpeter as the crowd looks on. Through those they died to protect, these men of Banstead, will always be remembered.

Remembrance Day Service November 2009

Name *Cutts F. W. MC*

Rank *Captain 116480*

Service *Royal Artillery*

3AA Tractor Battery

Date of death *19/11/1946.*   Age *57*

Frederick William Cutts the son of John and Sarah Ann Cutts was born in 1889, his birth being registered in Woolwich. Two years later the census shows him living in Plumstead at which time his 61-year-old father was recorded as a Grocer Master. Frederick was educated at Duke of York's Royal Military School and enlisted as a boy soldier into the Royal Horse Artillery (RHA) on 10 September 1904 which eventually led him to spend the four years between 1910 and 1914 in India.

The RHA was responsible for light, mobile guns that provided firepower in support of the cavalry, and was the senior arm of the artillery. In 1914 the establishment was one battery to each brigade of cavalry. A battery had six 13-pounder field guns, and included five officers and two hundred men as well as over two hundred horses.

Frederick was about twenty-five years old when the Great War started and he returned to England in readiness for mobilisation with the 29th Division. The British 29th Division, led by General Ian Hamilton, and known as the 'Incomparable' Division, was a First World War regular army infantry division formed in early 1915 by combining various units that had been acting as garrisons around the British Empire. It was involved throughout the whole of the Gallipoli campaign in Turkey, making the first landings as part of the Mediterranean Expeditionary Force in April 1915. The Turks put up fierce resistance and both sides suffered heavy casualties. Attempts to sweep across the peninsula were unsuccessful and by the end of August the Allies had lost over 40,000 men.

In October Hamilton was replaced by General C C Monro. After touring all three fronts Monro recommended withdrawal, and the division was evacuated from Gallipoli to Egypt in January 1916. General Monro was to feature further in the story of *These Men of Banstead*, as it was he who unveiled the Banstead War Memorial in June 1921.

The Division was sent to France in March of 1916 but Frederick had another ambition to fulfill, which he did on 1 April 1916 when he married Rose Ellen East at Tooting.

He went into action in France and took part in the Somme offensive in July 1916 gaining a commission in February 1917. He served with the 88th Battery of the 14th Artillery Brigade attached to the British Fourth Army under Major General Budworth, and remained in that theatre of war throughout the rest of the conflict. He was injured twice at St. Quentin and won the Military Cross late in 1918. The citation overleaf was printed in the *Supplement to the London Gazette* dated 11 January 1919.

I congratulate you on your gallantry and devotion to duty
for which you have been awarded

THE MILITARY CROSS.

The photograph on the right shows the actual medal won
by Lt. F W Cutts which is still in possession of the family

'Lt. Frederick William Cutts, R.F.A., attd. 88th BY., 14th A. Bde.

*For conspicuous gallantry and devotion to duty. While the battery was being shelled
this officer, although wounded himself, went out under heavy fire to collect stretcher-
bearers to remove the wounded, and refused any treatment until all had been cared for.
Later in the day he took command of the battery, still under heavy shell fire, and set a
fine example of coolness and endurance to all.'*

Having survived the horrors of the Somme, Frederick returned to England where, for a
time, he was based at a garrison in Winchester. In September 1919 the family doubled in
size when twins John and Margot were born. After a brief spell in Orpington, the Cutts
moved to 69 Ferndale Road, Banstead. Frederick was quite an entertainer and certainly did
his bit for Banstead Village although things did not always go to plan. On the 6 February
1929 he was meant to sing a song for the Ferndale Road Concert Party. At the last minute,
he was unable to go, and Mrs Cutts had to deputize.

In 1935 Frederick joined the newly-formed Banstead Amateur Film Society. Their first
production, *The Not-So-Good Companions* was a simple tale about the adventures of three
sets of people who set off on their summer holidays from different places, and are brought
together by various comical situations. Frederick Cutts was one of these companions along
with Geoff Pushman and others. Filming took place at weekends, mainly along Chipstead

Road and Holly Lane, at a time when it was possible to spend a whole Sunday afternoon filming with hardly any interruptions from cars or other vehicles.

Captain Cutts was well known in Banstead and was involved with various committees. In the April edition of the 1937 Banstead Quarterly, he wrote:

Frederick Cutts (left), Nelson Hill and Jimmy Priest in a scene from The Not-So-Good Companions

'*Sir, At the request of several young people of Banstead, I am contemplating, the formation of a real good cycling club, not of the type which considers rowdyism and disorderliness the crowning joy of life's ambition . . .*

. . . A good cycle club insists on suitable attire with respectability, the workmanlike superiority and cleanliness of their cycles, orderliness on the road and amongst many other things (the most important) good general leadership.'

There surely can be nothing better than his own words to tell us what sort of man he was, a military man through and through.

By January 1938 Frederick Cutts had moved to 136 Great Tattenhams and started working on the formation of a new Community Centre as Honorary Organising Secretary.

The Captain was devoted to his children, twins John and Margot, and with his army background was strict on discipline. Donald Luff, Margot's husband, clearly remembers how the Captain could not stand his son having a lie-in.

Frederick Cutts was a leader of men and this made him ideal for one of his roles as Gym Instructor at Beechholme residential school in Fir Tree Road, Nork. Frederick did have a softer side and Thomas Chapman recalled how whilst he was at the home, he used to watch Captain Cutts making paper kites for the boys. Ted Bond and Geoffrey Robinson, both members of the Banstead History Research Group, remember the Captain. Ted Bond actually worked with John Cutts, the Captain's son, at The Prospect Garage, a mechanical engineering workshop on the Brighton Road.

Geoffrey remembered Captain Cutts because he had given him a boys' annual one Christmas. Another member recalls the day when a friend of the family gave his father and Captain Cutts a lift to work – apparently a collection of 'Nissen' huts on the same site as the present-day National Archives building in Kew.

During WWII, Frederick's military skills were again put to good use in the Royal Artillery with 3 Anti-Aircraft Tractor Battery, but eventually, the day arrived when the Captain had to retire from military service, an event that was recorded in a letter from the War Office dated 30 January 1946.

'*Now that the time has come for release from active military duty, I am commanded by the Army Council to express to you their thanks for the valuable services which you have rendered in the service of your country, at a time of great national emergency and to express regret that, owing to disability, it is no longer possible to use them in an active capacity.'*

Captain Cutts, as he was always called locally, did not have the opportunity to enjoy his retirement for long as he died the same year. Frederick is the oldest man listed on the Banstead War Memorial and only one of two men, the other being Bertram Ives, to have been involved in both WWI and WWII.

His death on 19 November 1946, at the age of fifty-seven, was sudden and completely unexpected, leaving his family totally devastated. The Captain had suffered a heart attack whilst out in the Tattenham Corner area, close to Epsom racecourse.

The manner and date of his death raises a puzzling question – why is Captain Cutts on the Banstead War Memorial? The Commonwealth War Graves Commission have him included in their casualty list and have also erected his headstone at All Saints Churchyard Banstead. In reply to an enquiry, the Commission states:

'Our records were formed from information received from the relevant service authority after the war. At some point Captain F W Cutts' death must have been deemed attributable to his war service but we do not have any records that can confirm this.'

Without doubt, the Captain served his country well over a long period of time, and it may be that the 'disability' mentioned in the letter from the War Office played a part in his untimely death. Frederick Cutts made a significant contribution to the village of Banstead and he will always be remembered together with the other men of Banstead who gave their lives for the freedom of their country.

Captain Frederick W Cutts MC
All Saints Churchyard
Banstead
Surrey
Grave: south-east corner

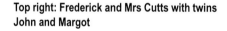

GVI RI

This scroll commemorates

Captain F. W. Cutts
Royal Regiment of Artillery

held in honour as one who
served King and Country in
the world war of 1939-1945
and gave his life to save
mankind from tyranny. May
his sacrifice help to bring
the peace and freedom for
which he died.

Top right: Frederick and Mrs Cutts with twins John and Margot

Above: The WWII King's Commemoration Scroll

Right: Captain Cutts in full uniform proudly displays the cap badge of the Royal Artillery

Sources:

Commonwealth War Graves Commission. Personal details and portrait photograph from Donald Luff (son -in-law) and other family members. Images of documents and medal, courtesy of Janet Cutts. Address details from local directories. Film details from *Focus on Banstead* by Val Randall.

Fact *file*

World War Two statistics from the Banstead War Memorial

There are fifty-six names on the Memorial

(D R Baple is a WWII casualty recorded on a WWI panel)

The first died 28 March 1940

Pilot Officer James Olliff Griffits

Royal Air Force aged 21

The last died 8 May 1947

Private Leslie Albert Stanley

Royal Pioneer Corps aged 28

The youngest was aged seventeen

Cadet Peter Cyril Francis Locatelli

Merchant Navy died 17 January 1941

The oldest was aged fifty-seven

Captain Frederick William Cutts

Royal Artillery died 19 November 1946

Captain Cutts also served in WWI

and was awarded the Military Cross

Note: These statistics are based on the fifty
WWII men who have been positively identified

EPILOGUE

Throughout this book I have sought to give some idea of the lives and sacrifices of thirty-four of the men of Banstead. But beyond those mentioned in these pages there are a further eighty-four men on the Banstead War Memorial, with additional names included on the plaques in the Lady Chapel in All Saints Church, and still more on the Garton Memorial in the churchyard. The Banstead memorial is one of many; more can be found within just a few miles of the village, and across the country, the continent, and indeed, the world.

It is hard to comprehend the scale of these conflicts; some thirty million service personnel are estimated to have been killed in the two World Wars, each one of those casualties having their own stories akin to the ones in this book.

Many of the memorials erected in their memory commemorate the fallen in the location where they breathed their last; we have seen that, even within our comparatively small group of thirty-four men, several have been laid to rest in places far from home. Despite this, they are still remembered by the people of those countries, like the schoolchildren in Chilliwack, British Columbia, at their annual blue hydrangea service, or the villagers of Mainneville in France, who maintain the three British soldiers' graves in their small cemetery.

Most readers of this book will immediately recognise the war cemeteries abroad, with their row upon row of white headstones cared for, and immaculately maintained, by the Commonwealth War Graves Commission. These belong to men who died overseas and whose bodies were never repatriated. But how many people realise that the same headstones can be found in British churchyards and cemeteries? Take a look around your local churchyard and you may see the distinctive white headstones dotted here and there. There are sixteen in All Saints Churchyard in Banstead, commemorating men who died or were killed in the United Kingdom.

The widows, family, and friends of those buried overseas had nowhere to visit and mourn their loved ones, and it was for this purpose that names were added to family headstones, and memorials were erected and unveiled across the country.

To date, the records of the Banstead War Committee have not been found, and it is hard to establish the criteria used to accept a man's name for inclusion. Most of the men whose names are listed on the Banstead memorial lived locally, but by no means all. Some had relatives who lived near to the memorial, and they no doubt wanted a place to remember their loved ones. Some names were added years after the unveiling or the WWII rededication, whilst some men are not on any local memorial, such as Private Robert Monk of Lambert Road, who was shot by the Japanese in Burma when he refused to abandon his beloved pack animals.

How or why the names came to be on the memorial, or were left off, makes no difference, as each Remembrance Day, the people of Banstead, joined by many visitors, gather at the memorial to remember all the men from Banstead, and elsewhere, who made the ultimate sacrifice.

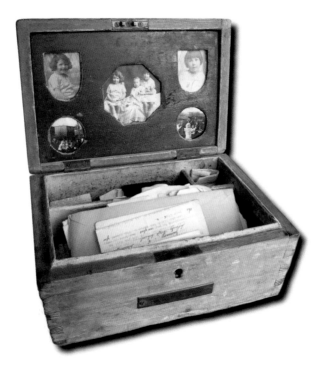

There are always more hidden treasures to be found like this box belonging to Leading Seaman Bertram Ives, now in the possession of his grandson Jonathan.

It was cleverly constructed with a 'lip' on the inside to keep it watertight and was recovered from the sea after the *St Achilleus* hit a mine and sank whilst taking part in the 'little ships' evacuation at Dunkirk in June 1940.

To learn more about the contents of this box visit www.bansteadhistory.com

A RESEARCHER'S WORK IS NEVER DONE

In the introduction, I asked whether it was possible to learn anything about the men listed on the Banstead War Memorial, working merely from surnames and initials. As this book draws to a close, there is no question that I, and now you, know a great deal more about the thirty-four men whose lives have been touched on in these pages.

'They shall grow not old, as we that are left grow old . . .'

Seeing photographs of the men brings new meaning to these words, recited at Remembrance Day services around the world, and ensures that those of us who pass the memorial will no longer view it in the casual way we perhaps once did.

As each year passes, fewer and fewer people remain who knew these men personally. For the younger generations it grows increasingly difficult to connect with the reality of war on such a huge scale and to appreciate the sacrifices made by their forefathers. If this book helps in that respect, it will have done its job, but if it also encourages even one reader to start researching a soldier in their family, or on a local memorial, that would be even better.

Four years of research has taught me that the information is out there and that time and patience will eventually reap rich rewards. Just days before this book went to print I received news of an old wooden box, belonging to Leading Seaman Bertram Ives, that was recovered after his ship hit a mine and sank at Dunkirk. It is full of letters, photographs, certificates and other documents and, although too late to be included here, information about its contents will be added to the website of the Banstead History Research Group. There you will also find more stories about many of the other men listed on the memorial.

The research goes on, and you can help. If you have more information about any of the men in this book or any others whose names are on memorials in the vicinity of Banstead, please get in touch with a member of the Banstead History Research Group or the Banstead History Centre at the library.

If there is no local record of the men listed on a memorial in your area, try to find them on the Commonwealth War Graves Commission on-line database and ensure the additional information you find is easily available to others via the British Legion or perhaps your local library or history centre. By the time you have added a few photographs and maybe spoken to local residents, or relatives, you will be well on your way to compiling a permanent record such as *These Men of Banstead*.

INDEX

Page numbers in **bold** refer to illustrations

NAMES ON THE BANSTEAD WAR MEMORIAL

Names in **bold** indicate that the man's story is in this book.

Correct surnames and initials have been shown here irrespective of inscriptions on the memorial.

Right hand column shows panel reference: WWI = Top Panels

WWII = Bottom Panels

(except Baple)

Armstrong R.W.	WWII BP 2	**Cutts F.W.**	WWII BP2	**Muggeridge S.**	WWI TP1
Arthur H.B.C.	WWI TP3	Daniels G.	WWI TP3	Nash A.	WWI TP6
Bailey J.E.	WWI TP5	**Davis F.G.**	WWI TP1	Nash G.	WWI TP4
Baker G.	WWII BP1	Duce C.G.	WWII BP4	**Nash W.J.**	WWI TP6
Balchin A.A.W.	WWI TP5	Durrad I.	WWII BP2	**Needham A.S.**	WWII BP1
Baldwin J.H.	WWI TP2	Eason D.B.	WWII BP2	Oliver W.E.	WWI TP6
Baple D.R.	WWII TP7	Eason K.W.	WWII BP4	**Parkes P.D.**	WWII BP4
Barnes R.C.A.	WWII BP2	Edwards G.	WWI TP3	**Paterson S.**	WWI TP4
Barton A.	WWII BP4	Everett A.H.	WWII BP1	**Peasley E.J.**	WWII BP3
Bates H.	WWI TP7	**Excell L.W.**	WWII BP2	Pidgeon A.A.	WWI TP6
Baugh J.H.	WWII BP2	Farley W.	WWI TP4	Plowright R.E.	WWII BP4
Bell K.T.	WWII BP3	Fletcher D.J.	WWII BP1	Powell G.H.	WWI TP6
Best R.S.	WWII BP3	Garton E.C.	WWI TP7	**Reeder R.C.**	WWII BP4
Biles W.R.C.	WWII BP1	Garton H.W.	WWI TP7	Rees M.O.	WWII BP3
Bissett Johnson E.O.	WWII BP2	Gatland J.	WWI TP4	**Remané C.C.**	WWII BP4
Blunt G.	WWI TP4	Griffits J.O.	WWII BP3	Reygate C.H.	WWI TP4
Blunt P.	WWI TP5	Griffits P.G	WWII BP3	Reygate S.	WWI TP5
Boobier A.	WWI TP3	**Grimwood E.N.**	WWII BP2	**Riches L.P.**	WWII BP1
Botting E.H.	WWII BP1	Guest A.	WWI TP2	Roberts H.W.	WWII BP4
Bown V.	WWI TP4	Gurney T.	WWI TP3	Scull S.M.	(see Cull)
Brown J.	WWII BP3	**Hammond J.L.G.**	WWII BP4	Seal L.H.	WWII BP1
Buckle A.S.	WWI TP7	Harden H.	WWI TP2	**Sharman C.**	WWI TP5
Buckle C.C.	WWI TP7	Harding H.	WWI TP1	Skelton A.	WWI TP2
Burberry W.	WWI TP3	Hart R.J.	WWII BP3	Skelton T.	WWI TP1
Burr J.J.K.	WWII BP2	**Hayward L.A.**	WWII BP4	Sopp E.	WWI TP5
Butler G.	WWI TP6	**Hillman J.**	WWI TP6	Stanley L.A.	WWII BP3
Butler W.W.	WWII BP1	**Hobden K.**	WWII BP1	Stemp A.E.	WWII BP2
Caselton R.M.	WWI TP3	**Hobden W.**	WWII BP1	Sturt R.	WWI TP3
Clark J.E.	WWII BP3	**Hobson C.A.**	WWII BP2	Sumner S.D.	WWI TP2
Couchman C.E.	WWI TP4	**Hoslin L.C.**	WWII BP3	Sutehall P.	WWII BP2
Cross E.J.	WWI TP7	**Hunt G. W.**	WWI TP2	Taylor A.J.R.	WWI TP6
Croxall J.F.	WWII BP3	**Ives B.H.**	WWII BP1	Taylor J.W.	WWI TP4
Cull S.M.	WWII BP1	Jenkins J.E.	WWII BP4	Tichener G.	WWI TP7
Curtis A.	WWI TP5	Johnson A.W.H.	WWII BP1	Tonge A.G.	WWI TP2
		Johnson E.O.B. (see Bissett Johnson)		Wallis W.A.	WWI TP3
		Kennard A.	WWI TP1	Waters A.	WWI TP5
		King Stevens L.E.	WWI TP2	Weller E.	WWI TP2
		Knight S.	WWI TP1	White D.J.	WWII BP2
		Lawrence S.P.	WWII BP4	Wigglesworth G.	WWI TP6
		Lee E.	WWI TP5	Wingrove G.S.	WWI TP1
		Lintott J.P.M.	WWII BP4	Wiscombe F.	WWI TP7
		Locatelli P.	WWII BP1	Wright A.J.	WWI TP1
		Low F.	WWI TP1	**Yeomans S.R**	WWII BP4

The thundering line of battle stands,
    And in the air death moans and sings;
But Day shall clasp him with strong hands,
    And Night shall fold him in soft wings.

Concluding verse of *Into Battle,*
a poem by Julian Grenfell (1888–1915)